# PRESERVING PRIVILEGE

# PRESERVING PRIVILEGE

## California Politics, Propositions, and People of Color

*Jewelle Taylor Gibbs*
*and Teiahsha Bankhead*

Westport, Connecticut
London

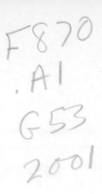

F870
.A1
G53
2001

**Library of Congress Cataloging-in-Publication Data**

Gibbs, Jewelle Taylor.
    Preserving privilege : California politics, propositions, and people of color / Jewelle
Taylor Gibbs and Teiahsha Bankhead.
      p.  cm.
    Includes bibliographical references and index.
    ISBN 0–275–96991–6 (alk. paper)
    1. California—Ethnic relations.  2. California—Race relations.  3. Minorities—
Government policy—California.  4. Multiculturalism—California.  I. Bankhead,
Teiahsha.  II. Title.
F870.A1G53  2001
323.1′794′0904—dc21        00–061175

British Library Cataloguing in Publication Data is available.

Library of Congress Catalog Card Number: 00–061175
ISBN: 0–275–96991–6

First published in 2001

Praeger Publishers, 88 Post Road West, Westport, CT 06881
An imprint of Greenwood Publishing Group, Inc.
www.praeger.com

Printed in the United States of America

The paper used in this book complies with the
Permanent Paper Standard issued by the National
Information Standards Organization (Z39.48–1984).

10 9 8 7 6 5 4 3 2 1

**Copyright Acknowledgment**

The author and publisher gratefully acknowledge permission for use of the following material:

Material from J.T. Gibbs, *California Crucible: Toward a New Paradigm on Race and Ethnic Relations* (San Francisco: Study Center Press, 1998). Courtesy of Study Center Press.

To Sharon M. Ikami for your support, your loyalty, and your friendship. (J.T.G.)

To my partner, Angelo Lamont Butler, who shares a vision of social justice, cultural diversity, and economic equity. (T.B.)

# Contents

# Preface

In the twentieth century, the state of California epitomized the American dream for millions of restless migrants, ambitious entrepreneurs, and hopeful immigrants. Seeking freedom and opportunity to build new lives and break the bonds of old traditions, these newcomers created a dynamic new society that embraced egalitarianism, innovation, and materialism. By mid-century, California had become the most ethnically and racially diverse state in the nation, welcoming thousands daily to fuel the state's expanding economy and to establish ethnic enclaves in the state's urban and rural areas. By 1985, demographers predicted that California would become the first state in the continental United States to have a non-white majority in the first decade of the twenty-first century.

The response to this dramatic prediction of California's population has been similar to the classic stages of grief over the loss of a loved one or a traumatic personal injury: first there was "shock" at the disclosure, followed by "denial" of the data, then a stage of "bargaining" to try to modify the facts or change the outcome. By the 1990s, those politicians and power brokers who were ambivalent about the emerging majority of people of color and unwilling to accept its inevitability launched a series of initiatives that would effectively turn back the clock on the socioeconomic progress of minorities and immigrants in the state by undermining their civil rights, eroding their civil liberties, and restricting their access to educational, employment, and entrepreneurial opportunities. We maintain that these initiatives—Propositions 184, 187, 209, and 227—were not random, spontaneous movements of the state's electorate to address a series of voters' concerns, but rather were carefully conceived and orchestrated measures to manipulate voters to adopt reactionary public policies. We further contend that these policies in the areas of criminal justice (Proposition 184), illegal immigration (Proposition 187), affirmative action (Proposition 209), and bilingual education (Proposition 227) represent a form of "bargaining" by their sponsors and supporters who hope to slow the rapid growth of people of color in California or, failing that result, intend to limit their socioeconomic mobility and weaken their potential political power.

In 1994, the first two of these initiatives appeared on the November statewide election ballot as Proposition 184 (the "Three Strikes, You're Out" initiative) and Proposition 187 (the "Save Our State" initiative). Both of these initiatives were enthusiastically supported by then Governor Pete Wilson, who was running for reelection for a second term, and generously financed by the Republican Party. The "Three Strikes, You're Out" initiative was promoted as an anti-crime measure with a media campaign targeting middle-class, white voters concerned about urban crime, but it was also used as a wedge issue to polarize "soft-on-crime" liberals and "law and order" conservatives. Its supporters were fully aware that Proposition 184 would have a severe, disparate impact on African American and Latino males in the state's criminal justice system.

The "Save Our State" initiative was even more clearly used as a wedge issue by Governor Wilson's reelection campaign, as it explicitly targeted immigrants of color from Mexico and Central America. In this case, the campaign manipulated both the anxieties of working-class voters about economic security and the prejudices of middle-class voters toward "illegal aliens." The Republican Party also endorsed and generously financed Proposition 187, apparently unconcerned about alienating the state's growing number of Latino voters.

In 1996, following the successful passage of Propositions 184 and 187, Governor Wilson played a crucial role in supporting Proposition 209, the California Civil Rights initiative. Having secured his second gubernatorial term with the help of two ethnically divisive initiatives, he made a calculated decision to use affirmative action as a wedge issue to advance his presidential ambitions. Once again, the Republican Party endorsed and funded Proposition 209, aggressively launching a campaign to disavow the intent and the principles of affirmative action and to retreat from three decades of civil rights legislation in California.

In 1998, Proposition 227, the "English for the Children" initiative, was launched by Ron Unz, another Republican politician aspiring to statewide office. This measure, which substantially eviscerated the state's bilingual education programs, targeted California's public school pupils with limited English proficiency, 80 percent of whom were Spanish-speaking. The Republican Party, as well as many of the same conservative organizations and individuals who had endorsed and financed the previous three initiatives, pledged their allegiance to this ballot measure. Latinos interpreted the passage of Proposition 227 as yet another assault on their community and a significant threat to the educational opportunities of their children.

In this book, we first intend to trace briefly the major historical, social, economic, and political events of the past fifty years (1948–1998) that laid the foundation for the impetus of these ethnically and racially divisive initiatives. During this period, as the demographic, technological, and economic changes have transformed the social and cultural landscape of California, interethnic and interracial tensions have accompanied them. These tensions have frequently escalated into conflicts over economic resources, employment opportunities, educational policies, religious practices, and political power. Unscrupulous community leaders and unprincipled politicians have all too often manipulated the anxieties and prejudices of the public to advance their own parochial agendas and political ambitions.

Second, we examine each of the four propositions that form the core of this book, describing and analyzing the background factors leading to their development, the pro and con arguments of their advocates and opponents, their major financial contributors, their campaign strategies, their ethnic voting patterns, the implications of their implementation, and the overall evaluation of their disproportionate impact on people of color.

Third, we discuss the role of the initiative process itself in California as a pace-setter and role model for other states in formulating public policies that represent a backlash against the liberal-progressive policies of the 1960s and 1970s, such as prison reform, immigration rights, affirmative action, and bilingual education. The inherent limitations of the initiative process are also examined. National trends are then compared to international trends in these same areas, which have emerged as some of the most controversial public policy issues in many of the Western industrialized countries. It is instructive to examine the national and international perspectives on these issues in order to place the California developments in a much broader, comparative context.

Fourth, we examine the trend toward "identity politics" in the California political culture as an example of its prominence in political discourse throughout the nation. Each of the four initiatives provides examples of the complex interplay of ethnicity, gender, socioeconomic status, and political affiliation in shaping voters' perceptions, attitudes, and decision making. As ethnicity becomes a more salient factor in voter behavior, political parties and their candidates may find themselves held hostage by large blocs of minority, white, or suburban voters.

Finally, we conclude the book with a discussion of the values that should guide public policy debates in a multiethnic, multicultural society. Adopting these values as a framework, we propose specific policy alternatives to address the issues of crime prevention and control, illegal immigration, affirmative action, and bilingual education. In proposing these alternative policies, our intention is to reframe the contemporary debates from an ethnocentric, exclusionary perspective to a multicultural, inclusive perspective on the future of California as a state and the welfare of the United States as a nation as it moves toward a society that will be divided equally between whites and people of color by the middle of the twenty-first century.

Historians note that the state of California was colonized by Spanish soldiers, Christianized by Spanish missionaries who proselytized the indigenous Indians, and developed by the labor of Mexicans and racially mixed mestizos and mulattoes before it became a state in 1850. It is not without considerable irony that 150 years after statehood, these same groups are emerging as the majority of California's residents, poised to reclaim their heritage and to reassert their right to determine the future course of their native state. The key question for the electorate is whether or not California will ultimately serve as a crucible for the explosion of a reactionary backlash, interethnic "wars," and urban riots, or as a laboratory for the development of an authentic multicultural and egalitarian society in America.

# Acknowledgments

This book has been a collaborative process since 1996 when we became increasingly concerned about the impact of several ballot initiatives on immigrants of color and ethnic minority groups in California. In order to gather the extensive political, demographic, and sociocultural information for this book, we enlisted the assistance of many organizations, professionals, community leaders, and students throughout the state. We owe all of them a debt of gratitude for the gracious gift of their time, their information, and their insights.

In particular we wish to express our sincere thanks to the following individuals, organizations, and groups: the Zellerbach Family Fund in San Francisco for their generous financial support of an endowed chair for the senior author and annual research grants since 1993 to support the research for this book in California, England, and Canada; Eddie Williams, President of the Joint Center for Political and Economic Studies in Washington, DC, and his staff for supporting my research on Afro-Caribbean youth in England, while I was a Distinguished Visiting Scholar at the Center in 1991–1992 (J.T.G.); Professor John Solomos at Birkbeck College, University of London in England, for his helpful insights and constructive suggestions about the Afro-Caribbean community during my affiliation as a Visiting Scholar at the College in the spring of 1992 and summer of 1993 (J.T.G.); Daphne Stratham, Director of the National Institute of Social Work in London, England, and her staff for facilitating my research on Afro-Caribbean youth in England during my affiliation as a Visiting Scholar at the Institute in the spring of 1992 (J.T.G.); Acting Dean Marion Bogo and the staff at the Faculty of Social Work, University of Toronto in Toronto, Canada, for facilitating my research on Afro-Caribbean youth in Canada while I was a Visiting Professor at the University in the fall of 1994 (J.T.G.); directors, staff members, and clients of social service and community agencies in Toronto, Canada, and in Birmingham, London, Liverpool, and Manchester, England, who graciously consented to lengthy interviews on the status of Afro-Caribbean youth for research conducted in their respective communities in 1992, 1993, and 1994; staff members of governmental agencies in Toronto, Canada, and London, England, who provided demographic data and information on social welfare services, the criminal justice system, employment, education and health services for the Afro-Caribbean community, particularly the Commission for Racial Equality (London) and Statistics Canada (Toronto); Dean James Midgley and colleagues at the School of Social Welfare, University of California at Berkeley, for their encouragement and scholarly support of this project; the staff of the Center on Juvenile and Criminal Justice and the Justice Policy Institute, particularly Vincent Schiraldi and Dan Macallair; the staff and Board of Directors of the American Civil Liberties Union (ACLU) of Northern California, especially Phillip Mehas, Roberta Speikerman, Irving Hockman, and Florence Moore; professional colleagues and community leaders in the San Francisco-Oakland Bay Area who were interviewed for this book for their helpful observations and insights about racial and ethnic relations in California; numerous reference archivists at the California State Archives, a division of the Office of the Secretary of State, Bill Jones, in Sacramento, California, for their help in retrieving information about the initiatives and the election results for three election cycles; graduate student researchers Laura Abrams, Virginia Duplessis, Sandra Owens Kane, and Joseph Merighi for their thorough, competent, and timely assistance with a variety of challenging assignments; James Steele, Assistant Dean for Administration, and his competent and cooperative office staff for their logistical support in facilitating this project; Sharon M. Ikami for her enthusiasm, efficiency, and unfailing good humor in preparing many versions of this manuscript; James Lowell Gibbs, Jr. for his long-term commitment to my professional development and his unflagging devotion as my lifelong partner and best friend (J.T.G.); Sandra Bankhead, my politically progressive mother, for her creative and grounding reinforcement (T. B.); Angelo Lamont Butler, criminal defense attorney, legislative analyst, civil libertarian, loving husband and impassioned friend, for his unyielding support and encouragement (T. B.).

Finally, we offer heartfelt thanks to our extended families, colleagues, and numerous friends who, throughout the past four years, have provided us with advice, guidance, thoughtful ideas, and suggestions, including

Lowell D. Gibbs, Geoffrey T. Gibbs, Shirlee Taylor Haizlip, Veronique Thompson, S. Omowale Fowles, NaNotchka Chumley, Facile Retta, Colleen Floyd- Carroll, Michael Carroll, and Vernon Mouton.

Some of the ideas developed in this book were first aired in my 1997 Gerald J. Seabury Lecture at the School of Social Welfare. The lecture was later issued as a short monograph (*The California Crucible: Towards a New Paradigm on Race and Ethnic Relations* by J. T. Gibbs, San Francisco: Study Center Press, 1998). I wish to acknowledge the contribution of Marjorie Beggs and the staff of the San Francisco Study Center to that monograph, as well as the support of the Zellerbach Family Fund, for its publication and dissemination (J.T.G.).

# CHAPTER 1

# The California Crucible:
# Melting Pot or Cauldron?

> The new nativism we see in California—expressed through the attempt to pass the English-only proposition, and more recently in the passage of Proposition 187 and the introduction of the California Civil Rights Initiative—reflects a sense of loss of white control over the affairs of the state.
> —Patricia Zavella (1997, 136)

In the last decade of the twentieth century, California has become the battleground on which the dwindling white populace has staged a last stand against an emerging non-white majority whom they view as a growing threat to their Anglo-American culture, economic dominance, and political control. As California has reluctantly faced the prospect of becoming the first state in the continental United States to have a majority of people of color, white Californians have increasingly mirrored the fears and anxieties of the dominant culture that these ethnic minorities, darker-skinned immigrants, and refugees will engulf them in an inevitable tide of unfamiliar and undesirable values and mores, that they will dilute or destroy the traditional American middle- class way of life, and that they will (God forbid!) mongrelize the society through interracial marriage, mating, and miscegenation. Thus, as the largest and most ethnically diverse state, it is not surprising that California has become the battlefield for the opposing forces of monoculturalism versus multiculturalism, white privilege versus affirmative action, "English only" versus bilingualism, inclusion versus exclusion.

These opposing forces have drawn their battle lines in four political campaigns in the 1990s, the decade in which the electorate witnessed epic struggles over four controversial statewide initiatives on the California ballot: Proposition 184, the "Three Strikes, You're Out" initiative, and Proposition 187, the "Save Our State" initiative, both passed in 1994; Proposition 209, the California Civil Rights initiative, passed in 1996; and Proposition 227, the "English for the Children" initiative, passed in 1998. Those four initiatives have come to symbolize the struggle between the old guard and the new majority emerging in California politics, the conflict between liberals and conservatives, and the widening gulf between the powerful and the powerless.

These four propositions are not new issues in the history of California's ambivalent treatment of its ethnic minorities and immigrants of color. Since California joined the Union in 1850, the state's politicians, power brokers, and labor leaders have alternated between welcoming people of color and demonizing them, largely reflecting the cycles of economic prosperity and depression. More recently, conservative politicians and business leaders have advanced their own elitist and self-serving agendas by financing the campaigns behind this series of nativist and exclusionary initiatives. In an era of "wedge issues," the California electorate has proven itself to be woefully misinformed and easily manipulated by monied interests and the media.

California, as the nation's trendsetter of social, cultural, and political movements, is a bellwether state in forecasting social change in the rest of the United States. Since California has successfully adopted these four propositions that impact disproportionately and negatively on minorities and immigrants of color, over two dozen states have launched similar initiatives or passed similar legislation in one or more areas of criminal justice, immigration reform, affirmative action, or bilingual education. California has proven to be the crucible in which these issues have generated extreme heat, have inflamed the voters, and have survived the test of public approval. As California goes, will the nation blindly follow? Or will voters in other states examine these issues with more information, more objectivity, and greater understanding of the serious long-term implications of public policies that will increase hostilities between whites and people of color and threaten the delicate fabric of racial and ethnic reconciliation and cooperation?

In this book, we examine all of these provocative issues and also compare the trends in California to similar trends emerging in Canada and England, two English-speaking countries also struggling to incorporate immigrants and refugees whose ethnic backgrounds and cultural heritages are quite different from their native-born populations. In both of these countries, as in the United States, ethnic and cultural differences are often perceived as a threat to the integrity of the country's traditional culture and homogeneous society, yet Canada and England both have developed rational policies and programs to promote inclusion while respecting diversity. An examination of current Canadian and British policies toward immigrants and ethnic minorities provides a useful framework for a discussion of alternative policy options in our own society, which we propose at the end of this book.

## DEMOGRAPHIC TRENDS

If the 1990's are any indication, the coming years are likely to bring great volatility and rancor in the public debate about immigration. Indeed, race, ethnicity and immigration status, and the intersection of these increasingly overlapping characteristics, may prove to be the social dividing lines in the United States for the foreseeable future.

Kevin R. Johnson (1997, 166)

Since 1970, the United States has undergone a social and cultural transformation that is surpassed only by the waves of European immigration in the peak years from 1840 to 1930 and the mass migration of millions of African Americans from the rural South to the urban North and West from 1910 to 1940. These newer immigrants and refugees have profoundly altered the racial and ethnic demographic profile of the country, reducing the proportion of non-Hispanic whites from 79.8 percent in 1980 to 71.8 percent in 2000 (est.) (U.S. Bureau of the Census, 1999). By the year 2010, Hispanics/Latinos are predicted to become the largest minority group, displacing African Americans whose proportion of the population has remained relatively stable, ranging from 11.5 percent in 1980 to 12.2 percent in 2000 (est.), but predicted to grow at a slower rate by 2010. However, within the Hispanic/Latino population, estimated at 31.3 million on July 1, 1999, growing diversity is reflected in greater differentiation between the needs and priorities of the older, better established immigrant groups such as Cubans, Mexican Americans, and Puerto Ricans versus those of the more recent immigrants and refugees from Central and South America (Hispanic, 2000).

Asians and Pacific Islanders, the fastest-growing minority population, increased nearly 150 percent from 3,563,000 in 1980 to 8,715,000 in 1995 and grew to an estimated 10.8 million by July 1, 1999 (U.S. Bureau of the Census, 1999; Hispanic, 2000). Fueled by three waves of Vietnamese and Southeast Asian refugees after the end of the Vietnam War, this rapid growth in the Asian/Pacific Islander population has also revealed some schisms among the forty-four groups who make up this broad census designation, raising valid questions about classifying such disparate groups as Chinese, Hawaiians, Filipinos, Indonesians, and Pacific Islanders in the same broad ethnocultural category. As the Japanese population has declined (due to

3

low birth rates and high rates of interracial marriage), there have been contrasting increases in the growth of the Korean, Filipino, and Southeast Asian groups. South Asians from India and Pakistan, a minuscule part of the Asian population in 1980, now account for 11.2 percent of Asian Americans (U.S. Bureau of the Census, 1999). Unlike some previous groups of Asian immigrants, South Asian immigrants came into the United States with a high proportion of people with professional and technical skills, found stable employment in high-technology firms, and have dispersed themselves geographically throughout the nation's major metropolitan areas, but disproportionately in areas of high technology industries such as Silicon Valley in Northern California.

Filipinos, the second largest group of Asians in America, are, in some ways, the most acculturated when they arrive. As a former protectorate of the United States, the Philippines has long had an ambivalent relationship with the United States, but its citizens grow up in a very Americanized culture, speaking English as a second language. Filipinos, like Japanese Americans, have high rates of intermarriage and have avoided the residential segregation that other Asian groups have experienced.

African Americans, who have been the nation's largest ethnic minority group since before the Civil War, estimated at 34.8 million on July 1, 1999, have had to confront some internal and external challenges to this claim (Hispanic, 2000). Despite the widespread perception that blacks constitute a homogeneous population, there is a great deal of diversity beyond the usual class and regional divisions. As a consequence of the economic and political upheavals in Africa and the Caribbean during the 1980s and 1990s, the population of African and Caribbean American blacks has swelled, particularly in major metropolitan centers in the East and Midwest. These groups brought their own cultural attributes with them, creating an uneasy alliance with American-born blacks. Further, the growth of interracial marriages, which more than doubled from 651,000 in 1980 to 1,392,000 in 1995, has fueled a debate about racial identity and racial classification that has serious implications for estimating the size of the group (Gibbs, 1998).

For most of the twentieth century, American Indians, the smallest of the four major ethnic groupings, estimated at 2.3 million on July 1, 1999, have been in the unfortunate position of being the most economically disadvantaged, most isolated, and most marginalized of the minority groups (Hispanic, 2000). This overall description does not, however, do justice to the diversity and complexity among the 330 federally recognized Indian tribes and the many smaller bands recognized by state and local governments throughout the country (LaFromboise & Low, 1998). Indian tribal groups also represent a broad range of cultures, lifestyles, social organizations, and levels of acculturation. Inspired by the American Indian Movement (AIM) of the 1970s, Indian leaders have become increasingly assertive about reclaiming their ancestral lands, fishing and mineral rights, and protecting their sacred burial places. Since the early 1980s, several Indian tribes have established gambling casinos on their reservations, a development that has been both a boon and a bane to their communities.

Since 1980, when demographers began calling attention to the rapidly increasing proportion of non-whites in the U.S. population, social scientists, politicians, educators, and business leaders have been discussing and debating the implications of these changes for the society. In the early 1980s, these discussions focused primarily on the impact of these changes on the educational system and the labor force, highlighting the potential problems and challenges for educators and employers in absorbing and integrating students and workers from diverse racial and ethnic backgrounds. By the late 1980s, the focus shifted from the issues of racial and ethnic diversity to the issues of immigration, with particular concern about immigrants of color from "third-world" countries such as those in Africa, Asia, the Caribbean, and Latin America, who were frequently portrayed in the media in stereotypical images as a threat to the stability and sanctity of American society (Borjas, 1990, 1999; Brimelow, 1995).

## CALIFORNIA: THE CRUCIBLE OF CHANGE

> Latino and Asian political empowerment is a certainty, one way or another. As we get closer to the presidential election (in 2000), people are looking at these numbers and they're seeing what the future is. The key to California is getting the support of these groups.
>
> Peter Morrison (cited in McLeod, 1998, 22)

While these demographic changes were igniting racial and ethnic tensions in various areas of the country, nowhere were they more apparent than in the state of California, the largest and most diverse state in the nation. As of 1990, California symbolized the ethnic and racial transformation of American society with a total population base of nearly thirty million, including 57.3 percent non-Hispanic whites, 25.8 percent Hispanics/Latinos, 7.4 percent African Americans/blacks, 8.5 percent Asians/Pacific Islanders, 1 percent of "others" (Johnson, 1999).

Demographers and policy analysts have suggested that the Hispanic population is very fluid, and probably underestimated in California and other border states, as many of the undocumented workers frequently travel between the states and Mexico or Central America for extended periods of time. African Americans and Asians may also be underestimated due to the methodological difficulties in obtaining reliable estimates of inner city and immigrant populations. Despite the potential undercounting of ethnic minorities, at the end of the 1990s, people of color clearly constituted about half of California's population, and in the year 2000 they exceeded the white population of the state by a slight majority (Johnson, 1999).

In the year 2000, California became the first minority-majority state in the nation, with people of color constituting 52 percent of the population and non-Hispanic whites 48 percent (est.) (Johnson, 1999). Currently 60 percent of the public school students in California are from ethnic minority groups (39 percent are Latinos), speaking over 100 languages and dialects. As California goes, so goes the nation, with demographers predicting that by 2020, other states such as Texas, New Mexico, Arizona, and Florida will also have minority-majority populations.

Throughout the state of California, there has been frequent media speculation over the precise moment when non-Hispanic whites would become a "minority" population, fueled by talk- show hosts, op-ed articles, and political commentators. These media commentaries reflected an underlying anxiety about the demographic shifts and their implications for the schools, the workplace, economic development, political power, and community life. A prominent theme running through the debate was the perceived threat to America's cultural identity, the fear of the majority being swallowed up, overwhelmed, and absorbed by a creolized minority (Maharidge, 1996).

> They [Los Angelenos] talk of non-white immigration . . . the way the Egyptians must have spoken about the inflictions of Jehovah. All that's missing are the biblical categories for the disaster. A plague of wetbacks? (Rieff, 1991, 132)

## ETHNIC DIVERSITY AND PUBLIC POLICY

> [T]he increased visibility of new immigrants, the sight of veiled women in suburban supermarkets, the proliferation of mosques in large cities, the prevalent sound of Spanish in the streets, and the proliferation of small businesses with Korean, Indian, Arabic and other ethnic advertising have aroused middle-class resentment in the 1990's similar to that observed nearly a century earlier.
>
> Thomas Muller (1997, 109)

These demographic trends and evidence of increasing tensions between whites and non-whites in California, as well as potential conflicts between native-borns and immigrants, obviously have important implications for the development of public policy in California, particularly for the four issues of public policy that have been heated topics of debate in California in the 1990s, and they will assume greater significance as national issues in the twenty-first century. These issues include "three strikes" laws, affirmative action, immigration reform, and bilingual education, all of which impact disproportionately on ethnic minority groups, and two of which are specifically targeted at non-English-speaking immigrants.

These concerns escalated after the Los Angeles civil disturbances of 1992, particularly in Southern California where the immediate impact of the riots was so devastating and so divisive. However, the impact of those riots on race relations in Los Angeles reverberated throughout the state and nation in terms of their long-term threat to the balance of power between majority and minority groups, between the "haves" and the "have nots," and between the powerful and the powerless (Gibbs, 1996; Gooding-Williams, 1993; Hahn, 1996).

Given that all of these issues have been part of the political discourse in California for some time, waxing and waning with the economic trends and the political power blocs in the state, a convincing argument can be made that all of these ballot initiatives became more socially salient, more politically viable, and more strategically possible because of the powerful xenophobic and racist fears aroused throughout the state in the aftermath of the 1992 Los Angeles riots (Maharidge, 1996; Schrag, 1998).

In fact, Proposition 184, known as the "Three Strikes, You're Out" law, was passed by the California voters in 1994, two years after the riots, by a majority vote of 72 percent, despite the opposition of most law enforcement agencies, labor unions, women's groups, and civil rights organizations (California Secretary of State's Office, 1995). As the prison population in California is disproportionately African American and Latino, the passage of this bill was predicted to have an extremely punitive effect on minority males, who generally tend to be arrested, charged, and convicted at higher rates than whites for comparable offenses (Walker, Spohn, & Delone, 1996).

In 1994, the California electorate also decisively supported the adoption of Proposition 187, the "Save Our State" initiative, by a vote of 59 percent versus 41 percent (Armbruster, Geron, & Bonacich, 1995). This initiative provided for the denial of basic health care, social services, and public education to undocumented immigrants as a way of discouraging a further influx of illegal Mexican and Central American immigrants. Although there is no hard evidence to link the passage of this anti-immigrant legislation to the 1992 riots, one can speculate that the television images of Latinos looting the stores, destroying property, and taunting the police, beamed around the state for four days and nights, might have contributed at least marginally to voter dissatisfaction and anger at Latinos whom they perceived as lawbreakers and ungrateful trespassers (Gooding-Williams, 1993; Hahn, 1996; Maharidge, 1996).

In 1996, California voters adopted Proposition 209, the "California Civil Rights Initiative" (CCRI), to eliminate affirmative action in public employment, state university and college admissions and hiring, and state contracting by a majority vote of 55 percent versus 45 percent (Chavez, 1998). The immediate impact of Proposition 209 on admissions to the professional schools at the University of California resulted in a precipitous drop in minority admissions, particularly at the two most selective campuses at

Berkeley and Los Angeles. Combined with an earlier ruling of the Board of Regents to eliminate race, ethnicity, and sex as criteria for admission to the university, undergraduate admissions of minority students also plummeted the following year at several of the most competitive campuses.

Buoyed by their string of victories in 1994 and 1996, conservative politicians and organizations launched another assault on immigrants in 1998 with Proposition 227, "English for the Children," the initiative that severely restricted access to and participation in bilingual education programs in California public schools. As in the three previous ballot initiatives, this proposition was supported by a coalition of organizations and prominent individuals with ties to right-wing causes with a documented history of opposition to school integration, immigration, gun control, prison reform, and other progressive policies. Proposition 227 was adopted by a margin of 61 percent of the California electorate, although the majority of Latino voters rejected it (Asimov, 1998).

Despite its reputation for tolerance and diversity, California has developed its own home-grown conservative movement, harbored its fair share of right-wing groups, and nurtured a Western brand of nativism that often borders on paranoia (Stefancic, 1997). California is also the birthplace of the John Birch Society and two Republican presidents, Richard Nixon and Ronald Reagan, both self-styled moderates who were elected on conservative party planks in 1968 and 1980, respectively. From the early Spanish missionaries, who laid the foundation for the missions that spawned the major cities along the California coast, to the latter day politicians who exploit the public's anxieties about urban crime and immigrant labor, California has been the site of both accommodation and conflict between Anglo-Americans and people of color, between native-born and foreign-born, between migrants and immigrants. In the 1990s, these unresolved conflicts seemed to escalate, unleashing the fears and anxieties of whites about racial violence, fueling the flames of racial prejudice, and generating an unprecedented backlash of punitive and divisive public policies (Maharidge, 1996; Schrag, 1998).

## OVERVIEW: PAST, PRESENT, AND FUTURE ISSUES

In order to provide a context for understanding these four initiatives, in Chapter 2 we provide a brief history and contemporary portrait of the migrants and immigrants who comprise the California mosaic of ethnic and racial groups, describing their diverse pathways to California, their strategies of adaptation and acculturation, and their patterns of mobility and migration.

In Chapter 3 we focus on Los Angeles as the quintessential example of a multicultural, multiethnic city and examine how it responds to massive demographic changes that have threatened to destroy it as a community. We also discuss the seismic impact of the 1992 disturbances in Los Angeles after the acquittal of three of the four police officers accused of assaulting Rodney King, assessing the direct and indirect effects of those disturbances on race and ethnic relations in Los Angeles. We also analyze the spillover impact of those riots throughout the state of California in terms of polarizing whites and non-whites, fueling the conservative social agenda, and fostering punitive public policies.

In Chapter 4 we examine the complex relationship between race, ethnicity, and crime in California that influenced the passage of Proposition 184, the "Three Strikes, You're Out" initiative, as well as how that relationship is socially constructed by the media and political demagogues to reinforce the public fears and stereotypes about violence, even in the face of dramatically declining crime rates.

Media images and political rhetoric are explored in Chapter 5 along with major factors that may have contributed to the passage of Proposition 187, the "Save Our State" initiative, such as scapegoating of immigrants due to economic insecurity, technological changes, and social dislocation of native-born working class and white-collar workers in the transformation of the California economy from a predominantly agribusiness and industrial state to a high-technology, information processing and service economy.

An analysis of the Proposition 209 campaign for the "California Civil Rights Initiative" and the severity of its impact on state university admissions in California is discussed in Chapter 6, as well as its long-term implications for California's changing labor force and economic productivity in the twenty-first century.

In Chapter 7 the debate about Proposition 227, the "English for the Children" bilingual education initiative, is discussed, as well as the broader issue of the role of language and ethnicity in framing debates about cultural identity, equality of educational opportunity, acculturation, and assimilation in American society.

California's influential role in the spread of these policies to other states is discussed in Chapter 8, which also employs a comparative perspective on policies of race and ethnic relations in the United States with similar policies in Canada and England. The racial and cultural conflicts in American society between whites and people of color are analogous to those in Canadian and British societies, but these countries have responded with programs and policies that provide alternative models of dealing with diversity, models that are generally more inclusive, less ethnocentric, and less divisive.

In Chapter 9 we analyze the four propositions from the perspective of ethnic identity politics, examining the proposition that these controversial initiatives collectively represent a concerted attempt by the Anglo-American majority to maintain their traditional position of economic, political, and cultural dominance by limiting the access, the opportunity, and the mobility of immigrants of color and ethnic minority groups in California. The responses of people of color to these initiatives are viewed from the prism of their perceived ethnic interests, needs, and priorities to assert their rights and privileges to full membership in American society.

Chapter 10, the final chapter, addresses the implications of these four new laws for the future of racial and ethnic relations in California and, by extension, to the rest of the nation. Proposals are offered for alternative public policies that would be more humane, more inclusive, and more progressive to promote a more harmonious and productive multiethnic and multicultural society in the twenty-first century.

Throughout this book we also develop four major themes. First, we describe and evaluate arguments of the advocates and opponents of these four propositions, illustrating how special interest groups, sometimes facilitated by partisan representatives of the media, manipulated each of these controversial issues through misinformation and sensationalism. We document their political and financial support and follow the money trail to demonstrate the intricate web of relationships among the supporters of these propositions, in an effort to determine whether these coalitions simply reflect a nativistic ideological view of American society or whether they reflect a coordinated conservative public policy agenda for the twenty-first century.

Second, we examine the immediate impact of the four propositions on people of color and immigrant groups, who have been targeted by these initiatives in a number of ways to limit significantly their civil rights, their civil liberties, and their access to social, economic, and educational resources that afford equality and foster mobility in American society. We also assess the potential adverse effects of these laws with respect to potential long-term consequences for these groups, such as educational failure, economic impoverishment, long-term incarceration, deprivation of civil rights, and political disenfranchisement.

Third, we assess the short-term effects of these propositions on race and ethnic relations between whites and people of color in California. This is particularly salient as the proportion of non-whites and Hispanics emerges as a majority of people of color at the beginning of this century. Public policies and legislation that exacerbate tensions between whites and people of color are not likely to promote cooperation and constructive relations between these groups. Even more troubling is the prospect that the "culture wars," predicted in the 1990s by Pat Buchanan and other icons of the far right, will erupt as ethnic groups assert their cultural identities and resist the evanescent promise of the mythical melting pot, which has never truly materialized for people of color in America.

Fourth, we extrapolate from these issues and trends in California to the rest of the nation by showing how California has already set a dubious example in race/ethnic relations by adopting a set of policies that can be characterized as conservative, regressive, divisive, and punitive rather than liberal, progressive, inclusive, and rehabilitative. If other states continue to follow California's lead in its policies toward immigrants and minorities of color, the nation will find itself confronted by a series of "ethnic wars" or intensive ethnic conflicts as the burgeoning population of these people of color assert their rights to equal education, equal employment opportunity, equal rights, and equal justice in a multiracial, multicultural democracy in the twenty-first century.

California can be viewed as a crucible where these intense issues of race, ethnicity, and culture are heating up as people of color challenge the dominant Anglo-American establishment over economic control, political power, and cultural dominance. California can also be viewed as a metaphor for the maelstrom of social and cultural changes that are taking root and rapidly spreading throughout the nation, hastening the creolization of American society in nearly every dimension through interracial/interethnic marriage, spicy ethnic foods and exotic restaurants, hip hop urban dress and music, salsa and reggae from the Caribbean, yoga and the martial arts from Asia, herbal medicines and Hindu temples, Muslim mosques, and myriad transcultural transformations. Above all, California has always been the harbinger of new trends, new ideas, and new values, and as California goes, so goes the nation. California has become the battleground, at the dawn of the millennium, where the issues of race, class, and culture are being played out on a giant media screen, projected instantaneously by satellite around the nation and to the world where people of color are an overwhelming majority, looking to America for leadership in creating viable solutions for a brave new world.

## REFERENCES

Armbruster, R., Geron, K., & Bonacich, E. (1995). The assault on California's Latino immigrants: The politics of Proposition 187. *International Journal of Urban and Regional Research, 19*(4), 655–663.

Asimov, N. (1998). Big victory for measure to end bilingual education. *San Francisco Chronicle*, February 25, A12.

Borjas, G. J. (1990). *Friends or strangers: The impact of immigrants on the U.S. economy*. New York: Basic Books.

Borjas, G. J. (1999). *Heaven's door*. Princeton, NJ: Princeton University Press.

Brimelow, A. (1995). *Alien nation: Common sense about America's immigration disaster*. New York: Random House.

California Secretary of State's Office. (1995). *Financing California statewide ballot measures: 1994 primary and general elections*. Sacramento, CA: Political Reform Division.

Chavez, L. (1998). *The color bind: California's battle to end affirmative action*. Berkeley: University of California Press.

Gibbs, J. T. (1996). *Race and justice: Rodney King and O. J. Simpson in a house divided*. San Francisco: Jossey-Bass.

Gibbs, J. T. (1998). Biracial adolescents. In J. T. Gibbs & L. N. Huang (Eds.), *Children of color: Psychological interventions with culturally diverse youth* (pp. 305–333). San Francisco: Jossey-Bass.

Gooding-Williams, R. (Ed.). (1993). *Reading Rodney King/Reading urban uprising.* New York: Routledge.

Hahn, H. (1996). Los Angeles and the future: Uprisings, identity, and new institutions. In M. Dear, H. Schockman, & G. Hise (Eds.), *Rethinking Los Angeles* (pp. 77–95). Thousand Oaks, CA: Sage Publications.

Hispanic and Asian populations expand. (2000). *New York Times,* August 30, A15.

Johnson, H. (1999). How many Californians? A review of population projections for the state. *California Counts: Profiles and Trends, 1*(1), 10–15.

Johnson, K. R. (1997). The new nativism: Something old, something new, something borrowed, something blue. In J. F. Perea (Ed.), *Immigrants out! The new nativism and the anti-immigrant impulse in the United States* (pp. 165–189). New York: New York University Press.

LaFromboise, T., & Low, K. G. (1998). American Indian children and adolescents. In J. T. Gibbs & L. N. Huang (Eds.), *Children of color: Psychological interventions with culturally diverse youth* (pp. 112–142). San Francisco: Jossey-Bass.

Maharidge, D. (1996). *The coming white minority: California, multiculturalism and America's future.* New York: Vintage Books.

McLeod, R. G. (1998). Minority majority well on its way in state. *San Francisco Chronicle,* September 4, p. 22.

Muller, T. (1997). Nativism in the mid-1990s: Why now? In J. F. Perea (Ed.), *Immigrants out! The new nativism and the anti-immigrant impulse in the United States* (pp. 105–118). New York: New York University Press.

Preston, M. B., & Lai, J. S. (1998). The symbolic politics of affirmative action. In M. B. Preston, B. E. Cain, & S. Bass (Eds.), *Racial and ethnic politics in California. Vol. II* (pp. 61–198). Berkeley: Institute of Governmental Studies Press, University of California, Berkeley.

Rieff, D. (1991). *Los Angeles: Capital of the third world.* New York: Simon & Schuster.

Schrag, P. (1998). *Paradise lost: California's experiences, America's future.* Berkeley: University of California Press.

Stefancic, J. (1997). Funding the nativist agenda. In J. F. Perea (Ed.), *Immigrants out! The new nativism and the anti-immigrant impulse in the United States* (pp. 119–135). New York: New York University Press.

U.S. Bureau of the Census. (1999). *Statistical abstract of the United States* (119th Ed.). Washington, DC: U.S. Department of Commerce.

Walker, S., Spohn, C., & Delone, M. (1996). *The color of justice.* Belmont, CA: Wadsworth.

Zavella, P. (1997). The tables are turned: Immigration, poverty and social conflict in California communities. In J. F. Perea (Ed.), *Immigrants out! The new nativism and the anti-immigrant impulse in the United States* (pp. 136–161). New York: New York University Press.

# CHAPTER 2

# Coming to California:
# Chasing the Dream

[My mother] told me California was a special place where people judged you
on what you did and nothing else. So I worked hard and studied hard. I've always believed California is a very special place. . . . It's a place where if you
work hard . . . you can set your goals high and not only dream dreams, but
you and your children can then go out and realize them.
—Tom Bradley, Mayor of Los Angeles (qtd. in Rieff, 1991, 62)

## SAN FRANCISCO: GATEWAY TO ASIA

If one visits the International Terminal at the San Francisco Airport (per-
petually under construction since the 1960s to accommodate the ever increasing flow of immigrants, refugees, businessmen, and tourists), one
can see the hundreds of Asians and Pacific Islanders arriving daily, tired
but excited, speaking rapidly in a cacophony of musical languages, with
children, aging parents, and precious possessions in tow. As they fly in
low over the Pacific Ocean, the pilot will graciously point out the Golden
Gate Bridge, as much a symbol of freedom and opportunity to them as the
Statue of Liberty was for the millions of European immigrants who
streamed through the turnstiles of Ellis Island in the early years of the
twentieth century.

As the hub of the second largest metropolitan area in California, San Francisco epitomizes the tolerance, sophistication, and optimism of Northern California with its proximity to two world-class universities, Silicon Valley, and expensive suburban satellite communities. From the early days of the Gold Rush and the transcontinental railroad, San Francisco has attracted Asian immigrants as laborers, skilled craftspersons, and small entrepreneurs. After the Vietnam War, the San Francisco Bay Area was one of the major ports of disembarkation for thousands of Southeast Asian refugees, who added more spice and style to the city's ethnic salad bowl. In more recent years, the growth of the corporations and the telecommunications industry has spurred a new wave of immigrants from East and South Asia, spawning a new breed of entrepreneurs and the upscale services to cater to their cultural preferences.

Although the heterogeneous Asian population has become the largest ethnic minority group in San Francisco, the City-by-the-Bay has also witnessed the influx of sizable groups of immigrants and refugees from Central America, East Africa, Eastern Europe, and the Middle East, testing both its ability to absorb so many ethnic groups and its flexibility in adapting to such diverse cultures.

In 1997, non-Hispanic whites were only 39 percent of the city of San Francisco's population, compared to 35 percent of Asians, 17 percent of Latinos, 11 percent of African Americans, and less than 1 percent of "others" (Johnson, 1999). While Los Angeles reflects a distinctive Latino culture, San Francisco owes its predominant international flavor to Asia. In just over 25 years, the population of the San Francisco Bay Area (including the six counties surrounding San Francisco to the north, south, and east) shifted from a non-Hispanic white majority population of 77 percent in 1970 to a bare majority of 54 percent in 1997. In 1997, Asians and Latinos in the Bay Area metropolitan region each constituted 19 percent, African Americans 9 percent, and American Indians only 1 percent of the people of color, but non-whites are predicted to become the majority of the Bay Area's population by 2008.

> It is a dramatic change, but what is happening today is much more in keeping with the state's history than that brief period in the mid-century when it seemed like the only people who came here were whites from other states. (Hans Johnson, cited in McLeod, 1998, 22)

## THE LURE OF GOLD MOUNTAIN

California, with its lure of gold, its abundant land, and its balmy climate, has attracted immigrants, adventurers, and visionaries ever since it was explored by Spanish missionaries in the eighteenth century. The Golden State has been a magnet for many looking for a new opportunity, a changed lifestyle, a new start. Successive waves of migrants and immigrants have arrived to seek their fortune in the gently rolling hills, the verdant valleys, the pristine lakes, and the sun-baked desert of California. The latter-day migrants came as pioneers in movie making, computers, television, and communications with their theme song "California Dreamin'" and their inchoate yearnings to find their own places in the sun—dreams of land, wealth, power, success, and fame.

From its earliest days as part of the northward expansion of the Spanish conquest of Mexico, California has cultivated close ties with Mexico and reflected the Spanish-Indian culture in its language, its land grants, its religion, and its architecture. The missions founded by Father Junipero Serra in his travels from Baja, California, north along the Pacific Coast bore the Spanish names of San Diego, Los Angeles, Santa Barbara, San Jose, and San Francisco, all destined to become major centers of commerce, industry, and culture in the new state of California (Starr, 1985).

European immigrants and native-born discontents, searching for adventure and opportunity, many eager to escape the social conventions and economic constraints of the East and South, flocked to California during the gold rush fever of the 1850s. Soon joined by imported Chinese laborers, these whites and Asians provided the sweat and sacrifice that fueled the growth of the gold country, created the prosperity of San Francisco, and spread the image of Northern California as "Gold Mountain" to beckon countless generations of Asian immigrants.

While Northern California was developing into a center of commerce, banking, and industry, Southern and Central California welcomed white Southern migrants and immigrants from China, Japan, and the Philippines to develop their vast agricultural lands. The expansion of the railroads created another incentive for imported labor to Northern and Southern California. Mexican laborers found year-round opportunities as they moved from the fertile fields of central California to the vineyards of Napa and Sonoma Counties in Northern California, where Italian farmers were developing a domestic wine industry (McWilliams, 1946; Starr, 1985).

As each wave of immigrants and migrants settled into its own economic and cultural niche in California, the state developed its own map of ethnic heterogeneity. Northern California, especially the San Francisco Bay Area, was a welcoming beacon for Asians, Europeans, and Mediterranean immigrants. Los Angeles, with its proximity to Baja California and the Southwest, was a convenient magnet for Mexicans, Southern whites, and African Americans, while the Central Valley was a haven for Middle Eastern immigrants, Midwestern farmers escaping the "Dust Bowl," and cowboys searching for the last frontier. As communities were confronted with streams of non-white immigrants in escalating numbers, the early-arriving white immigrants and migrants became increasingly restive and resentful about the minority groups who, in their view, were encroaching upon their land, competing for their jobs, and straining their public schools and social services (Davis, 1992; Schrag, 1998).

## Scapegoating "Strangers and Outsiders"

Politicians, always seeking issues to exploit, were quick to sense the ambivalence and anxieties of the white farmers, small businessmen, and blue-collar workers who were concerned about depressed wages, rising land prices, and inflated consumer products. Whenever these anxieties surfaced in California communities, the politicians all too quickly and eagerly found a new immigrant group (nearly always ethnic minorities) who could be blamed for the community's problems. During periods of severe economic depression and wartime hysteria in California, the scapegoating of "strangers and outsiders" was reinforced and legitimized by state and national legislation and further justified and endorsed by the mass media (Daniels & Olin, 1972).

"Strangers and outsiders" were code terms, all too often affixed as pejorative labels to people of color, people who came from non-European countries, people who spoke English with an accent, if at all. These people did not look like the golden-haired models and the tanned lifeguards smiling seductively from the magazine ads and billboards welcoming newcomers to California. No, they looked foreign, spoke foreign languages, and belonged to foreign cultures, thus they could not possibly be mistaken for "real Americans" or treated as equals (Perea, 1997).

Against this backdrop we can understand the motives underlying the Chinese Exclusion Act of 1904, the deportation of thousands of Mexican nationals in the 1930s and 1950s, the restricted entry of Japanese laborers and the alien land laws in the early twentieth century, and the internment of Japanese Americans in relocation camps during World War II (Takaki, 1994). During the Korean War years (1950–1953), the Koreans, who had been imported to fill the agricultural and manufacturing jobs left vacant by the exclusion of the Chinese and Japanese, found themselves targeted as the new "Yellow Peril" by the American public (Kim, 1993).

African Americans, who first migrated to California in small numbers as freed slaves after the Civil War, flocked in groups during the depression years and the Great Migration from the South between the 1920s and 1950s. Most blacks headed straight across Route 66 from Texas and Louisiana to Bakersfield, Los Angeles, and the Central Valley, where they sometimes competed with Mexican migrants for menial service and agricultural jobs. But the majority of blacks preferred urban communities where opportunities for blue-collar jobs and higher wages were available. However, after the Great Depression in 1929 when thousands of Southern whites also fled from the ravages of the dust bowl in Oklahoma, Arkansas, and Texas, demographic changes altered the dynamics of race relations, particularly in Southern and Central California (McWilliams, 1946). The Southern white migrants, socially displaced and economically impoverished, found some measure of misplaced pride and fragile dignity in asserting their Southern norms of racial superiority and separation to distinguish themselves from their black fellow migrants, thereby signaling to prospective employers, realtors, and entrepreneurs that they expected and deserved preferential treatment in employment, housing, and consumer services (Horne, 1995). Skin color superseded all other salient characteristics as a ticket to claim a share of the California pot of gold.

## RACE, WORK, AND POLITICS

There were a series of racial incidents in Southern and Northern California that epitomized the conflicts between whites and non-whites in the decade between 1940 and 1950. These included:

1. the boycott of white-owned Los Angeles businesses in the 1940s by African Americans who protested racial discrimination in hiring;
2. the "Zoot Suit" riots in June 1943 when angry young Mexican American *pachucos* brawled in the streets of East Los Angeles with Anglo-American sailors who had verbally abused them with racial epithets;
3. the mutiny of black sailors at the Port Chicago naval depot in 1944 after an explosion killed 202 of their comrades who were engaged in loading ammunition onto ships;
4. the protests over segregated housing and restrictive covenants; and
5. the chronic complaints about racial incidents in restaurants, hotels, and public accommodations throughout the decade (Davis, 1992; Horne, 1995).

These protests, demonstrations, and riots were dramatic and divisive, but they probably represented the tip of the iceberg of deepening despair and frustration among people of color toward equally frustrated and angry whites who perceived some threat to their way of life, their economic security, and their cultural dominance.

Before and after World War II, successive waves of Chinese, Japanese, and Filipino laborers had experienced racial discrimination, economic exploitation, and social exclusion as their numbers grew and their needs for housing, schools, and social services increased. The leaders of the emerging labor union movement, who viewed them as a threat to white workers' job security, launched a campaign of racist propaganda against them, joined forces with nativist politicians, and succeeded in removing the majority of them as competition for jobs in the expanding economy (Daniels & Olin, 1972). It was the first time, but not the last, when organized labor would team up with conservative politicians in California to keep a minority group in its place or, more to the point, to challenge its right to have a place at all.

Meanwhile, other European groups were arriving in California, themselves looking for a chance to win the brass ring. Italians settled in San Francisco, attracted first by the potential of the commercial fishing industry and later moving into construction, the restaurant industry, and small businesses. Portuguese fisherman established a niche in the east side of San Francisco Bay, settling in small towns near Oakland where they could replicate the cottages and gardens of their native Portugal. Armenians and Greeks gravitated to the Central Valley, where they brought small farms and small businesses to rural areas that reminded them of home. When these newcomers from the southern Mediterranean and middle-Eastern countries arrived, most were olive-skinned and dark-haired, with prominent features unlike the fair-skinned Irish, English, and Germans who had preceded them. In recent discussions of the evolution of white ethnic identity, several writers have asserted that these darker immigrants were hardly considered "white" in America and were rarely treated as social or cultural equals by those from Northern and Western Europe (Alba, 1990). In fact, they were viewed as socially inferior, treated as foreigners or "white ethnic groups" before that term was in vogue, and tolerated as long as they did not compete directly with the ruling elite of Anglo-Americans who had formed the vanguard of the white settlers in California.

However, unlike Asians, Hispanics, Indians, and African Americans, these European ethnic groups were generally allowed to buy property, establish businesses, and engage in commercial and professional activities without fear of exclusion, deportation, or overt discrimination. There was an unwritten and unspoken gentleman's agreement that these newer immigrants, at the very least, were still Europeans and thus should be treated with greater respect and dignity than people of color, no matter how many generations they had been in America.

By the beginning of World War II, industries in Southern and Northern California had begun to recruit blacks in order to replace the white workers who were joining the armed services. For the first time in their lives, many of these blacks had the opportunity to move into high-paying skilled and semi-skilled manufacturing jobs in the shipbuilding, airplane manufacturing, and other defense-related industries, creating a solid working-class group among urban African Americans in California (Davis, 1992; Horne, 1995).

At the end of World War II, returning black veterans whose families had bought small homes and created a thriving African American community during the war, found that they were no longer valued workers as defense industries in Northern and Southern California downsized or were transformed into peacetime manufacturing plants (Glasgow, 1980; Horne, 1995). African Americans were not part of the postwar prosperity in California, but part of the postwar surplus. Once again, in an all-too-familiar cycle, blacks were the first fired and the last hired when the economy slowed down and the privilege resurfaced.

## THE CALIFORNIA MULTICULTURAL MOSAIC

After the Korean War and the Hungarian uprising, two new groups of immigrants arrived in California to compete for their place in the sun. Prior to World War II, the Koreans had a small community in Los Angeles, but this community rapidly expanded from the 1960s to the 1980s (Kim, 1993). Korean shopkeepers soon saw opportunities to expand as middle-man entrepreneurs to other areas around the state, creating a series of small Koreatowns in San Francisco, San Jose, and other cities. During the 1960s and 1970s, Hungarians and other immigrants from Eastern Europe fled repressive Communist regimes to seek political asylum and economic security in the United States, with California as one of the their favored destinations.

In the mid- to late 1970s, after the end of the Vietnam War, California welcomed yet another group of refugees from Vietnam, Cambodia, and Laos, introducing a new culture from Southeast Asia to cities like San Jose, Stockton, Sacramento, and Long Beach (Reimers, 1985). As a reward for their military assistance to the United States during World War II, these Southeast Asian refugees, many of whom were illiterate and unskilled from traditional peasant cultures, were afforded an array of economic benefits and social services such as low-cost loans for housing and small businesses, employment training programs, and classes in the English language and American culture. The government's efforts to acculturate and incorporate these refugees into American society stood in striking contrast to their benign neglect of previous immigrants from Asia, Mexico, and Latin America. Within a decade, with the active assistance of government aid, these Southeast Asian refugees had established thriving communities with a commercial infrastructure, social institutions, and political organizations. They, too, had bought into the "California Dream," but would they see their dream turn into a nightmare?

In the 1980s and 1990s the California Dream continued to beckon to still newer groups of immigrants and refugees from El Salvador and Guatemala, fleeing political violence in Central America; from Eritrea and Ethiopia, seeking refuge from three decades of war and revolution in the Horn of Africa; from the chaos of revolution and the trauma of famine in West and Central Africa; from the fall of Communism in Russia and Eastern Europe; and from the poverty and corruption of the Caribbean Islands and South American dictatorships (Maharidge, 1996; Reimers, 1985; Rieff, 1991). Along with those escaping from intolerable social, political, and economic conditions are those immigrants from countries such as India, Pakistan, and South Asia seeking to parlay their technological and scientific skills into material success and professional achievement in California's preeminent high-technology industries and those from the Middle East, searching for freedom from religious and social fundamentalism.

In less than two decades, California has become the home of one of the largest groups of Muslims in the United States with about 150,000 in the San Francisco Bay Area alone. Often dressed distinctively with women in their *hijabs* (head scarves) and modest long dresses and men in their robes and sandals, groups of Muslims have established mosques in several communities, along with successful businesses, restaurants, and farms. Perhaps more than any other group of recent immigrants, Muslims have been the targets of religious prejudice, ethnic discrimination, and various forms of verbal and physical abuse. Viewed by some Americans as "outside the box" due to their traditional dress and unfamiliar religious practices, they are often lumped by association with Middle Eastern terrorists who have been accused of several devastating attacks on American embassies and tourists, airplanes, military installations, and private businesses (e.g., the World Trade Center bombing in New York). This "guilt by association" is frequently used as an excuse to justify the prejudice and discrimination against them by "real Americans," without exposing the underlying anxiety evoked by their "otherness" and the threat of being engulfed by their "exotic" culture and "alien" religion.

Since the end of World War II, in just 50 years, California has become the most racially and culturally diverse state in the nation, home to over 100 ethnic groups who speak even more languages and dialects, are affiliated with dozens of religious denominations and cults, practice a bewildering array of culturally diverse behaviors, and enjoy a variety of ethnic foods, music, dress, and leisure activities (Maharidge, 1996; Rieff, 1991; Schrag, 1998). California can no longer be characterized in simple stereotypes as the home of the Valley Girl, the Surfer, the Movie Starlet, or the Hippie. While all these images remain a part of the California gestalt, the state's current reality reflects a multicultural and multiracial mosaic of people of color and white ethnic migrants, immigrants, and refugees from around the world, alongside native-born sons and daughters, speakers of many languages, rural, urban, and suburban, rich and poor, skilled and unskilled, traditional and nontraditional.

This California mosaic of racially diverse people, ethnic cultures, and polyglot languages generates the energy that drives the expanding economy, creates the excitement that nurtures the creative arts, and provides the vision that fosters innovation in fields as discrete as fashion design and computer software. California is the benchmark for the rest of the country, the initiator of trends, the cradle of creativity, and the bellwether for change.

## CITIZENS AND OUTSIDERS: CYCLES OF NATIVISM IN CALIFORNIA

California has recently endured major injuries and upheavals—natural, social, and cultural. . . . The Rodney King affair was a social upheaval that many are still mourning. The cultural landscape of California is undergoing a profound transformation. Political minorities are fast becoming the numerical majority of the state. . . . The state has endured half a decade of severe economic stagnation. In a climate of frustration and malaise, those who are least like the dominant population—the new arrivals—have been singled out as the cause of all the chagrins.

M. M. Suárez-Orozco (1996, 158)

With so much promise and so much potential, how can one explain the darker forces in the California landscape? How can one understand the strong undercurrent of nativism, paranoia, and punitive social policies? What social, political, and economic factors are operating to promote racism and xenophobia against those perceived to be strangers and outsiders, those deemed different and unworthy to share the California Dream? What forces are in motion to reinforce racial separation, social exclusion, and economic inequality among these groups? What criteria are used to anoint those who are acceptable as citizens and to demonize those who are "outsiders," unacceptable to participate in the California vision?

It is instructive to note some parallels between the legislative and policy efforts to address these issues in the 1930s and 1940s and those that have surfaced in the 1980s and 1990s, half a century later. If we examine the periods of nativism and xenophobia in California history, we can rather quickly discern a pattern of cycles of exclusion, discrimination, and harassment of people of color, both native-born and immigrants. These cycles are closely tied to periods of economic downturns or instability, wars or hostile relations with other countries, and periods of rapid social and economic change (Smith & Tarallo, 1995; Stefancic, 1997; Takaki, 1994).

Whenever an Asian American is seen as too successful and acts too equal, watch out. We have the mark upon us . . . we become the "Yellow Peril" . . . and the "Model Minority" quickly becomes the "Indispensable Scapegoat." (Hata and Hata, 1990, 91)

The Chinese Exclusion Act of 1904, for example, was a response to demands of the emerging labor movement on the West Coast to stem the immigration of Chinese laborers who they blamed for undercutting their wages and working conditions (Takaki, 1994). Only twenty years later, all immigration from Asia was restricted by the passage of the National Origins Act in 1924, partially in response to the economic success of the Japanese on the West Coast and the fear of the Imperial Japanese government's growing political influence in the Asian-Pacific region. The Japanese had replaced the Chinese as the "Yellow Peril" long before the bombing of Pearl Harbor in 1941, but when the Japanese attack on Pearl Harbor catapulted the United States into World War II, the anti-Japanese hysteria escalated and was a major factor in the government's decision to "relocate" over 110,000 Japanese American citizens from the West Coast and confine them in internment camps for most of the war years (Takaki, 1994). The "Yellow Peril" had become a self-fulfilling prophecy, a threat to national security, and their rights were violated with impunity. Ironically, German and Italian prisoners of war held in American prison camps were often treated with more dignity and respect than Asian American, African American, and Latino citizens and servicemen during the war.

Attitudes toward Mexican immigrants have closely paralleled the rise and fall of the agribusiness industry in California. During the early years of the twentieth century, Mexican laborers were enthusiastically welcomed as the agriculture industry expanded and there were few other sources of labor. Later, during the depression, when the "Okies" and the "Arkies" were displaced from their land ravaged by the dust bowl, hostility grew toward Mexican laborers in the 1930s and they were harassed, attacked, and driven back across the border by the U.S. government by forced repatriation (Carrasco, 1997).

During World War II, Mexican workers were again in demand as whites were enlisted for the war effort, for it was essential for someone to grow the vegetables and fruits to feed the civilian and military populations. With most of the Japanese farmers and laborers interned during World War II, Mexican and Filipino farm laborers were indispensable in California's fields. However, when the Anglo-American soldiers returned to California after the war, it was not long before Mexican farm workers were being called "wetbacks" and politicians found it expedient to call for stricter controls on the borders between California and Mexico, triggering "Operation Wetback," another U.S. government campaign to deport thousands of Mexicans in the late 1940s (Carrasco, 1997).

Over the last forty years, the official immigration policies have often been at odds with the practical needs of California farmers, leaving Mexican farm laborers caught in a bind between ideology and expediency. From 1942 to 1964 for example, California and other Western states cooperated with the federal government to pass legislation for a "Bracero Program" in which Mexicans were recruited under contract to work as seasonal farm laborers, then they would be returned to Mexico (Carrasco, 1997). But the honor system didn't work after these workers got a taste of the American way of life, and many of them remained on this side of the border and disappeared into the barrios and farm hamlets of Southern and Central California.

Just three decades later, many of the same politicians who had supported the "Bracero Program" were leading the fight against "illegal aliens," supporting a renewed "Operation Wetback" to deport undocumented workers, and advocating harsh measures for those Mexicans who had entered the United States illegally as labor shortages eased after the Korean War ended (Carrasco, 1997). The alternating pattern of leniency and punitiveness toward Mexican "illegals" clearly parallels periods of economic expansion and economic recession in the California agribusiness cycles. Unfortunately, Mexican farm laborers seeking relief from their own stagnant economy are not able to predict these economic shifts or fathom their political implications, so they simply keep coming across the border trying to support their families and to make their own dreams come true.

## COLOR AND CLASS: AFRICAN AMERICANS IN THE INNER CITY

Just as ambivalent attitudes toward Mexican and Asian immigrants have waxed and waned for much of the twentieth century in California, so too have attitudes about the treatment of African Americans evolved between poles of inclusion and exclusion. For the first half of the twentieth century, the African American population in California was minuscule, located primarily in the urban areas, and not a visible threat to the majority. Perceptions of blacks began to change after World War II as they became more numerous, more visible, and more assertive about their rights to decent jobs, fair housing, and good schools (Bunch, 1990; Horne, 1995).

After World War II, African American veterans returned to California expecting just rewards at home for "fighting for democracy" abroad. They soon found themselves confronted with inadequate housing stock, downsized manufacturing plants, and persistent and pervasive racism in higher education, public accommodations, and bank lending practices. The promise of democracy was unfulfilled and their own California Dream was unrealized. Despite some tense demonstrations in Los Angeles and San Francisco in the 1940s and 1950s, African Americans were still the victims of discrimination in education, employment, housing, and public accommodations in California, which had always prided itself as a state that was more liberal and more progressive about race relations than the rest of the country (Horne, 1995; Preston & Lai, 1998).

In the early 1960s, buoyed by the liberal administration of Governor "Pat" Brown and the booming California economy, the California legislature passed several progressive pieces of legislation, including the Rumford Fair Employment Practice Act, forerunners of federal laws to outlaw discrimination in public accommodations and housing (Schrag, 1998). Although this legislation was difficult to monitor and to enforce, California had finally sent a positive signal to the rest of the nation that African Americans would receive equal treatment and equal opportunity in this state. It was a message that did not go unheard or unheeded, as more African Americans headed west to seek the California Dream. Despite the repeal of the Fair Housing Act in 1964 by Proposition 14, blacks still believed that California promised unlimited opportunities; from 1960 to 1990, the African American population in California nearly doubled, the major growth occurring in the metropolitan areas of Los Angeles, San Francisco-Oakland Bay Area, Sacramento, San Diego, and San Bernardino (Johnson, 1999).

In 1965, the black community of Watts, in South Los Angeles, erupted in a six-day riot after the Los Angeles police assaulted a young black man stopped for a traffic violation (Horne, 1995). The riot's heavy toll in economic damages, death, and injuries reflected the pent-up anger of a community with high unemployment, poor schools, inadequate social services, and chronic police brutality. The Watts Riots served as a trigger to urban riots throughout the nation, forcefully calling to the attention of politicians and business leaders the not-so-benign neglect of the inner cities. Once again, California was in the vanguard of social change through social protest.

But as African Americans tried to claim their share of the pie, they found themselves competing more and more not just against Anglo-Americans and Latinos, but against other "newcomer" groups such as Africans, Arabs, South Asians, and Southeast Asians who often arrived in California with money to invest in small businesses, technical skills, and social support networks to facilitate their adjustment and their absorption into the mainstream society (Johnson & Oliver, 1989). As the economy downsized again in the 1970s and 1980s, many of the low-skilled African Americans began to view themselves (and to be viewed) as superfluous labor, unable to compete for the high-technology jobs, unable to afford the inflated housing costs, and unable to secure safe schools for their children. Their frustrations increased as they witnessed special loan programs for Southeast Asian refugees, special praise for "model minorities" who had been victimized by a previous generation of political demagogues, special aid programs for developing countries, special incentives for the high technology companies, special quotas for skilled immigrants, and diminishing resources for disadvantaged and disenfranchised black Californians.

## WINDS OF CHANGE: POLITICAL ORGANIZING AND PROTEST OF PEOPLE OF COLOR

In the mid-1960s Cesar Chavez, a charismatic community organizer from Los Angeles, helped to organize the Latino agricultural workers into the United Farmworkers Union to protest the low wages and inhumane working conditions prevailing in the farms of California (Maharidge, 1996). Against all odds and with very limited resources except their determination and dedication to improve their status and living conditions, the farmworkers' movement gained national support from other unions, civil rights organizations, liberals, and college students for their 1975 strike against the grape and lettuce farmers, eventually forcing the agribusiness leaders in California to negotiate a favorable contract with them. Moreover, this movement achieved other less obvious goals in awakening the consciousness of Mexican Americans in California to their potential as a political and economic force, as well as serving notice on the Anglo-American establishment that the winds of change had finally swept away the passivity and patience of the state's largest ethnic minority group.

These winds of change had also ruffled the California Japanese American community, which had been politely seeking reparations for the families who had been abruptly uprooted and involuntarily placed in internment camps during World War II. In the wake of the success of the black civil rights protests and the Latino farmworkers' boycott, the Japanese American civil rights organizations became more assertive and more confrontational in their demands for reparations. Once again, a movement that began in urban areas of Los Angeles and San Francisco spread throughout California and the West Coast, eventually enlisting the support of Japanese Americans throughout the nation, many of whom had deliberately chosen to move out of "Japantowns" in the nation's largest cities in order to assimilate and to become nearly invisible Americans. Although their campaign took nearly forty years, the U.S. Congress finally granted reparations in 1988 to those families who had actually survived the humiliation and the heartache of internment (Takaki, 1994). For the Japanese American leaders who had refused to abandon their cause, the paltry sum of $20,000 per survivor was a pyrrhic victory but an important symbol of healing and reconciliation to a group who had become the "model minority" in a society always seeking visible scapegoats.

Hailed by the liberal activists and civil rights advocates who had worked so tirelessly to obtain some redress for the Japanese American community, these reparations were met with some criticism and bitterness by African Americans and Native Americans who had never received any compensation for their enslavement, exploitation, or extermination by American citizens and their government.

## Urban Riots: A Reprise and a Revelation

On April 29, 1992, four years after reparations were granted to Japanese American internees, African Americans in South Central Los Angeles erupted again in response to police brutality and racial injustice after the acquittal of three of the four white police officers who were accused of brutally assaulting Rodney King, a young black man arrested for drunk driving. Even more destructive than the Watts Riots, the 1992 riots lasted for over four days and were fueled by the anger and frustrations of blacks,

Latinos, and Asians, some of whom used the opportunity to loot the stores and taunt the police (Gibbs, 1996; Gooding-Williams, 1993). The explosion of anger and rage of these people of color not only sent a powerful signal of social discontent, but also raised the consciousness level about racism, police brutality, and unequal justice throughout California and the nation. Arguably, these 1992 riots also heightened the fears and aroused the anxieties of white Californians that these multi-ethnic riots represented a harbinger of greater militancy and violence of people of color, protesting the status quo and challenging the dominance of the state's entrenched elite power brokers, traditional leaders, and dominant institutions.

By the last decade of the twentieth century, the California Dream had turned into a bittersweet myth for many of the ethnic minority groups who had been early settlers and early arrivals to the Golden State. When demographers announced in the early 1980s that people of color and Hispanics/Latinos collectively would constitute a majority of the state's population early in the twenty-first century, this prediction seemed to set off alarm bells and reawakened the nativists to reassert their claim on California.

## THE EROSION OF THE DREAM

By the close of the decade, the conservative and right-wing forces had galvanized their base of political and financial support and devised a series of propositions that would have very significant and negative consequences for California's people of color. These four propositions represent a direct assault on those immigrants and ethnic minorities who, perceived to be a threat to the Anglo-American "way of life," are demonized as a threat to public safety (Proposition 184), stigmatized as unworthy recipients of public welfare (Proposition 187), stereotyped as unqualified for higher education and competitive jobs (Proposition 209), and deprived of the right to learn in their native languages and celebrate their cultural identities (Proposition 227).

Do these series of propositions simply reflect the public's impatience with criminal offenders, welfare cheats, unqualified students, and poor schools, or do they represent a resurgence of nativistic and xenophobic attitudes about minorities and immigrants of color? Are these initiatives fueled by underlying anxieties about "outsiders and outlaws," or are they attempts to scapegoat the most vulnerable groups in the population and to displace the blame on them for economic instability, income inequality, rapid technological change, and rapid social and political change? Will these laws be used to maintain and reinforce white privilege and power in economic, political, and cultural spheres of California society? Or are these laws intended to serve as temporary stopgaps to stem the flow of undocumented immigrants, to deter violent crime, to establish English as the primary language in the schools, and to raise the achievement level of minority students to enable them to compete successfully for slots in the meritocracy?

Whatever the answers to these questions, in subsequent chapters we examine the implications of these four propositions in terms of their impact on the civil rights and civil liberties of these targeted populations, their access to opportunities for educational and economic mobility, and the goal of their inclusion and full participation in the society. The negative impact of these laws in fostering the maintenance of cultural identity and facilitating a sense of ethnic community in a multicultural society cannot be overestimated.

Before we turn to a discussion of these issues, we take a closer look at Los Angeles, the quintessential multicultural community, and the legacy of the 1992 South Central riots on the political, economic, and social structures of the City of Angels and the state of California. If we wish to understand one of the major precipitating factors in this series of repressive and reactionary political initiatives, it is crucial to delineate the connections between those destructive riots and the backlash that followed them.

## REFERENCES

Alba, R. D. (1990). *Ethnic identity: The transformation of white America*. New Haven: Yale University Press.

Bunch, L. G. (1990). A past not necessarily prologue: The Afro-American in Los Angeles since 1990. In N. Klein & M. J. Schiesl (Eds.), *20th century Los Angeles: Power, promotion and social conflict*. Claremont, CA: Regina Books.

Carrasco, G. P. (1997). Latinos in the United States: Invitation and exile. In J. F. Perea (Ed.), *Immigrants out! The new nativism and the anti-immigrant impulse in the United States* (pp. 190–204). New York: New York University Press.

Daniels, R., & Olin, S. C., Jr. (1972). *Racism in California: A reader in the history of oppression*. New York: Macmillan.

Davis, M. (1992). *City of quartz*. New York: Vintage Books.

Gibbs, J. T. (1996). *Race and justice: Rodney King and O. J. Simpson in a house divided*. San Francisco: Jossey-Bass.

Glasgow, D. G. (1980). *The black underclass: Poverty, unemployment, and entrapment of ghetto youth*. San Francisco: Jossey-Bass.

Gooding-Williams, R. (Ed.). (1993). *Reading Rodney King/Reading urban uprising*. New York: Routledge.

Hata, D. T., & Hata, N. I. (1990). Asian-Pacific Angelinos: Model minorities and indispensable scapegoats. In N. M. Klein & M. J. Schiesl (Eds.), *20th century Los Angeles: Power, promotion, and social conflict* (pp. 61–99). Claremont, CA: Regina Books.

Horne, G. (1995). *Fire this time*. Charlottesville: University Press of Virginia.

Johnson, H. (1999). How many Californians? A review of population projections for the state. *California Counts: Profiles and Trends, 1*(1), 10–15.

Johnson, J. H., Jr., & Oliver, M. L. (1989). Interethnic minority conflict in urban America: The effects of economic and social dislocations. *Urban Geography, 10,* 449–463.

Kim, E. (1993). Home is where the Han is: A Korean-American perspective on the Los Angeles upheavals. In R. Gooding-Williams (Ed.), *Reading Rodney King/Reading urban uprising* (pp. 215–235). New York: Routledge.

Maharidge, D. (1996). *The coming white minority: California, multiculturalism and America's future.* New York: Vintage Books.

McLeod, R. G. (1998). Minority majority well on its way in state. *San Francisco Chronicle,* September 4, p. 22.

McWilliams, C. (1946). *Southern California country: Island on the land.* New York: Duell, Sloan & Pierce.

Perea, J. F. (Ed.). (1997). *Immigrants out! The new nativism and the anti-immigrant impulse in the United States.* New York: New York University Press.

Preston, M. B., Cain, B. E., & Bass, S. (Eds.). (1998). *Racial and ethnic politics in California. Vol. II.* Berkeley: Institute of Governmental Studies Press, University of California, Berkeley.

Preston, M. B., & Lai, I. S. (1998). The symbolic politics of affirmative action. In M. B. Preston, B. E. Cain, & S. Bass (Eds.), *Racial and ethnic politics in California. Vol. II* (pp. 161–198). Berkeley: Institute of Governmental Studies Press, University of California.

Reimers, D. (1985). *Still the golden door: The third world comes to America.* New York: Columbia University Press.

Rieff, D. (1991). *Los Angeles: Capital of the third world.* New York: Simon & Schuster.

Schrag, P. (1998). *Paradise lost: California's experiences, America's future.* Berkeley: University of California Press.

Smith, M. P., & Tarallo, B. (1995). Proposition 187: Global trend or local narrative? Explaining anti-immigrant politics in California, Arizona, and Texas. *International Journal of Urban & Regional Research, 19*(4), 664–676.

Starr, K. (1985). *Inventing the dream: California through the Progressive Era.* New York: Oxford University Press.

Stefancic, J. (1997). Funding the nativist agenda. In J. F. Perea (Ed.), *Immigrants out! The new nativism and the anti-immigrant impulse in the United States* (pp. 119–135). New York: New York University Press.

Suárez-Orozco, M. M. (1996). California dreaming: Proposition 187 and the cultural psychology of racial and ethnic exclusion. *Anthropology and Education Quarterly, 27*(2), 151–167.

Takaki, R. (Ed.). (1994). *From different shores: Perspectives on race and ethnicity in America* (2nd ed.). New York: Oxford University Press.

# CHAPTER 3

# Los Angeles:
# The Legacy of Rodney King

Along Wilshire Boulevard and Melrose Avenue, in Brentwood Park and Los Feliz, the faces behind the counters were Han and Dravidian, Korean and Persian, Mixtec and Ethiopian—anything except black and white. . . . Ready or not, the Third World was coming to Los Angeles . . . coming in numbers that defied the imagination, coming fast.

—David Rieff (1991, 144)

Los Angeles has been called a "third world city" by David Rieff in his book *Los Angeles: Capital of the Third World* (1991), a provocative and prescient portrait of the current racial and cultural balkanization of the City of Angels. In their recent book *Rethinking Los Angeles* (1996), Michael Dear and his colleagues graphically describe the city's demography: "In social terms, Los Angeles is now characterized as a 'First World' city flourishing atop a 'Third World' city. This postmodern metropolis is increasingly polarized along class, income, racial and ethnic lines. The disadvantaged classes are overwhelmingly people of color" (11). Los Angeles is emblematic of the social transformation taking place in the cities and suburbs of California, a crucible of social change where people of color find themselves separated from whites in complex patterns of vertical and horizontal segregation.

In this chapter we briefly describe the social demography of Los Angeles as a "third world city" and will show how these patterns of separation evolved into ethnic enclaves throughout the city. Further, we examine the factors that contributed to the buildup of tensions between the white community and the people of color, the minorities and the immigrants, as well as the conflict and competition among these groups.

We look at the role of the police and the criminal justice system in Los Angeles to maintain "law and order" and preserve the status quo of the Anglo-American establishment through repression, reactionary policies, and social control of minority communities. Such tactics have generated among minorities deeply entrenched feelings of anger and outrage at the criminal justice system, disrespect and cynicism toward the rule of law, and cycles of protest and rebellion in the Watts Riots of 1965 and the South Central riots of 1992 (Gibbs, 1996; Gooding-Williams, 1993).

Finally, we analyze the impact of the police beating of Rodney King, the subsequent acquittal, and the violent response of the South Central community to those highly publicized events. We suggest that these 1992 riots had a much greater impact than has traditionally been assumed and a much broader sphere of influence in terms of long-term consequences. In fact, we propose that these riots served to trigger off a conservative backlash not only in Los Angeles, but throughout the state of California, that unmasked the fears and anxieties in the white community of racial violence and cultural chaos, unleashed their latent feelings of racism and xenophobia, and transformed these fears and feelings into a political agenda to disadvantage, disenfranchise, and disempower these threatening people of color. The populist political feature of the ballot initiative in California would provide the mechanism to launch this agenda and the conservative right-wing groups would provide the money, the media exposure, and the manpower to promote it.

## THE MULTICULTURAL MOSAIC

The best thing about being Latino in L.A. is that everywhere you look, and everything you see and touch and feel, tells you that you belong here. The worst thing is that everyone else feels the same way, and it's turning L.A. into a battle zone.

Cheech Marin (qtd. in Rieff, 1991, 166)

Los Angeles is a city of balkanized neighborhoods, dissected by futuristic freeways; of gated communities patrolled by uniformed security guards; of rich and poor, separated by spatial and social barriers; of whites and non-whites, splintered into racial and cultural enclaves; of native-born and immigrants, searching for a sense of identity and community (cf. Davis, 1992; Rieff, 1991).

The demography of Los Angeles with its ethnic enclaves separated from each other by race, culture, and socioeconomic status is not an uncommon phenomenon in large American cities. Yet unlike many other cities, the wealthy and powerful whites in Los Angeles have little contact with the poor people of color (except as service and domestic workers), little interest in their lives, and little incentive to become involved with their fates.

Reveling in its reputation as the quintessential city of the future, Los Angeles with its vertical and horizontal segregation is also a city that resonates to rumors of crisis, that responds to racial demagoguery, and succumbs to paranoid fears of crime and gangs. Thus, Los Angeles is simultaneously laid back and on edge, subliminally waiting and watching for the next catastrophe, the next riot, the next earthquake. It is a city where conspiracy theories abound, where police helicopters are part of the urban landscape, where urban legends find fertile soil to take root (Davis, 1992; Rieff, 1991).

After the Watts Riots in 1965, the Mexican American community expanded its borders beyond East Los Angeles into Watts, then westward into South Central. By 1990 they had been joined by Central American immigrants and refugees, swelling the Latino community to nearly half of the South Central population and 40 percent of the city's population. These were the brown people who were the maids, the gardeners, the babysitters, and the handymen who daily greased the cogs in the machinery of middle-class Anglo-American life in Los Angeles. Invisible on the west side when their day's work was done, they were highly visible in South Central where their spreading presence was viewed with ambivalence and hostility, an unwelcome invasion into African American territory (Gooding-Williams, 1993; Horne, 1995).

The Asian Americans, who currently account for 10 percent of the city's population, had also multiplied beyond the familiar Chinese, Japanese, and Koreans, now including darker-skinned immigrants from India and Pakistan, hill people from Laos and Cambodia, Burmese and Thai in their silk camisoles, and Indonesians in their batik sarongs.

For many whites in Los Angeles, all the Asian groups were lumped together as unwelcome alien intruders, except when extraneous economic or political factors heightened their awareness that one group might pose a greater threat to their welfare at any given time. Thus, the Chinese, Japanese, and Koreans alternately assumed the roles of scapegoats, victims, and allies throughout most of the twentieth century, but the Southeast Asian refugees, the most recent arrivals, evoked American sympathy and charitable impulses after the fall of Vietnam. The newer Asian images were more varied and more exotic, but the stereotypes were similar. Even as they grumbled about the flood of immigrants, the native Angelenos praised these Southeast Asian newcomers for their industriousness, their politeness, and their willingness to work long hours for low wages (Rieff, 1991).

Although maintaining a low profile throughout the Korean War years, by the late 1970s the Korean commercial community had mushroomed in Los Angeles until it was bounded by Hoover Street on the east, Crenshaw Boulevard to the west, Jefferson Boulevard to the south, and Beverly Boulevard to the north (Rieff, 1991). Their small stores were also scattered throughout South Central Los Angeles, a predominantly African American area, and relations between the two groups were very strained. The explosive growth of the Korean community followed the earlier patterns of the Chinese and Japanese immigrants, but they had moved south and west of the traditional Asian neighborhoods, thus they were both more visible and more vulnerable targets for blacks and Hispanics whose communities had developed an uneasy symbiotic relationship with Korean shopkeepers, described by Blauner as "middle-men" minority entrepreneurs, the voluntary immigrants who create a buffer zone between whites and "colonized" minorities such as blacks and American Indians (Blauner, 1972).

While working-class whites were fleeing to the small satellite communities around Los Angeles, middle-class whites were moving to the San Fernando and San Gabriel Valleys, and wealthy whites (business executives, corporate lawyers, the movie industry elite) were building their own version of the Hollywood dream in the wooded hills and canyons of West Los Angeles and along the scenic shores of the Pacific Coast. Although their high-status jobs required frequent, if not daily, commuting to the high-rise office towers in downtown Los Angeles, Century City, or Hollywood, these managers and moguls hardly ever ventured off the freeways during their business weeks and spent their weekends as far away as possible from the inner city, rarely encountering the people and problems of the "other Los Angeles" (Davis, 1992). Most suburban whites were far removed from the political realities of governing this multiethnic city, thus they were hardly interested in the problems of poverty, homelessness, crime, police brutality, or immigration issues; not at least until they felt personally menaced by any of these urban dilemmas.

## THE LEGACY OF THE WATTS RIOTS

After the Watts Riots in 1965, African Americans and Latinos began to see that they had much common ground for coalition building in terms of economic exclusion, housing segregation, and lack of political representation (Hahn, 1996). In addition to Black–Mexican alliances in Watts, Mexican American leaders began to establish civil rights organizations such as MECHA and MALDEF (Mexican American Legal Defense and Educational Fund), patterned closely after black civil rights organizations such as the Urban League and the NAACP-Legal Defense Fund. However, the African American community was gaining more political power and greater political sophistication, symbolized by the election of Tom Bradley as mayor of Los Angeles in 1973.

After the Watts Riots, Los Angeles was also desperately seeking political leadership to bridge the racial and class barriers and to heal the racial wounds that had been exposed by the riots. Tom Bradley, a former police officer and a city councilman, emerged from the pack to challenge Mayor Sam Yorty, an abrasive and calculating conservative who had turned deaf ears to the black community's legitimate grievances and supported the repressive tactics of the Los Angeles Police Department against the minority communities (Davis, 1992; Hahn, 1996). Running on a platform to root out police brutality and revitalize the inner city, Bradley lost in his first mayoral campaign, but soundly defeated an increasingly erratic and divisive Yorty in 1973, becoming the first African American mayor of a predominantly white city in the United States. Bradley's election as mayor of Los Angeles symbolized the emergence of an effective coalition of white liberals, labor unions, and minorities who maintained control of city politics for twenty years despite escalating tensions between liberals and conservatives over land use and economic development, between labor and management, over wages and benefits, and between whites and non-whites over integration and civil rights.

## Civil Rights versus Law and Order

[T]he local television stations were overly concerned with the daily body count in Watts or in the Mexican barrios of East Los Angeles. . . . Moreover, the fear of the South Central gangs and the fear of drugs were constantly being stirred up by Los Angeles officials, notably by the current chief of police, Daryl Gates, and his predecessor, Ed Davis.

David Rieff (1991, 39)

Los Angeles is a city where black gangs, headquartered in Watts and South Central Los Angeles, rose to prominence in the 1970s and 1980s, capitalizing on the mushrooming trade in drugs, guns, and contraband in the inner city (Davis, 1992). Though less violent and less hierarchical than the Latino gangs, which were formed after World War II, the loosely organized super gangs of the "Bloods" and the "Crips" managed to invoke fear and revulsion in the African American community. For these young black men, the gangs replaced their often dysfunctional families, offered them identity, social status, income, and a sense of security and solidarity against a hostile and uncertain world. Rarely venturing beyond the narrow confines of their set's neighborhood, these gang members were extremely isolated, fostering their intense feelings of anti-white, anti-police, and anti-establishment hatred and paranoia—feelings that would later play a major role in fanning the flames of rage and rebellion in the wake of the acquittal of the police officers in the Rodney King assault case (Gibbs, 1996).

The militarization of the Los Angeles police department from Chief Parker's tenure in the 1950s to Chief Daryl Gates's reign in the 1980s paralleled the spread of black and white gangs in Watts, South Central, and East Los Angeles (Davis, 1992). Capitalizing on the growing angst of the middle-class voters and downtown business leaders about crime, gangs, and drugs, the LAPD used a combination of sophisticated weaponry, modern surveillance techniques, and aggressive street policing to intimidate and control the inner-city minorities, the poor immigrants, the homeless, and the deviant. Successive leaders of the LAPD, fanning the paranoia of the white community, justified their blatant violation of civil rights and routine police brutality by inflating crime statistics, exaggerating gang membership, and using the media to promote a mythic image of their integrity and invincibility as "Blue Knights" (Christopher Commission, 1991).

For many years, the conservatives in Los Angeles, as in other cities and suburbs of California, had invoked the code term "law and order" to excuse chronic tactics of police harassment and misconduct toward immigrants and people of color as a form of social control. There had been numerous charges of police brutality against the LAPD, but few officers had ever been punished or fired for egregious public displays of excessive force, fatal beatings, and unexplained deaths in policy custody (Davis, 1992). There had been a long-time gentleman's agreement, an implicit social contract, between the police and the politicians: in return for keeping the crime rate down and the streets safe, the politicians would provide cover for aggressive police tactics directed against the unwanted and undesirable segments of society, that is, the minorities, the poor, and the powerless. As the anger and outrage against police brutality escalated in the ghettos and barrios of Los Angeles, astute observers predicted that it would only take a minor spark to set off a major community conflagration, a reprise of the Watts Riots in 1965.

Unfortunately those traumatic riots had actually reinforced these messages as the community's fear quotient rose and their willingness to tolerate repressive policies and harsh police tactics increased. Ironically, it was not until these police-community tensions exploded again in the South Central riots of 1992 that Bradley, confronting the reality of his fractured coalition and his own political demise after five terms in office, was finally able to force changes in the leadership and policies of the LAPD only after the Christopher Commission documented a pervasive pattern of police brutality and misconduct that had been ignored or tolerated for over fifty years (Christopher Commission, 1991).

However, a fairly benign state of homeostasis prevailed in this multilayered metropolis until March 1991, when the televised beating of Rodney King, a young black man, by four white Los Angeles police officers made it

34

impossible for the mainstream establishment to continue to ignore the problems in the inner city, to deny the existence of police brutality, or to dismiss the threat of escalating inter-ethnic and inter-racial tensions to the stability of the total community. The riots following the acquittal of the police officers in April 1992 perceptibly altered the balance of power, perhaps only temporarily, between the police and the gangs, and between blacks and whites, rich and poor, native-born minorities and immigrants (Gooding-Williams, 1993).

## UPRISING IN SOUTH CENTRAL: NO JUSTICE, NO PEACE

Watching the fires burning on TV, I understood immediately why people resort to violence. When you feel helpless and angry and there's nowhere to turn for help, you strike out at anybody. . . . If we have to do what we did in Watts in 1965 to let the Los Angeles Police Department, the city and the Government know that we're not going to tolerate this kind of travesty, then I say we have to make our point any way we can.

Terry McMillan (1993, 238)

The riots that broke out in South Central Los Angeles on the late afternoon of April 29, 1992, shortly after news of the verdict in the Rodney King beating case, were the second set of violent upheavals in Los Angeles in less than three decades. In contrast to the Watts Riots twenty-seven years earlier, these were multiethnic "equal opportunity" riots, involving hundreds of Asians, African Americans, Latinos, and even some whites, groups from neighborhoods throughout the city from Hollywood in the north to Parker Center police headquarters in the downtown core of the city. What started at the corner of Florence and Normandie, the flashpoint of the violent uprising in South Central, spread throughout the city and raged for four days and four nights before the combined forces of the LAPD and the National Guard finally brought it under control on May 3, 1992 (Gooding-Williams, 1993; *Los Angeles Times*, 1992).

Even more destructive and traumatic than the Watts Riots in 1965, these riots resulted in nearly $1 billion in property damage and looting, over 1,000 businesses burned or destroyed, over 2,500 people injured, and fifty-two fatalities directly attributed to the violence (*Los Angeles Times*, 1992). The motives of the rioters were far more varied and complex than the media reported, as they shifted depending on the person, the place, and the day of participation. In the initial stages of the riots, the action was primarily in South Central, the rioters mainly black, and the motive clearly anger and outrage at the perceived injustice of the officers' acquittal by a predominantly white jury in Simi Valley. The enraged protestors were seeking revenge on whites, Korean shopkeepers, and outsiders in the community in a spontaneous uprising fueled by a long history of racial discrimination, economic injustice, and police brutality (Gibbs, 1996; Gooding-Williams, 1993).

On the second and third days of the riots, blacks were joined by Latinos and a few low-income whites in the poorest neighborhoods for wholesale looting of the stores for food, household goods, clothes, and items that poor people coveted but could not afford. In the final phase of the riots, the crowd was rainbow-hued, more youthful, and socially upscale, joining in the vandalism, looting, and skirmishes with the police as if they were committing fraternity pranks at a homecoming game, or participating in an antiwar protest march (Gooding-Williams, 1993).

The city was in a state of emergency, its leaders suffering from shell-shock, its major streets cordoned off in battle zones, and its residents experiencing symptoms of post-traumatic stress. More than any single consequence, those riots would forever change the image of Los Angeles as a beacon of tolerance and a haven of multicultural harmony. The impact of the 1992 riots would reverberate for years throughout the city, the state, and the nation (Hahn, 1996; Maharidge, 1996). Although these riots would give the lie to those who championed California as the model of diversity for the rest of the nation, the riots would also put the rest of the country on notice that minorities were fed up with unfulfilled promises of equality and justice and they were simply "not going to take it anymore."

The 1992 civil disorders in Los Angeles dramatized the underlying tensions among whites and people of color, among African Americans and Latinos against Koreans, and among the immigrants and native-born citizens. These riots also exposed the "fault lines" in Los Angeles in the competition over economic resources, the jockeying for political power, the fears and anxieties over cultural dominance, and the vested interests of the "haves" and the "have nots" in preserving the status quo of the traditional social institutions of the community (Gibbs, 1996; Gooding-Williams, 1993).

For residents of California, the riots had a more subtle and sinister meaning, for the violence signaled a new militant phase in the awakening of ethnic consciousness and dissatisfaction with the status quo. The riots polarized whites and non-whites, but they also gave new meaning to the term "identity politics" as African Americans, Latinos, and Asians viewed the aftermath of the riots through their distinctive cultural prisms and from the vantage point of their own community's self-interest. Ironically, the riots served both as a harbinger of change for ethnic minority groups and a symbol of resistance for whites in the emerging struggle for political, economic, and cultural dominance in the state of California at the end of the twentieth century.

## THE LEGACY OF THE 1992 LOS ANGELES RIOTS

> What happened in Los Angeles—the police brutality, the unjust verdict, the angry response—are part of an ancient spiral. The spiral will continue in the absence of fundamental change. Any fundamental long-term change will have to result in power, political and economic, for the African-American community. Without power there will be no solution, without strength there will be no justice, and without justice, there will be no peace.
>
> Tony Martin (1993, 35)

The 1992 riots were a cataclysmic event in the history of Los Angeles, the city of the silver screen, sunshine, and sandy beaches. They shattered the myth of community progress and multicultural harmony that had lulled the politicians and power brokers into complacency about the growing tensions and the widening social and economic inequities in the community. They threatened the image of glamour and glory projected by Peter Ueberroth and his elite committee only eight years earlier in 1984, as they presided over one of the most successful Summer Games in the history of the Olympics. After all the damage and destruction were calculated and all the police had withdrawn, the long-term effects of the riots, though difficult to quantify, exacted an incalculable toll on the public and private spheres of business, finance, education, politics, and the media, not only in Los Angeles, but throughout the state of California (Gooding-Williams, 1993).

The most obvious legacy of the 1992 riots was the immediate impact on the Los Angeles Police Department. Within a period of three months after the riots, the LAPD had a new African American chief, the city had passed a new charter amendment limiting the chief's autonomy and powers, and some important changes in police personnel and procedures had been instituted (Hahn, 1996).

But the changes extended far beyond the LAPD and its conservative constituency. The traditional coalition of minorities, white liberals, and progressive businessmen who had been the backbone of Mayor Tom Bradley's reign as the five-term Democratic African American mayor of Los Angeles had been torn asunder by the riots (Sonenshein, 1998). Prominent members of the coalition had engaged in a bitter round of blaming, name-calling, and scapegoating. African American and Latino leaders had accused the white liberals of complicity in supporting Chief Daryl Gates' policies of brutality and misconduct against their communities and excoriated the business leaders for failing to support the economic rebuilding of South Central. From their vantage point, the white liberals believed they had been betrayed by the more radical black and Latino spokespersons who seemed to be fomenting racial antagonisms and practicing racial politics with highly inflammatory rhetoric and divisive tactics. Business leaders, who had initially supported the goals of "Rebuild L.A.," chaired by

Peter Ueberroth, had become disillusioned with the daunting problems of investing in neighborhoods where the infrastructure was inadequate, the labor force was untrained, and the risk of doing business so uncertain (Gooding-Williams, 1993; Hahn, 1996; Regalado, 1998).

### Political Backlash to South Central Riots

The demise of this effective coalition resulted in the 1993 election of Richard Riordan, a wealthy white businessman, as the first Republican mayor of Los Angeles in twenty years (Sonenshein, 1998). Riordan was viewed by the conservative voters in the San Fernando Valley as a law-and-order candidate, by the liberals in West Los Angeles as a mediator, by the moderate business leaders as a good manager. Winning decisively in the nonpartisan election, Riordan actually managed to capture minorities of every voting bloc except African Americans and Latinos. It was ironic that Riordan's victory was won at the expense of Michael Woo, the first Asian American candidate for mayor of Los Angeles. In 1991, immediately following the beating of Rodney King, Michael Woo had been one of the few members of the City Council to call for the resignation of Chief Daryl Gates. The only tangible reward he received for his courage in confronting Chief Gates was the lukewarm support of the African American community, most of whom stayed home from the polls in an incomprehensible show of apathy and alienation over Bradley's successor.

The riots had achieved what twenty years of conservative opposition to Mayor Bradley's policies had not been able to accomplish—the defeat of a minority candidate in America's most multiethnic metropolis. With the election of a moderate white Republican mayor, the minority-liberal-progressive coalition relinquished its hold over the power and purse strings of the nation's second-largest city, a prophetic sign of the setbacks that would shape the destiny of the demoralized minority groups throughout California in the final decade of the twentieth century.

### Rebuild L.A.: The Hype versus the Help

The enthusiasm of corporate leaders and business executives who had originally rallied to the cause of rebuilding the inner city soon waned in the face of the overwhelming challenges of tackling the long-neglected neighborhoods of South Central Los Angeles. Despite the upbeat public pronouncements of Peter Ueberroth and the benevolent blandishments of Mayor Bradley, many of the business leaders who had pledged money and other resources to facilitate the economic development of South Central simply reneged on their promises and quietly returned to business as usual in the boardrooms and bistros of West Los Angeles and in the downtown financial firms and corporate law offices.

"Rebuild L.A." opened in 1992 with high expectations and maximum publicity, and like the Stealth fighter plane, simply faded away from public view in 1997, after waging an unsuccessful five-year battle to attract capital investment in the community (Park, 1996; Regalado, 1998). In fact, after five years, the staff of "Rebuild L.A." reported limited success in their efforts, taking credit for building a few new supermarkets, rebuilding some small businesses, and developing several new strip-malls in the area. However, by the end of 1996 an official survey of the riot-damaged area concluded that over 75 percent of the severely damaged businesses had been repaired or rebuilt (Sterngold, 1997). As was true after the 1965 Watts Riots, many of the small entrepreneurs whose businesses were destroyed either had insufficient insurance or lacked the motivation to rebuild, so the loss to the community in terms of convenient stores and services was enormous and, tragically, would never fully be replaced. Ironically, the people most seriously affected by the loss of neighborhood stores were the families and friends of those who displaced their rage over injustice in the criminal justice system on their own poor distressed community.

### African American and Korean Relations

They [Koreans] hadn't heard that there is no equal justice in the U.S. They had to learn about American racial hierarchies. They did not realize that, as immigrants of color, they would never attain political voice or visibility but would instead be used to uphold the inequality and the racial hierarchy they had no part in creating.

Elaine H. Kim (1993, 218)

Most residents in South Central did not mourn the destruction of the liquor stores that had sprung up on nearly every block of the commercial streets that crisscrossed the area. Before the 1992 riots it was estimated that there were over fifty stores that sold liquor within the twenty-square-mile South Central area (Oliver, Johnson, & Farrell, 1993). Although many of these stores were also convenience stores selling food and grocery items, liquor was a high volume item, attracting the unemployed, the addicts, and the antisocial segments of society who, in turn, harassed children, women, and the elderly and created environmental eyesores in the neighborhood. After the widescale destruction of these stores, minority members of the City Council used the opportunity to introduce legislation to rezone the area for fewer liquor stores. That many of these stores were owned by Koreans, who already had been doubly victimized by both the riots and the lack of police protection, fueled another confrontation between the Korean community leaders and the African American–Latino coalition on the City Council. After many bitter confrontations and protracted political negotiations, the City Council succeeded in passing a bill to limit the number of liquor stores in South Central by mandating a series of restrictive requirements for business licenses, including higher insurance coverage and higher penalties for violating numerous city ordinances. These excessive requirements undoubtedly further discouraged Korean merchants from returning to South Central, but the City Council's actions also further exacerbated the growing tensions between the Koreans and the two other major ethnic minority groups in Los Angeles.

Perhaps, on the other hand, these developments energized Koreans to participate more actively in the political arena, since they had been twice burned in the aftermath of the riots by their lack of political influence. The riots certainly increased the visibility of younger Korean American leaders such as Angela Oh, a lawyer who had been active in local Democratic party politics, and Bong Kwan Kim, the executive director of the Korean American Community Center, both of whom had established good relationships with younger leaders in the African American and Latino communities (Park, 1996).

While Angela Oh and Bong Kwan Kim were identified with liberal-to-moderate political positions, many of the older Korean immigrant leaders had allied themselves with conservative causes. After the riots, these leaders felt betrayed and angry toward the younger, mainly American-born, leaders who had promoted interethnic collaboration through organizations such as the Black-Korean Alliance and other multiethnic coalitions (Park, 1996). This anger and alienation may have contributed to the election of Jay Kim, the first Korean congressman to be elected in the United States. Jay Kim is a Republican who represented a predominantly white district in Orange County, adjacent to Los Angeles County and a bastion of conservative voters (Park, 1996). A 1997 investigation into his campaign finance committee by the Congressional Ethics Committee found a sufficient number of irregularities and illegal practices to indict him for breaking the law, derailing his hope for reelection in 1998. This investigation also revealed that his campaign had financial support from a large number of Korean contributors throughout the Los Angeles area and the state of California. How many of these contributions could have been fueled by the feelings of "han," the concept of internalized anger and resentment, that many Koreans felt after the devastation of their businesses during the Los Angeles riots? What effect would these bitter feelings of Korean voters toward the African American and Latino rioters have on their attitudes about Proposition 184, the "Three Strikes" initiative, and Proposition 209, the anti-affirmative action initiative? By the same token, how had the years of poor communication and exploitation from Korean merchants influenced the attitudes of black voters about Proposition 187, the anti-immigration initiative, and Proposition 227, the anti-bilingual education initiative?

### African American and Latino Relations

With traditional blue collar industries in Los Angeles . . . disappearing fast, with city jobs that had begun to offer another avenue of advancement . . . now being claimed by L.A.'s Hispanic population, blacks in L.A. . . . had actually seen their situation deteriorate.

David Rieff (1991, 143)

The riots also exposed the tensions between African Americans and Latinos in competing for attention and resources in South Central Los Angeles. Although this area was described in the media and stereotyped in the minds of most white Angelenos as an inner city black neighborhood, it had become increasingly diverse, with a large community of Mexican Americans and pockets of recent Central American immigrants making up nearly half of the area's population (Johnson & Oliver, 1989). They had established their own distinctively Latin culture with their own small shops, services, and restaurants, moved their extended families into the large, older, two-family homes and small bungalows lining the broad avenues with Spanish names like Figueroa, La Cienega, and Pico Boulevard, named after the last Mexican governor of California who was of mixed Spanish, Indian, and black heritage.

Although many Latinos were engaged in manual labor, service occupations, and unskilled work, they had strong networks that helped them to find the jobs that whites and blacks did not want, jobs that barely paid a minimum wage (or lower), had few benefits, and few opportunities for mobility (Johnson & Oliver, 1989). For those Latinos who were undocumented, Los Angeles represented the end of the fabled yellow brick road or the pot of gold at the end of the rainbow. Yet their aspirations collided with the African Americans in South Central who found themselves unemployed and obsolete with skills that were no longer useful in the age of information and high technology. The growing Latino presence in South Central was a daily reminder that blacks didn't own this corner of Los Angeles and that their political power would soon erode just as their economic viability had vanished.

Adding insult to injury, the rioters were portrayed by the media as primarily African American, yet these were equal opportunity riots where people joined in for many different motivations—some were angry at the police and the criminal justice system, some were angry about their frustrated lives, some were looking for an opportunity to get some free merchandise, and some were just having an antisocial adventure. The continuous television coverage of the four-day riots clearly shows Latinos, Asians, and even some whites joining in the general vandalism and looting of the stores. In fact, the majority of those arrested during the riots for looting and vandalism were Latinos, not African Americans (Oliver, Johnson, & Farrell, 1993).

Latino leaders complained that the police had selectively arrested Latinos because they were easy targets and, if found to be undocumented, they could be turned over to the INS for deportation. Further, the police realized that Latinos had far less political clout and fewer civil rights organizations to protect their interests and to protest their unfair treatment. After the Rodney King beating, the LAPD had cautioned its officers to be particularly careful about arresting African Americans, and this was reflected in plummeting arrest rates in predominantly black neighborhoods since mid-1991. So, it seemed to some Latino leaders that the police had ignored the illegal behaviors of blacks and pursued the Latino rioters because they were much more vulnerable. The fact that many of these looters were poor mothers of young children, who were stealing baby food, diapers, and groceries, did not mitigate the aggressive efforts of the LAPD to arrest and incarcerate them.

Images of these Latinos being herded into police vans were not as prominent in the media as images of African Americans, yet they made an indelible impression on the Latino community, not only in Los Angeles, but throughout the state. Those images may have helped to energize "the sleeping giant" of the Latino community, which had never been a major factor in local or state politics. Few of those who were registered to vote even showed up at the polls, so Latinos were generally not counted on by the politicians or consulted by the policy makers in major city or statewide elections. Yet in 1996, only two years after the passage of Proposition 187 and four years after the South Central riots, Loretta Sanchez, a relatively unknown Latina businesswoman, ran for Congress as a Democrat in a heavily Republican district in Orange County, defeating Representative Robert Dornan, a conservative Republican who had supported anti-immigrant and anti-affirmative action legislation (Schrag, 1998). Stunned by this unexpected victory of the daughter of Mexican immigrants over a better-known and better-financed white male incumbent, political analysts attributed the upset to the growing number of Latinos in Orange County, now 25 percent of the county's population. The "sleeping giant" was waking up with a vengeance!

The riots also exposed the fault lines between the African American and Latino communities, fissures that had been gradually widening just below the surface for several decades as political leaders in both communities jockeyed for power and patched up their fraying coalition for strategic reasons (Regalado,1998). Rooted in historic tensions over jobs and housing at the low end of the economic pyramid, African Americans and Latinos in Los Angeles had developed an ambivalent but accommodating relationship that reflected the mores and cultural realities of Southern California in the last half of the twentieth century. The African American community was more integrated than Latinos into the economic and cultural fabric of the mainstream society, despite the obvious patterns of housing and job discrimination. Moreover, African Americans had a growing middle class, a thriving business community, and a foothold on the American dream. By contrast, Latinos were commonly viewed as immigrants, often undocumented, hired primarily in unskilled and domestic service jobs, and treated as cultural outsiders.

### Politics Is Not All Local: Long-Term Reverberations of the South Central Riots

After years of an uneasy alliance, forged not out of natural affinities but out of political exigencies, the 1992 riots once again forcefully reminded African Americans and Latinos of how easily their differences could be manipulated by the media, the police, and the power brokers to serve their own entrenched interests. But the simmering tensions between the two communities were destined to erupt again in two statewide campaigns in the 1990s to limit the rights of immigrants and to eviscerate bilingual education programs in the public schools. While the interests of African Americans and Latinos certainly coincided over rejecting Proposition 209, the anti-affirmative action initiative that specifically targeted people of color, it was not at all certain that blacks would oppose Propositions 187 and 227, both of which targeted non-English-speaking immigrants. For some African Americans this would create a painful dilemma, that is, whether to oppose these discriminatory measures against other ethnic minority groups or whether to choose their own group's self-interest in limiting immigrants' access to jobs and education.

### FROM RIOTS TO REACTIONARY REFORMS

Greater Los Angeles is about to become the new Pacific Byzantium, with only a minority of whites, and a population exceeding Greater New York. Statistics on crime grow worse. The underclass grows steadily larger. . . . It is also becoming as primitive as many Pacific Rim cities, with new sweatshops, depleted medical services, and a two-tier segregated society increasingly more similar to many Pacific cities.

Norman Klein (1990, 31)

As the urban hub of Southern California, Los Angeles dominates the politics, the economy, and the culture of the most populated area of the state. Its media market is the largest on the West Coast, reaching more than twelve million people daily, controlling their access to information, shaping their opinions, and defining their images (*Los Angeles Times*, 1992). The Los Angeles riots in the spring of 1992 were literally seen and heard around the world, on television screens and in graphic newspaper and magazine images. These images were bound to inflame the emotions, distort the perceptions, and bias the opinions of Californians of all racial, ethnic, and social class groups. Those whites who had decried the beating of Rodney King and could empathize, if not condone, the uprising in South Central found themselves appalled and enraged by the unprovoked assault on Reginald Denny by a group of four self-described black gang members (Gibbs, 1996; *Los Angeles Times*, 1992). Their identification with Denny as one of their own group created even deeper empathy and triggered an angry backlash against the black rioters.

The impact of these violent and disturbing images exacerbated the pre-existing tensions between whites and non-whites, between Hispanics and non-Hispanics, between rich and poor. More importantly, these stark images of violence, looting, and civil disobedience in South Central Los Angeles may well have given conservative politicians in California powerful ammunition for them to launch sustained assaults on the most disadvantaged and vulnerable of the state's residents: minorities and immigrants.

Despite its laissez-faire ambience, Los Angeles often seems more in tune politically with its conservative past than with its innovative present. In Los Angeles there is a chronic undercurrent of fear and anxiety about crime and violence—what Mike Davis (1992, 224) calls "the social perception of threat"—that is easily manipulated by politicians and the police who have a vested interest in promoting harsh penalties for criminal offenders and perpetuating their own powerful institutions of social control. Thus, the majority of voters in Los Angeles became enthusiastic supporters of Proposition 184, the "Three Strikes" initiative, a measure that promised safe streets and social stability, perhaps heralding a return to a simpler, more homogeneous, community.

If crime could be brought under control, why not the flood of alien and troublesome immigrants who were overwhelming the infrastructure of Los Angeles, changing the character of their city, overburdening its welfare system? Proposition 187, intended to "Save Our State," seemed like a natural follow-up to reducing crime on the streets. After all, the television talk shows equated increased immigration with rising crime rates and the LAPD had warned citizens frequently about the alarming surge in Latino and Asian gang membership during the 1980s, so a hard-line against illegal aliens could easily be justified as a form of crime prevention and intensified social control (Davis, 1992; Maharidge, 1996).

Just two years later in 1996, two little-known college professors in Northern California launched a successful campaign to place Proposition 209, the "California Civil Rights Initiative," an anti-affirmative measure, on the statewide ballot (Chavez, 1998). This initiative revealed deep strains between the liberals who gave lip-service to equal rights for minorities and women and the conservatives who felt threatened by the growing presence of women and minorities in the elite schools and the executive suites

44

throughout the state. Rhetoric about meritocracy and quotas soon replaced rhetoric about equal opportunity and diversity in public discourse.

By the time Proposition 209 was placed on the ballot in the summer of 1996, the conservative forces in Southern California were well organized and confident of success. People of color had been identified as the enemy, as unworthy recipients of welfare benefits, and as unwelcome usurpers to reclaim California from its rightful heirs, those Anglo-American pioneers who had played by the rules, built the flourishing economy, and proved that they were qualified for the best universities and competent for the best jobs (Maharidge, 1996; Schrag, 1998). This was an easy sell for those white working- and middle-class California voters whose earning power had eroded and whose economic future was uncertain. Once again, minorities became the scapegoats for the political, economic, and social forces that the majority could neither control nor manipulate.

With the advent of Proposition 227, the "English Only" advocates stirred up the even deeper anxieties of these Los Angelenos about defining who they are and what American culture stands for (Maharidge, 1996; Rieff, 1991; Schrag, 1998). Facing the encroaching Latinization of Southern California, they made a defiant stand to resist the inroads of Spanish language and culture, hoping to hold back the tide just a few more years to assert their Anglo-American identity and to defend their Western heritage. The large voting blocs in Southern California were able to prevail over the more moderate and liberal voters in Northern California, as they had demonstrated in the three previous initiatives aimed at people of color.

History teaches us that single discrete actions of individuals and groups often have unintended, long-term multiple consequences. If we trace the trajectory of events from the routine arrest and subsequent beating of an unemployed laborer named Rodney King in the spring of 1991 to the riots in South Central Los Angeles just over one year later after a jury failed to convict three of his police assailants, it allows us to appreciate the enormous cost of that single act of police brutality (though part of a persistent and pervasive pattern of the Los Angeles Police Department) in lost lives and destroyed buildings, in race and ethnic relations, in civic pride and political capital, in personal reputations and professional honor. Above all, the South Central riots contributed to widening the gulf between the major ethnic minority groups and the dominant political constituencies in Los Angeles. The riots also deepened the schisms between those who wished to protect the status quo and preserve the city's image as a multicultural melting pot versus those who wished to redistribute the power and privilege of the ruling elite and create a new reality of the city as a haven of multiethnic mobility. From these fundamentally contrasting views and visions of Los Angeles, we can begin to assess the profound impact of the 1992 South Central riots on the broader California electorate in terms of the hardening of political attitudes, the search for quick-fix solutions, and the adoption of draconian policies to resist change and to restore stability to a world spinning out of control.

## REFERENCES

Blauner, R. (1972). *Racial oppression in America*. New York: Harper & Row.

Chavez, L. (1998). The color bind: California's battle to end affirmative action. Berkeley: University of California Press.

Christopher Commission. (1991). *Report of the Independent Commission on the Los Angeles Police Department*. Los Angeles: Office of the Mayor.

Davis, M. (1992). *City of quartz*. New York: Vintage Books.

Dear, M. J., Shockman, H. E., & Hise, G. (Eds.). (1996). *Rethinking Los Angeles*. Thousand Oaks, CA: Sage Publications.

Gibbs, J. T. (1996). *Race and justice: Rodney King and O. J. Simpson in a house divided*. San Francisco: Jossey-Bass.

Gooding-Williams, R. (Ed.). (1993). *Reading Rodney King/Reading urban uprising*. New York: Routledge.

Hahn, H. (1996). Los Angeles and the future: Uprisings, identity, and new institutions. In M. Dear, H. Schockman, & G. Hise (Eds.), *Rethinking Los Angeles* (pp. 77–95). Thousand Oaks, CA: Sage Publications.

Horne, G. (1995). *Fire this time*. Charlottesville: University Press of Virginia.

Johnson, J. H., Jr., & Oliver, M. L. (1989). Interethnic minority conflict in urban America: The effects of economic and social dislocations. *Urban Geography, 10*, 449–463.

Kim, E. (1993). Home is where the Han is: A Korean-American perspective on the Los Angeles upheavals. In R. Gooding-Williams (Ed.), *Reading Rodney King/Reading urban uprising* (pp. 215–235). New York: Routledge.

Klein, N. M. (1990). The sunshine strategy: Buying and selling the fantasy of Los Angeles. In N. M. Klein & M. J. Schiesl (Eds.), *20th century Los Angeles: Power, promotion, and social conflict*. Claremont, CA: Regina Books.

Los Angeles Times. (1992). *Understanding the Riots*. Los Angeles: The Times-Mirror Company.

Maharidge, D. (1996). *The coming white minority: California, multiculturalism and America's future*. New York: Vintage Books.

Martin, T. (1993). From slavery to Rodney King: Continuity and change. In H. R. Madhubuti (Ed.), *Why L.A. happened: Implications of the '92 Los Angeles rebellion* (pp. 27–40). Chicago: Third World Press.

McMillan, T. (1993). This is America. In H. R. Madhubuti (Ed.), *Why L.A. happened: Implications of the '92 Los Angeles rebellion* (pp. 237–240). Chicago: Third World Press.

Oliver, M. L., Johnson, J. H., Jr., & Farrell, W. C., Jr. (1993). Anatomy of a rebellion: A political-economic analysis. In R. Gooding-Williams (Ed.), *Reading Rodney King/Reading urban uprising* (pp. 117–141). New York: Routledge.

Park, E.J.W. (1996). Our L.A.? Korean Americans in Los Angeles after the civil unrest. In M. J. Dear, H. E. Schockman, & G. Hise (Eds.), *Rethinking Los Angeles* (pp. 153–168). Thousand Oaks, CA: Sage Publications.

Regalado, J. A. (1998). Minority political incorporation in Los Angeles: A broader consideration. In M. B. Preston, B. E. Cain, & S. Bass (Eds.), *Racial and ethnic politics in California* (pp. 381–409). Berkeley: Institute of Governmental Studies Press, University of California, Berkeley.

Rieff, D. (1991). *Los Angeles: Capital of the third world*. New York: Simon & Schuster.

Schrag, P. (1998). *Paradise lost: California's experiences, America's future*. Berkeley: University of California Press.

Sonenshein, R. (1998). Jewish participation in California politics: A revisit in the 1990s. In M. B. Preston, B. E. Cain, & S. Bass (Eds.), *Racial and ethnic politics in California* (pp. 109– 136). Berkeley: Institute of Governmental Studies Press, University of California, Berkeley.

Sterngold, J. (1997). 5 years after Los Angeles riots, inner city still cries out for jobs. *New York Times*, April 28, A1.

# CHAPTER 4

# California's Three Strikes Initiative: The Politics of Crime and Corrections

Not since the days of the all white juries and state-sponsored discrimination under Jim Crow laws has the United States seen such a dramatic display of systematic overrepresentation in its public policies. "Three Strikes and You're Out" can truly be said to be California's apartheid.

—Davis, Estes, & Schiraldi (1996, 5)

On November 1, 1994 California voters passed Proposition 184, the so-called "Three Strikes and You're Out" initiative, a law requiring that all third-time felonious offenses carry a mandatory twenty-five-years-to-life sentence. California's "Three Strikes" initiative was voted into law by greater than a two to one margin (72 percent versus 28 percent). Although an exact copy of the voter-approved "Three Strikes" legislation had already passed the California legislature and been signed by Governor Pete Wilson earlier that year, the initiative's supporters wanted the proposition to be taken to the voters so that overturning it would require a constitutional amendment.

The presumptive goals of the California "Three Strikes" initiative were to deter repeat felony offenders from engaging in future serious crimes by mandating stiffer penalties for third-time convictions for any type of felony offense. Conviction would carry a twenty-five-year minimum sentence with offenders being required to serve at least 80 percent of that time in prison, rather than the usual 50 percent of the sentence if the prisoner engages in rehabilitation efforts and maintains good behavior (California Secretary of State's Office, 1994). Moreover, the sentence would be doubled for a person convicted of a second "strike," even for a minor felony, that is, not classified as violent or serious, such as rape, robbery, or burglary.

Voters supporting this "tough on crime" measure reported being concerned with their safety. A series of *Los Angeles Times* polls conducted from 1991 through 1994 found that in two years (1992–1994) there was a 300 percent increase in residents reporting crime and gangs as the most significant problem facing California (Weintraub, 1994), although in the same poll, 72 percent of the respondents were unwilling to cut funds for public education to finance prison maintenance. Support for the "Three Strikes" initiative carried it to victory, despite the reality that actual crime rates had been declining in nearly every category throughout the state of California since 1992 (Schrag, 1998).

The political, social, and economic climate during California's 1994 preelection campaign facilitated the climate for a chain of conservative propositions having a disproportionate impact on ethnic minorities, immigrants, and women. In the first state positioned to become a minority-majority state by the early twenty-first century, the backlash to three decades of progressive legislation began with Proposition 184.

## POLITICS AND PROPOSITION 184: BACKGROUND ISSUES

In January of 1994, an election year, California Governor Pete Wilson had been informed of two comprehensive reports that documented statewide reductions in crime. Notwithstanding these reports, Governor Wilson called a special legislative session to address the public's increasing concerns over crime and public safety. Governor Wilson's focus on crime in California just happened to coincide with his decline in the polls during his 1994 reelection campaign against Kathleen Brown, a popular Democratic gubernatorial candidate and the daughter and sister of two former California governors (Schrag, 1998). Wilson's advocacy of harsh penalties for chronic offenders sharpened his image as a conservative "law and order" candidate and gave him a powerful platform against a liberal candidate associated with a "soft on crime" perspective. During that session, an Assembly Bill (AB 971) commonly referred to as the "Three Strikes" initiative was introduced, passed the legislature, and was signed into law by the governor. A series of other "tough on crime" measures followed in the same year. Five additional targeted bills on "three strikes" were brought to the legislature in 1993–1994. Legislation stipulating life sentences for first-time sex offenders, sometimes referred to as the "one strike and you're in" law, was implemented.

The legislative analyst, a nonpartisan state bureaucrat, estimated that the increased costs of incarcerating nonviolent felons convicted of second and third strikes under AB 971 would swell the prison operating budget by $3 billion by the year 2003 and $6 billion by the year 2026, exclusive of the additional billions needed to build more prisons to house the expanding prison population (California Secretary of State's Office, 1994). Moreover, the Rand Institute issued two reports predicting that the anticipated costs for the correctional budget would increase from about 8.5 percent of the state's budget in the mid 1990s to about 20 percent by 2004–2005, leaving less than 7 percent in the general fund for nonmandated programs such as higher education, the court system, the highway patrol, and other essential state services (Greenwood et al., 1994; Shires, 1996).

Behind the political manipulation of the public's perception of increased crime and the hysteria over imagined threats to the public safety was the cynical exploitation of the tragic murders of two California girls, Kimber Reynolds and Polly Klaas, slain in random acts of violence (Schrag, 1998). Both were Caucasian, middle-class, adolescent girls with promising futures, a network of support, and loving families. Both of the girls' fathers, Mike Reynolds and Marc Klaas, became crusaders as a direct result of their daughters' deaths. These two fathers, united by tragedy, played very different but crucial roles in providing the rationale for the initial legislation, but eventually diverged in their positions on Proposition 184.

The "lock 'em up" philosophy was appealing to Mike Reynolds, father of slain Kimber Reynolds. Prior to sponsoring Proposition 184, Mike Reynolds founded an organization called Crime Victims United in an effort to ensure that other potential victims would not face the tragic fate that his daughter faced. In an effort to avenge the violent murder of his 18-year-old daughter in 1992, Mike Reynolds began the organizing efforts for Proposition 184 after he had been successful in lobbying for the passage of AB 971 in the California State Legislature (Schrag, 1998).

The 1993 abduction and murder of 12-year-old Polly Klaas by Richard Allen Davis spawned activism in Petaluma, California, the small suburb of the Klaas family's residence, and gripped the nation. In memory of his abducted and murdered daughter, Marc Klaas worked to establish both the Polly Klaas and Marc Klaas Foundations. The goals of these volunteer-based, nonprofit organizations are to assist parents and communities to recover missing children, to disseminate child safety guidelines, and to lobby in support of child safety legislation. Marc Klaas initially supported the "Three Strikes" initiative but eventually opposed it because he believed that it offered an inadequate solution to crime reduction. In his words, "the measure is too soft on hard crime and too hard on soft crimes" (Schiraldi, Sussman, & Hyland, 1994).

Notwithstanding Marc Klaas's change of heart about the "Three Strikes" initiative, Governor Pete Wilson, who had initially shown little support for the punitive legislation, recognized its political potential as a way to invigorate his faltering campaign. Since voters were horrified by the Polly Klaas kidnap murder and public sentiment was clearly coalescing around the need for anticrime legislation, the Wilson campaign joined the bandwagon and rode it to victory in the November elections.

After several unsuccessful attempts to pass the law, the bill was revived and widely endorsed after Polly Klaas was murdered. With Governor Wilson's enthusiastic advocacy of this strong law and order legislation, the bill easily passed in the state legislature. On March 7,1994, the same day Governor Wilson signed Assembly Bill 971 into law, Mike Reynolds' Crime Victims United organization submitted an identical initiative to the California Secretary of State with enough signatures to qualify for the November ballot as Proposition 184 (Schiraldi, Sussman, & Hyland,1994). It was a fairly auspicious beginning of a series of voter-initiated ballot propositions that would change the legal, social, and cultural landscape of California in the final decade of the twentieth century.

### "Three Strikes" Initiative: Pro and Con Arguments

Proponents of Proposition 184 emphasized the high rates of repeat offenders in the criminal justice system, while pledging legislative action that would purportedly turn the situation around. The legislative intent of Proposition 184 was to deter individuals with multiple felony offenses from committing future crimes and becoming a drain on the prosecution arm of the criminal justice system. This policy was presumably designed to reduce the revolving door effect of so-called career or repeat offenders. With fewer repeat offenders out of custody, the expectation was that overall rates of violent crime would decrease in major metropolitan areas and communities would be improved. This emphasis on greater punishment and longer prison sentences would effectively shift the allocation of county and state resources over time from rehabilitation and treatment to long-term incarceration and punishment of repeat offenders through an increased need for financing of larger prisons and constant jail construction and maintenance.

Opponents of Proposition 184 argued that its implementation would have a disproportionate negative impact on people of color and focused on the many flaws in its provisions. They also contended that the popular political discourse on 184 did not present the legislation accurately. For example, one argument in support of Proposition 184 was that it would make communities safer by removing violent offenders from neighborhoods. However, the blanket legislation is written such that the law does not apply only to violent offenders, but to anyone who has committed three felony offenses. Additionally, the law includes some felonies committed by juveniles over the age of 16. This component was controversial because some voters who were likely to vote for the "Three Strikes" initiative may have been less critical of adolescent criminal behavior and surprised to find that the legislation covered youth under 18 years of age, who are under the supervision of juvenile court policies and procedures.

The "Three Strikes" law would target those youths who are most at risk for becoming involved in illegal activities, that is, those who are young, minority, and high school dropouts. Among youthful offenders, over 40 percent are illiterate and one-third are unemployed upon arrest, suggesting that these youth need education and training for productive employment rather than arrest and incarceration in nonproductive prisons. Moreover, opponents of Proposition 184 pointed out the relative irreversibility of the legislation as it would take a constitutional amendment to change the law.

Lobbying efforts against Proposition 184 focused on its high cost of implementation, absence of an evaluation component, disproportionate impact on people of color and consensus of opposition among criminal justice experts. Opponents also noted that states that had previously adopted "Three Strikes" laws such as Tennessee, New Mexico, Colorado, and North Carolina had chosen not to implement them at all. Critics of these state laws overwhelmingly contend that "Three Strikes" laws are ineffective and discriminate by equating vastly different criminal charges, thus severely limiting judicial discretion based on the scope and severity of the individual felony (Schiraldi & Ambrosio, 1997).

As the campaign for Proposition 184 progressed, nearly every major politician in the state jumped on the bandwagon to demonstrate their law and order credentials, including Democratic Senator Diane Feinstein and gubernatorial candidate Kathleen Brown, both of whom were considered moderate-to-liberal on the issue. In dramatizing the need for strong anticrime measures, the advocates for "Three Strikes" legislation used Mike Reynolds and Marc Klaas as their poster boys for victims' rights. However, Marc Klaas and his family had second thoughts about Proposition 184 when they saw some of the early cases of young men who received the harsh sentence for nonviolent crimes. The Klaas family disavowed its initial support for Proposition 184, but not before Polly Klaas's death had been exploited in the press and manipulated by the members of the "Three Strikes" campaign committee (Schiraldi, Sussman, & Hyland, 1994; Schrag, 1998). By the eve of the November election, many of the California legislators who had voted for AB 971 and most of the major newspapers in the state were now opposing Proposition 184.

## FINANCING THE CAMPAIGN FOR PROPOSITION 184

The prison guard's union, former Congressman Michael Huffington, and the National Rifle Association (NRA) were the major financial contributors to Proposition 184. In total, these three far-right, conservative, "tough on crime" interests fueled the pro-"Three Strikes" initiative campaign to the tune of about half a million dollars. The California Republican Party contributed an additional $428,000 in the month preceding the November 1994 election. Of all political action committees, the California Correctional Peace Officers' Association (CCPOA) was number two in political contributions for 1992, giving over $1 million to various candidates. This group has publicly taken credit for putting Governor Pete Wilson in office by giving almost $1 million to his gubernatorial race, the largest independent campaign contribution in California's history (Schiraldi, 1994). In 1990, CCPOA made campaign contributions of almost $2 million, which was double that of the California Teachers Association, a group that has ten times as many member on its roles. In the "Three Strikes" arena, CCPOA was the second largest contributor at $101,000, after Congressman Huffington who cosponsored the bill and contributed $300,000, perhaps pledged in an effort to advance his hopes of unseating the incumbent U.S. senator, Democrat Diane Feinstein of California (California Secretary of State's Office, 1995). Additionally, the NRA made a cash contribution to Mike Reynolds's organization, the Crime Victims United group that was involved in spearheading the organizing efforts for Proposition 184. The NRA can be credited with partial responsibility for the passing of Proposition 184 as it donated advertising space, offered financial support, and shared grass-roots organizing methods to increase dissemination of pro-Proposition 184 campaign materials to its membership. Mike Reynolds himself contributed $221,508 to the campaign for Proposition 184 (California Secretary of State's Office, 1995).

The infusion of strategically placed campaign contributions suggests multiple agendas and potentially conflicting politics. For example, Michael Huffington's $300,000 contribution to the "Three Strikes" campaign and cochairmanship of the bill offered a tough-on-crime avenue for Congressman Huffington to introduce himself to the entire state while running for the U. S. Senate seat then held by Senator Diane Feinstein (Schiraldi, 1994). The prison guards' union (CCPOA) contribution of $101,000 signaled its desire to support the state's fastest growing industry and to increase the number of corrections officers by supporting Governor Wilson's platform, as they had donated record amounts to his previous campaign. It is unlikely that the CCPOA was genuinely committed to deterring criminal activity as its growth and expansion is dependent upon increases in the prison inmate population.

The NRA's direct cash contribution of $40,000 coupled with undisclosed amounts of in-kind material and human resource donations may seem inexplicable at first glance. Yet, the NRA's powerful lobbying body reflects the conservative agenda of a constituency that advocates gun ownership as a constitutional right, yet sees no inconsistency with the burgeoning rates of death and disability from gun-related accidents, suicides, and homicides in American society. Although these major contributors to the Proposition 184 initiative may have believed their interests were best served by passage of "Three Strikes" laws, another lesser known entity has reaped enormous benefits from California prison expansion.

Aggressive lobbying efforts of CCPOA officials have resulted in its phenomenal, rapid expansion and significant political clout. In little more than a decade, CCPOA has increased its largely high school-educated membership by 500%, successfully negotiating compensation packages that average $50,000 a year (Schiraldi, 1994). Their salaries are the highest in the nation for corrections officers, rivaling highway patrol officers, far exceeding public school teachers, and even greater than some tenured professors at the University of California. This union collects $8 million annually in dues and spends about one-fourth of that on campaign endorsements. It is no wonder that the California legislature and Governor Pete Wilson were responsive to their agenda. In fact, various conservative political interest groups and media have exploited the society's anxiety about crime in an effort to counteract mounting evidence of the overall decline in crime rates.

There were few organizations that reported contributions over $10,000 to the campaign against Proposition 184. These included the American Friends Service Committee, a Quaker organization, for $10,292; the California Teachers Association Issues PAC for $10,000; and a grass-roots coalition called Taxpayers for Effective Crime Prevention for contributions of $31,070 (California Secretary of State's Office, 1995). Among the other organizations that registered their opposition to Proposition 184 by making contributions under $10,000 to the campaign to defeat it were the California Democratic Council, the ACLU Foundation of Northern California, the California Democratic Socialists of America, the Alameda County Public Defenders' Association, and the Santa Cruz County Defense Bar Association. Well-known civil rights activists such as State Senator Tom Hayden, Eva Patterson, and Vincent Schiraldi also contributed to the opposition campaign. Liberal advocacy groups such as the Pacific Center for Violence Prevention and the Center on Juvenile and Criminal Justice provided educational information to the campaign. Although numerous groups and individuals with moderate to liberal views on prison reform contributed small amounts of money and in-kind services to defeat the initiative, the supporters spent nearly thirty times the funds spent by the opponents of Proposition 184 ($1,295,791 versus $45,419) who were out-spent, out-maneuvered, and out-matched in the campaign (California Secretary of State's Office, 1995).

Organizations that opposed Proposition 184 included the American Civil Liberties Union, the NAACP-Legal Defense Fund, MALDEF, the League of Women Voters, and many labor unions, civil rights groups, religious organizations, and teachers' organizations. Educators were particularly concerned over the budgetary implications of Proposition 184 for the California public schools, already underfunded and overcrowded. Civil rights groups opposed the initiative because they feared it would have a disparate impact on ethnic minority young people, who would be most at risk for arrest and harsh penalties. Labor unions opposed it because the use of cheap prison labor in certain manufacturing operations undermine union wages and working conditions. Proposition 184 was opposed by religious groups on the grounds that it would lead to cruel and inhumane treatment of offenders, who could receive sentences that were disproportionate to their crimes.

Although individual Democratic candidates opposed Proposition 184, the California Democratic Party was unusually mute on this measure, fearing that they would alienate many of their working-class and suburban constituents by taking a stand against it. Even Willie Brown, the confrontational Speaker of the California Assembly, who had voted against the "Three Strikes" bill in the assembly, did not try to mobilize his Democratic colleagues to offer any organized opposition to it (Richardson,1998). Efforts to mount a statewide campaign against the initiative were simply too little and too late.

## THE CAMPAIGN FOR PROPOSITION 184

The campaign for Proposition 184 was waged with a ferocity that belied the actual declining crime rate in California. Supporters of the "Three Strikes" initiative shared the conservative view that criminals deserve punishment and retribution for their crimes, not empathy and rehabilitation. But their motivations were varied and sometimes incomprehensible. The Republican Party, which contributed directly and through indirect in-kind contributions to the campaign, was primarily concerned with reelecting Pete Wilson as governor, thus they supported an issue that would create controversy, polarize conservatives and liberals, and attract some independent voters. The Wilson campaign exploited the close filial relationship between Democratic gubernatorial candidate Kathleen Brown and her brother, former Governor Jerry Brown, who had opposed the death penalty during his term in office and was viewed as "soft on crime." Moreover, Pete Wilson reminded voters that Jerry Brown had appointed Rose Bird to be Chief Justice of the California Supreme Court, an appointment so controversial that she was removed by the voters in 1986 over her ultra-liberal views and persistent failure to uphold the state's death penalty (Schrag, 1998). Thus, Wilson projected onto Kathleen Brown the political baggage of her brother, pressuring her to declare lukewarm support for Proposition 184 near the end of the campaign.

The prison guards' union, CCPOA, saw Proposition 184 as a measure that would generate hundreds of jobs and increase the power and prominence of their union in the state. They had lobbied aggressively for AB 971, the "Three Strikes" bill passed in March 1994 by the California State Legislature, but they realized that Proposition 184, as a constitutional amendment, was an insurance policy against legislative repeal and for their own economic security (Schiraldi, 1994). Republican Congressman Michael Huffington, who contributed $300,000 to the campaign for Proposition 184, hoped it would gain him votes of moderate Democrats and independents in his contest to defeat incumbent Democratic Senator Diane Feinstein, but she neutralized his strategy by speaking at the memorial service for Polly Klaas, assuring a wide audience of her own anticrime credentials (Schrag, 1998).

Corporate contributions to the pro-Proposition 184 campaign reflected the interests of California's large businesses in promoting law and order in their communities, creating conditions conducive for attracting capital and labor. Safe streets and crime-free neighborhoods were not only appealing to homeowners, but became marketing slogans for real estate developers, entrepreneurs, local politicians, and community leaders.

The National Rifle Association supported the "Three Strikes" initiative as part of their broader strategy to win friends and influence people over the controversial issue of gun control. Through advocating harsher penalties for the victims of crime, the NRA used an effective strategy of diverting attention away from the public's easy access to guns, which are the weapons of choice for most criminals.

Ultimately Mike Reynolds turned a personal tragedy into a political crusade, using his slain daughter Kimber as a symbol of all the victims of violent crime. His success at mobilizing the media and the legislature to respond to the murder of his daughter laid the foundation for his later successful advocacy for Proposition 184. The timing of his initiative just happened to coincide with Pete Wilson's search for a wedge issue that would galvanize voters behind his campaign, a fateful coincidence for the criminal justice system in California.

## Opposing Views on Proposition 184

Among the organizations that went on record to oppose Proposition 184 during the campaign were a number of lawyers' and judges' groups such as the California Attorneys for Criminal Justice, the California Public Defenders Association, the California Judges Association, and the Los Angeles District Attorney. Additionally, organizations such as the American Civil Liberties Union, the California Drug Policy Reform Coalition, and the League of Women Voters of Orange County also opposed it and were united in their warnings about the long-term costs of the "Three Strikes" provisions, as well as the damage that would be inflicted on education and social programs in the state of California.

Opponents to Proposition 184 marshaled their arguments against the "Three Strikes" initiative on ethical, financial, and humane grounds. First, they pointed out that the provisions of the law would have a disparate impact on minority males, especially on African Americans who had committed felony offenses as juveniles (Davis, Estes, & Schiraldi, 1996). Many of these offenses were nonviolent drug-related crimes, but any felonies committed after age 16 could be counted as a first or second strike.

A second major objection to the bill was the increased cost of long-term imprisonment of these nonviolent offenders. These prison operating costs were predicted to escalate to at least $6 billion by 2020, consuming a major share of the state's annual budget, to the detriment of funds for education, health, and welfare, and environmental programs (California Secretary of State's Office, 1994). Under Governor Wilson, the state's allocation for corrections had already increased to 8.5 percent in the 1997–1998 budget, the highest level of the three previous California governors (Taqi-Eddin, Macallair, & Schiraldi, 1998).

Third, civil libertarians argued that the "Three Strikes" law is antithetical to our system of criminal justice, as it violates the principle of proportionality as articulated by the Eighth Amendment of the Bill of Rights. This amendment expressly forbids the infliction of "cruel and unusual punishments" that are out of proportion to the offense committed. Yet, under "Three Strikes," offenders can be sentenced to lengthy prison terms for a second or third nonviolent felony offense such as petty theft or passing bad checks (Morain, 1994a). By removing judicial discretion from sentencing, the law does not take into account the severity of the offense or any mitigating circumstances of the offender.

Fourth, there was a humanitarian concern for the high percentage of prisoners who would age in prison, creating excessive costs for medical care due to increasing physical and mental disabilities. The estimated $60,000 annual cost of maintaining an older prisoner is three times more than for a younger prisoner at $20,000 per year, but most crimes are committed by men in the fifteen to twenty-four age range, with only 1 percent of all serious crimes committed by people over age sixty (Zimbardo, 1994). However, as these young prisoners age, the "Three Strikes" law will create an explosion in California's geriatric population, which will be an enormous burden on the state's taxpayers (Morain, 1994b).

Finally, these critics of Proposition 184 expressed skepticism that the draconian measures of the "Three Strikes" law would be an effective deterrent to serious crime, particularly since it focused exclusively on punishment and retribution rather than treatment and rehabilitation (Davis, Estes, & Schiraldi, 1996; Zimbardo, 1994).

## Public Opinion and "Three Strikes"

By early March of 1994, public opinion polls indicated that crime was the top concern for California voters, who expressed overwhelming support (by an 8 to 1 ratio) for the "Three Strikes" legislation proposed in Assembly Bill 971 to lock up repeat offenders for their third felony crime (Schiraldi, Sussman, & Hyland, 1994). In the absence of any opposing views, the public easily succumbed to the alarmist claims of the bill's supporters, paving the way for the smooth passage of Proposition 184.

However, by the time Proposition 184 was placed on the ballot and voters were facing the prospect of adopting an amendment to the state's constitution in the November election, the public had become more educated about the impact of the law on nonviolent offenders and they had become more cautious about the long-term implications of the initiative. Support for Proposition 184 had declined in the wake of criticism by Marc Klaas and his family against its draconian provisions, so the polls showed that voter approval was about 2 to 1 in favor of the initiative (Schiraldi, Sussman, & Hyland, 1994). However, 85 percent of those polled preferred that a "violent-crime-only" provision be included in the proposition.

## IMPACT OF PROPOSITION 184: RACIAL DISPARITIES AND EXCESSIVE COSTS

The two most tangible consequences of "Three Strikes" implementation today are the growing and disproportionate rates of incarceration of African Americans and Latinos and the high cost of warehousing nonviolent third strikers.

The incarceration rates for African American men in California is 3,700 per 100,000, compared to 681 per 100,000 in South Africa (Davis, Estes, & Schiraldi, 1996). By 1994 California's inmate population had already exploded to 200,000, which roughly equals the combined prison populations in England, France, Italy, Spain, Sweden, Switzerland, and Finland.

In their paper on "Three Strikes: The New Apartheid," Davis, Estes, and Schiraldi (1996) discuss how African Americans do worse and Caucasians fare comparatively better under the new "Three Strikes" law. They note that while African Americans are 7 percent of the California state population they constitute 23 percent of felony arrests, are 31 percent of the state prison population, and 43 percent of third-strike prisoners. Comparatively, whites represent 53 percent of the state population, constitute 33 percent of felony arrests, are 29.5 percent of the state prison population, and 24.6 percent of the third-strike prisoners. This data illustrates how African Americans are grossly overrepresented as third-strike prisoners and whites are underrepresented relative to their proportions in the general population; blacks are 4.7 times more likely to be arrested than whites, 7.8 times more likely to be imprisoned than whites, and 13.3 to 17 times more likely to be third strikers than whites. In Los Angeles, for example, black male offenders were 17 times more likely than whites to be charged under the "Three Strikes" law, although there is no credible evidence that blacks actually commit more total offenses than whites. It has been proposed that blacks are more likely to be vulnerable to police surveillance and arrest, since they are more likely to commit street crimes in inner-city neighborhoods, but middle-class whites who are more likely to commit white-collar crimes and suburban crimes are less likely to be apprehended and convicted (Poe-Yamagata & Jones, 2000).

One of the particularly troubling aspects of the law allowed prosecutors to take into account a juvenile offense as the "first strike," even though juvenile offenses had previously not been counted against an adult defendant in deciding his penalty. Moreover, this provision would clearly have a greater negative impact on African American and Latino males, who were more likely than whites or Asians to have been arrested and convicted for minor violations of the law as juveniles and for petty drug crimes or nonviolent felonies as young adults.

A three-year follow-up of the implementation of the "Three Strikes" law showed that the disproportionate representation of African Americans and Latinos in the inmate population is reversed for high-level prosecutors in the criminal justice system in California (Davis, Estes, & Schiraldi, 1996). Seventy percent of three-strike inmates come from Los Angeles, Orange, San Bernardino, Sacramento, and San Diego counties, where 82 percent of the prosecuting attorneys are white. The counties that prosecute three-strike cases most aggressively can also be characterized as those with disproportionate numbers of Caucasians in high-level supervisorial positions.

## California's Prison Population Explosion

With the prison population expected to continue to soar, as the result of the "victories" of the war on drugs and gangs . . . California is creating a time-bomb of multiple-Attica potential. Lacking minimal educational, job-training or drug-treatment resources, the prisons of today have all but abandoned the pretense of "rehabilitation."

Mike Davis, (1992, 289)

During the fifteen-year period from 1977 through 1992, the California Department of Corrections prison population had increased by 500 percent (Foote, 1993). The inmate population in 1977 was less than 20,000 but had grown to levels greater than 100,000 by 1992. This corresponds to an incarceration rate of 87 persons per 100,000 in 1977 to 358 per 100,000 in 1993. State correction facilities in 1992 were at 170 percent of capacity with 80 percent of inmates in county jails incarcerated in overcrowded facilities.

According to criminologists, the United States has the highest rate of incarceration on the planet (Davis, Estes, & Schiraldi, 1996). This rate surpasses China, West Germany, South Africa, and the Soviet Union. South Africa's rate of incarceration is 311 of every 100,000 people compared with the United States rate of 455 prisoners for every 100,000 adult Americans. Most developed countries have incarceration rates of about 70 per 100,000.

California's prison system is the largest in the country and the second largest in the world with 12.5 percent of all U.S. prisoners residing in California. Prisons are so dense in California that one could drive from Sacramento to Los Angeles, a seven-hour journey, and never be more than forty minutes from a corrections facility (Davis, Estes, & Schiraldi, 1996).

In an effort to house the rapidly expanding prison population in California, budget allocations had to be increased for prison construction and maintenance. During the fourteen-year period from 1980 to 1994, California prison spending rose from $300 million to $3 billion dollars. These figures take into account one-time construction costs, but can only provide an estimate of the rising costs of ongoing prison operations which in 1993 were about $25,000 annually per inmate bed. In 1993 alone, an additional 1,000 beds were added to California prisons and jails to capture the overflowing population.

### California's Fastest Growing Industry

The prison system is not only very large but has spawned a very lucrative industry. In 1994 California spent about $4 billion on prisons and jails. A RAND study of Proposition 184's cost to California taxpayers concluded that its implementation would increase the state's prison budget from $3 billion to $5.5 billion annually and cost each taxpayer approximately $300 a year (Greenwood et al., 1994). The majority of the budget would be expansion dollars covering construction costs of twenty-five new prisons to compensate for the inmate population predicted to double to approximately 250,000 by the turn of the century. Other estimates suggested as many as eighty new prisons and expenditures of $21 billion would result from the "Three Strikes" law. This prison population explosion happened in a time when the number of serious and violent crimes was actually declining. In fact, during the initial six months of 1994, before Proposition 184 was voted on, but during the time it was signed into law as AB 971, there was a 7.7 percent statewide reduction in serious crimes as compared to the previous year. Despite these dire predictions, the state's prison population actually registered a small decline in late 1999 and was 161,401 by June 30, 2000, well below the projected increase (Terry, 2000). California corrections officials attributed this slower rate of growth to both the declining crime rate and alternative sentencing for nonviolent offenders such as drug rehabilitation programs and extended parole.

Corrections Corporation of America (CCA) is the largest private corrections operation in the United States and the fifth largest of the combined public and private sectors. This private, for-profit company was established in 1983, not coincidentally at the onset of the prison explosion. CCA has grown in fifteen years to own and/or manage seventy-eight facilities with 63,500 inmate beds (Corrections Corporation of America, 1998). Each of these beds requires about $25,000 per year in operating costs. A simple math calculation reveals that CCA has annual revenue of approximately $1.5 billion dollars. As a company that has boasted sequential profits with mass earnings and such rapid growth that it was once publicly traded on the stock market, during the period 1995–1998 CCA's revenue increased at an annual rate of 57 percent and earnings increased at an annual rate of 69 percent. Net company income for CCA has steadily risen from $4 million in 1993 to $54 million in 1997. These financial gains raise the issue of the extent to which the profit motive competes with a rational social welfare perspective or humane correctional philosophy among supporters of "Three Strikes" legislation.

Proprietary interests supporting Proposition 184 create a mass of conflicts that complicate effective, unbiased, and nondiscriminatory assessment of the impact of any legislation. When private, for-profit corporations become involved in the business of prison operations there is an inherent conflict of interest. A corporation may have the best humanitarian intentions about rehabilitative efforts for a prison population, but that same corporation must ultimately answer to its shareholders whose primary interest, as capital investors, is profitability. Because these private corrections companies are often publicly traded, with CCA's net worth being greater than the remaining companies combined, there exists the unique opportunity for individual investors to gain financial benefit from the human tragedy and hardship of the incarceration of others. There seem to be no ethical considerations for contracting out such services, particularly in an industry that has had astronomical expansion that cannot be explained solely by a proportional increase in demand; for example, the California crime rate for all crimes has remained relatively constant over the last 25 years at about 100 per 100,000, yet the incarceration rate has steadily risen from about 100 per 100,000 in 1973 to about 350 per 100,000 in 1991. By 1994 that rate had risen to 626 per 100,000 (Foote, 1993).

### Warehousing the Recidivists: Costs of "Three Strikes"

As three strikers age in prison, they will increasingly require more sophisticated, complex, and costly medical services. Psychiatric services, rehabilitation, and reintegration services will consume prison costs with unknown potential consequences for the state. The aging prison population will increase dramatically in the coming years, driving up prison operation costs and medical costs, and aggravating the problem of prison and jail overcrowding (Zimbardo, 1994). The current California prison population of about 20,000 inmates over the age of fifty will rise to approximately 126,000 by the year 2020 due almost completely to the "Three Strikes" law (Foote, 1993). If three strikers convicted later in life survive to serve their full sentences, an average twenty-five-year sentence begun at age fifty and served until age seventy-five will cost taxpayers $1,000,500 per inmate. In essence, the prison population will expand because those convicted of crimes will stay in prisons much longer than they would have in the past given greater judicial discretion. While some three strikers will die in prison, many will emerge from jail bitter after having lost what may seem like a lifetime, yet still unrehabilitated and unprepared to participate productively in a high-tech economy.

Professor Philip Zimbardo (1994) of Stanford University suggests that the "Three Strikes" law essentially transforms prisons into corrections facilities for the elderly, illustrating how the inflexible sentencing regulations will necessarily mean that inmates will grow old in prisons. As such, tremendous costs not yet anticipated will need to be factored into the operations equations for inmates. The current estimate of $25,000 to $30,000 could rise to upwards of $60,000 annually for each prison inmate. As a society we could pay for the four-year college education of each of these inmates with one to two years of the cost needed to place him or her behind bars.

## EDUCATION VERSUS CORRECTIONS

Considering the cost of corrections and college together may seem like comparing apples and oranges; however, the legislation of Proposition 13 passed in 1978, coupled with Proposition 184, ensures that California will sacrifice education for corrections in the coming years. Proposition 13 was a landmark ballot initiative that assessed a flat 1 percent property tax rate, restricting increases to assessed property values and requiring a two-thirds voter authorization to levy additional tax increases (Schrag, 1998). Proposition 13 thus reduced the state and local government's ability to raise funds, which has most directly impacted education in a state with increasing public education demands related to its general population expansion. Proposition 184 will inevitably result in geometric increases in the cost of prison operations and maintenance, while Proposition 13's result will continue to be decreases in funding for public education.

Over the past two decades, the corrections budget in California has increased in inverse proportion to the dwindling education budget. The rate of corrections growth in the California budget is greater than all other major categories including health, welfare, and education. In fact, in 1996, California spent more funds on building and maintaining prisons than on its entire budget for schools and educating its students. From the state level, this fact sends a message to California citizens that education is competing with corrections and emerging a loser. Dramatizing this trend is the fact that in 1998 one African American male was enrolled at a University of California or California State University for every five African American men in prison, on probation, or on parole (Taqi-Eddin, Macallair, & Schiraldi, 1998). For every African American male University of California or California State University student who drops out of school, fifty-seven enter the corrections system. Although only 7 percent of the state population, African Americans are 31 percent of the state's prisoners but fewer than 6 percent of the students enrolled in state high schools and universities. Between 1990 and 1997, the Latino male population increased from 11 percent to 17 percent in the state's public universities, but grew from 31 percent to 35 percent in the state's correctional institutions.

These dismal statistics have provided fodder for the growing cadre of conspiracy theorists who contend that the legal intention of the "Three Strikes" laws is to remove all the potential black and Latino gang members, community organizers, and radical revolutionaries from the inner cities so that the ghettos and barrios can be easily contained and controlled in the event of a government decision to isolate minorities and to deprive them of their citizenship, as was forced on the Japanese Americans in World War II. An idea easily dismissed as a paranoid fantasy by most rational people, it nonetheless has gained considerable currency and dissemination in the African American community, where its proponents find supporting evidence in every questionable arrest, every unjustified police beating, and every law eroding the civil rights and civil liberties of the average citizen (Burris, 1999; Gibbs, 1996).

## IMPLEMENTATION OF THE "THREE STRIKES" LAW

After five years, the implementation of the "Three Strikes" law in California has come under close scrutiny and criticism. Studies have found disparities in the prosecution of the law across county jurisdictions in California, where county prosecutors vary from strictly enforcing the provisions of the law to virtually ignoring them (Males, Macallair, & Taqi-Eddin, 1999). A study by the Justice Policy Institute (Schiraldi, 1999a) found that there is no direct correlation between vigorous enforcement of the law and reduced crime rates, since violent crime rates in San Diego, where it was invoked eleven times more frequently, dropped less than crime rates in San Francisco, where it was rarely applied. One reason for these disparities is the ambiguity of the "third strike," which does not actually have to be a conviction of a *violent* offense, just a serious offense, thus creating confusion among prosecutors in different jurisdictions.

By September 1999, half of the more than 5,000 defendants who had received life sentences were nonviolent offenders. According to an op-ed piece by Schiraldi (1999a) in the *San Francisco Chronicle*, "more than twice as many people were imprisoned under 'three strikes' for drug possession and petty theft as for murder, rape, and kidnapping, combined" (A29). Some of the more bizarre "third strike" cases involved stealing one can of beer, a piece of cake, and a package of chuck steak, not exactly the type of felony offenses that threaten the social order.

In a recent study by Macallair (1999), crime rates in the over-thirty age group were the only rates to increase, despite the fact that this group comprised two-thirds of all the "three strikes" defendants and were eight to ten times more likely to be sentenced under the law than defendants under age twenty-eight. Thus, the harsh law did not seem to have the desired effect of deterring crime in the very age group with the highest rate of serious felony offenses.

In another study evaluating the impact of the "Three Strikes" law after five years, researchers at the University of California at Berkeley found that the law had almost no deterrent effect on repeat offenders (Chiang & Gledhill, 1999). In fact, those convicted under the "Three Strike" law were more likely to be arrested for violent offenses than other offenders, but they accounted for nearly the same proportion of arrests (12.8%) after the law was passed as they had before it took effect (13.9%). Although California accounted for 90 percent of all "Three Strikes" sentences in the nation from 1994 to 1999, the majority of prosecutors in the three counties studied (Los Angeles, San Diego, and San Francisco) were more likely to apply the "two strikes" penalties than the "three strikes" to felony offenders.

Moreover, the costs of endorsing the "Three Strikes" law are mounting enormously and threatening to overwhelm the state budget. In 1998, for the first time in its history, California spent more on prison construction and maintenance than on its entire higher education budget. California leads the nation with its over 165,000 inmates, which cost an average of $22,000 annually to incarcerate, yet conservative legislators, and even some moderates, continue to support billions of dollars for new prison construction in California (Taqi-Eddin, Macallair, & Schiraldi, 1998). Other studies have documented the cost effectiveness of drug treatment programs, alternative sentencing, and training programs, yet legislators are highly susceptible to the public's fear of crime and the political appeal of law and order platforms.

As Macallair (1999) has pointed out, "The current public policy of unbridled vengeance, as espoused by many of today's prosecutors, along with a political environment that scapegoats the vulnerable, ensures that reason, sensibility, and compassion will continue to lose out to the hysteria of the three-strike law" (B13).

## Critical Perspectives on Proposition 184

There are several major problems in the criminal justice system that demand critical scrutiny before harsher penalties can be justified and implemented fairly. First, a number of recent reports have documented persistent racial disparities and inequities in the juvenile justice system, where minority youth are overrepresented (Poe-Yamagata & Jones, 2000). In the report *The Color of Justice*, the Justice Policy Institute found that minority youth in California are more than twice as likely as white youth to be transferred from the juvenile justice system to be tried as adults, and concluded that:

> Discrimination against kids of color accumulates at every stage of the justice system and skyrockets when juveniles are tried as adults. California has a double standard: throw kids of color behind bars, but rehabilitate white kids who commit comparable crimes. (Males & Macallair, 2000, 18)

Further, the authors of the report noted that in Los Angeles County, the racial disparities increase at every phase of the process after a minority youth enters the adult court system. In fact, African American juvenile offenders were 18.4 times more likely to be sentenced to jail than their white counterparts, while Hispanic youth were 7.3 times and Asian youth, 4.5 times more likely to be imprisoned than white youth for similar offenses (Lewin, 2000).

An analysis of incarceration decisions for thousands of juvenile offenders in California by the National Council on Crime and Delinquency (cited in Schiraldi, 1999b) revealed that minority youth were locked up at higher rates than white youth even when their offenses and previous records were quite similar. Among youth who were arrested for violent offenses, for example, 47 percent of whites were detained as compared to 64 percent of African Americans and 61 percent of Latinos (cited in Schiraldi, 1999b).

These, and numerous other state and national surveys of the juvenile justice system, reflect systematic biases in the decisional pathways that result in the probability that minority youth will be less likely to be initially diverted from the system, less likely to receive alternative sentencing or probation, more likely to be sentenced to a correctional facility or jail, and more likely to receive a longer and harsher sentence than white youth who commit comparable offenses (Gibbs, 1988; Leonard, Pope, & Feyerherm, 1995).

Since the "Three Strikes" law in California allows prosecutors to disclose and use juvenile felony convictions as prior strikes, it is obvious that these laws will have a disparate negative impact on adult minority defendants accused of felony offenses. Without the resources to investigate the just application of the juvenile court's dispositions for these prior offenses, prosecutors and judges cannot be expected to be empathic or lenient in their application of the law.

Second, there has been a great deal of attention focused on the phenomenon of "racial profiling," the practice of police and highway patrol officers stopping, arresting, or harassing minority males while driving, walking through predominantly white residential areas, shopping in retail stores, or using public accommodations (American Civil Liberties Union, 1999). Frequently these encounters between police and minority males, particularly in traffic stops, escalate into violent confrontations, terminating in arrests or assaults. Under these circumstances, the police officer's version of the encounter is accepted in the official report, despite the widespread complaints in the African American and Latino communities about unjustified stops, searches, harassment, and brutality. Minorities have reported numerous incidents of being unjustifiably arrested and charged with "resisting arrest," "assaulting an officer," or some other trumped-up charge to justify the officer's misconduct. Unfortunately, such arrests may result in a felony conviction of the falsely accused defendant and make him vulnerable for a later "three strikes" conviction if he should commit any further real or alleged serious offenses. In June 1999, the American Civil Liberties Union of Northern California filed a lawsuit against the California Highway Patrol, charging racial discrimination targeting minority drivers (ACLU, 1999).

Third, serious charges of police misconduct and brutality have been lodged against urban police forces in California for the past fifty years (Burris, 1999; Davis, 1992; Gibbs, 1996; Skolnick & Fyfe, 1993). The LAPD, in particular, has been the focus of at least three major reports on police misconduct since the Watts Riots of 1965 (California State Assembly, 1992; Christopher Commission, 1991; McCone Commission, 1965), all of which documented a pervasive pattern of abuse and misconduct aimed at minorities. In late 1999 the most recent scandal broke out, exposing widespread misconduct and abuse in the Rampart Division of the LAPD, which had escalated by March 2000 to the most horrific charges of framing innocent people, planting drugs and guns, and beating and shooting suspects, resulting in deaths and disabling injuries (Cohen, 2000). While the LAPD reports of misconduct have received the most media attention, police forces in other California cities from San Francisco to San Diego have also been accused of biased treatment against minorities (Skolnick & Fyfe, 1993). With a plethora of such documentation of police misconduct, questions of the veracity and reliability of police arrests of minority offenders are certainly relevant to the fair operation of the criminal justice system. How many of these arrests are actually valid and justified? How many minority offenders have been advised by their lawyers to "plead out" for a guilty plea rather than risk a longer prison sentence in a jury trial? How many minority men in California have been wrongly convicted under a "Three Strikes" law that does not have any mechanism to account for prior wrongful arrests, prior wrongful convictions, and unjustified periods of incarceration based on the actions and testimony of corrupt police officers?

In the current investigation of misconduct in the Los Angeles Police Department, District Attorney Gil Garcetti had thrown out nearly one hundred wrongful convictions by August 30, 2000 and his office was eventually expected to investigate up to 4,400 cases, involving eighty or more police officers (Cohen, 2000; Terry, 2000). He admitted that this scandal was "the most important case I have seen this office handle in my 31 years here. It goes to the heart of police misconduct" (Deutsch, 2000, 3B).

## FIRST STRIKE IN RACE-BASED POLITICS: THE DOMINO EFFECT

> The media ... ceaselessly throw up spectres of criminal underclasses and psychotic stalkers. Sensationalized accounts of killer youth gangs high on crack and shrilly racist evocations of marauding Willie Hortons ... the moral panics that reinforce and justify urban apartheid.
>
> Mike Davis (1992, 226)

Proposition 184, the "Three Strikes" initiative, was the very first of a series of initiatives passed by the California voters that have far reaching consequences in ethnic minority communities. In some ways, these newly developed laws unravel a web of equity-building politics that were fragile and not designed to withstand a backlash against the slight, though significant, progress made by people of color in California since the late 1960s. The backlash against people of color in California has already launched a wave of racist, xenophobic sentiment sweeping the country, as exemplified in the proliferation of hate crimes against minorities, repressive legislation against immigrants, and legislative efforts to rescind or restrict programs such as affirmative action, desegregation of schools, and fair housing.

Whether intentional or accidental, the new wave of legislation begun with "Three Strikes" initiatives across the country disproportionately impacts against minorities and women in a number of negative and significant ways. Women are the fastest growing inmate population in California and are usually convicted on drug-related charges. Similar in demographic characteristics to their male counterparts, female offenders in California are disproportionately low-income, poorly educated, and people of color. Since many of these women are repeat offenders due to a toxic combination of drugs, prostitution, and domestic violence, they will swell the rank of third-strike inmates, quickly requiring new and expanded facilities to house them.

Recent national legislation abolishing the Aid to Families with Dependent Children (AFDC) program contains an article that excludes parents who are convicted drug felons from accessing the new replacement program Temporary Aid to Needy Families (TANF) (Adams, Onek, & Riker, 1998). This provision discriminates against women, children, and minorities who are overrepresented as recipients of public welfare benefits. In effect, the law punishes parents and their children with a *lifetime* ban on accessing welfare benefits for mothers who are convicted drug felons. It also channels serial offenders into the prison system rather than into treatment programs that are more cost effective and would preserve families, rehabilitate substance abusers, and save long-term costs of incarceration.

California's "Three Strikes" law raises fundamental questions about how we as a society should allocate our resources. Should we invest taxpayers' dollars into front-end programs such as crime prevention strategies by boosting education, employment training, affordable housing, and treatment programs? Or should we invest dollars at the back end in punitive programs such as incarceration, boot camps, and probation? The "Three Strikes" initiative is a law of lost hope and desperation for society, as it does not even attempt to address crime prevention strategies and early intervention programs but rather indiscriminately allocates seemingly endless tax dollars into prison construction and containment of those who are the most disadvantaged, disenfranchised, and dysfunctional in our society, who might be served more effectively by programs addressing their social, health, and employment needs.

On October 1, 1998, about 2,500 high school students converged on the East Bay town of San Leandro, a suburb of Oakland, to protest the spending cuts for California public schools (Lee & Fernandez, 1998). As they chanted "education, not incarceration," several speakers noted that the California state budget had increased by 60 percent in that same period. Student speakers also complained that recently built prisons had state-of-the-art computer equipment and recreation facilities compared to the outdated and inadequate resources in their schools. These student protestors clearly understood that the state's politicians valued prisons over schools, punishment over rehabilitation, incarceration over education, and that governmental resources were allocated accordingly. As a young Latina organizer reminded the marchers, "The need isn't to build more prisons, it's to build better schools" (Lee & Fernandez, 1998, A1).

The criminal justice system is simply a mirror of the underlying systemic racism and pervasive inequities that permeate nearly every institution of American society, resulting in the reproduction of inequality from generation to generation. If minorities do not have access to equal education and employment opportunities in American society, African Americans and other people of color will continue to be overrepresented in the criminal justice system, as legitimate avenues of social and economic mobility are blocked. If the problem of urban crime and the racial disparities associated with it are ever to be solved, there must be a coordinated strategy to eradicate poverty; to provide decent jobs, housing, and schools for low-income families; and to provide a set of family support policies for vulnerable families.

Finally, if this society is going to eliminate inequities in the criminal justice system, we must root out police misconduct and abuse and make police accountable to the community; we must monitor the media and insist on accuracy and objectivity in their portrayal of minority groups; and we must resist the rhetoric of politicians who thrive on demagoguery and division, and, when all else fails, will invoke the "race card" to create fear and anxiety in their constituents to win elections, and then interpret their victories as a "public mandate" for further repression against the poor, the people of color, and the powerless in our society.

## REFERENCES

Adams, R., Onek, D., & Riker, A. (1998). *Double jeopardy: An assessment of the felony drug provision of the welfare reform act.* Washington, DC: Justice Policy Institute.

Ambrosio, T. J., & Schiraldi, V. (1997). *From classrooms to cell blocks: A national perspective.* Washington, DC: The Justice Policy Institute.

American Civil Liberties Union. (1999). *Driving while Black: Racial profiling on our nation's highways.* New York: American Civil Liberties Union.

Burris, J. L. (1999). *Blue vs black: Let's end the conflict between cops and minorities.* New York: St. Martin's Press.

California Secretary of State's Office. (1994). *1994 California voter information: Proposition 184. Three strikes.* Sacramento, CA: author.

California Secretary of State's Office. (1995). *Financing California statewide ballot measures: 1994 primary and general elections.* Sacramento, CA: Political Reform Division.

California State Assembly. (1992). *Report of the Assembly Special Committee on the Los Angeles Crisis.* Sacramento, CA: Assembly Publications Office.

Chiang, H., & Gledhill, L. (1999). "Three Strike" law failing to deter crime, study says. *San Francisco Chronicle,* November 9, A5.

Christopher Commission. (1991). *Report of the Independent Commission on the Los Angeles Police Department.* Los Angeles: Office of the Mayor.

Cohen, A. (2000). Gangsta cops. *Time Magazine,* March 6, pp. 30–34.

Colvin, R. L. (1994). "3 Strikes" found hobbled by enormous prison costs: RAND says full implementation would cut crime by one-third but huge price tag makes that unlikely. *Los Angeles Times,* September 22, A1.

Corrections Corporation of America (CCA). (1998). *Crime & correctional statistics and untitled company information downloaded from Web.* Nashville, TN: author, pp. 1–15.

Davis, C., Estes, R., & Schiraldi, V. (1996). *"Three Strikes": The new apartheid.* San Francisco, CA: Center on Juvenile and Criminal Justice.

Davis, M. (1992). *City of quartz: Excavating the future in Los Angeles.* New York: Vintage Books.

Deutsch, L. (2000). 10 more convictions tossed out in scandal. *San Jose Mercury News,* Jan. 26, 3B.

Foote, C. (1993). *The prison population explosion: California's rogue elephant.* San Francisco, CA: Center on Juvenile and Criminal Justice.

Gibbs, J. T. (1996). *Race and justice: Rodney King and O. J. Simpson in a house divided.* San Francisco: Jossey-Bass.

Gibbs, J. T. (Ed.). (1988). *Young, Black and male in America: An endangered species.* Westport, CT: Greenwood Press.

Greenwood, P. W., Rydell, C. P., Abrahamse, A. F., Caulkins, J. P., Chiesa, J. R., Model, K. E., & Klein, S. P. (1994). *Three strikes and you're out: Estimated benefits and costs of California's new mandatory sentencing law.* Santa Monica, CA: RAND Institute.

Hewitt, C., Kubota, K., & Schiraldi, V. (1992). *Race & incarceration in San Francisco: Localizing apartheid.* San Francisco, CA: Center on Juvenile and Criminal Justice.

Koetting, M., & Schiraldi, V. (1994). *Singapore West: The incarceration of 200,000 Californians.* San Francisco, CA: Center on Juvenile and Criminal Justice.

Lee, H. K., & Fernandez, M. (1998). Rally in San Leandro. *San Francisco Chronicle,* October 2, A1.

Leonard, K., Pope, C., & Feyerherm, W. (Eds.). (1995). *Minorities in juvenile justice.* Thousand Oaks, CA: Sage.

Lewin, T. (2000). Racial discrepancy found in trying of youths. *New York Times,* February 3, A14.

Macallair, D. (1999). Is California striking out with its Three-Strikes law? *The San Diego Union-Tribune,* March 11, B13.

Males, M., & Macallair, D. (2000). *The color of justice: An analysis of juvenile adult court transfers in California.* Washington, DC: Building Blocks for Youth.

Males, M., Macallair, D., & Taqi-Eddin, K. (1999). *Striking out: The failure of California's "Three strikes and you're out" law.* Washington, DC: Justice Policy Institute.

McCone Commission. (1965). *Violence in the city: An end or a beginning?* Sacramento, CA: Office of the Governor.

Morain, D. (1994a). California elections: The propositions: Funds fuel Proposition 187 fight. *Los Angeles Times,* October 29, A23.

Morain, D. (1994b). Legislators vow to fight Wilson over prison funds. *Los Angeles Times,* October 21, A3.

Poe-Yamagata, E., & Jones, M. A. (2000). *And justice for some: Differential treatment of minority youth in the justice system.* Washington, DC: Youth Law Center.

Purdum, T. S. (2000). Justice Dept. warns Los Angeles police. *New York Times,* May 9, A14.

Richardson, J. (1998). The members' speaker: How Willie Brown held center stage in California, 1980–1995. In M. B. Preston, B. E. Cain, & S. Bass (Eds.), *Racial and ethnic politics in California* (pp. 137–158). Berkeley: Institute of Governmental Studies Press, University of California, Berkeley.

Schiraldi, V. (1994). *The undue influence of California's prison guards' union: California's correctional-industrial complex,* San Francisco: Center on Juvenile and Criminal Justice.

Schiraldi, V. (1999a). Five year old "Three Strikes" law needs closer look. *San Francisco Chronicle,* September 1, A29.

Schiraldi, V. (1999b). The bias of "color blind" juvenile justice. *Los Angeles Times,* June 27, 26.

Schiraldi, V., & Ambrosio, T. J. (1997). *Striking out: The crime control impact of "three-strikes" laws.* Washington, DC: Justice Policy Institute.

Schiraldi, V., Kuyper, S., & Hewitt, S. (1996). *Young African Americans and the criminal justice system in California: Five years later.* San Francisco, CA: Center on Juvenile and Criminal Justice.

Schiraldi, V., Sussman, P. Y., & Hyland, L. (1994). *Three strikes: The unintended victims*. San Francisco: Center on Juvenile and Criminal Justice.

Schrag, P. (1998). *Paradise lost: California's experiences, America's future*. Berkeley: University of California Press.

Shires, M. (1996). *The future of public undergraduate education in California*. Santa Monica, CA: RAND Institute.

Skolnick, J. H., & Fyfe, J. J. (1993). *Above the law: Police and the excessive use of force*. New York: Free Press.

Taqi-Eddin, K., Macallair, D., & Schiraldi, V. (1998). *Class dismissed: Higher education vs. corrections during the Wilson years*. Washington, DC: Justice Policy Institute.

Terry, D. (2000). Police case to be treated as mob case in Los Angeles. *New York Times*, August 30, A14.

Weintraub, D. M. (1994). The Times Poll: Residents balk when asked to pay for "3 Strikes." *Los Angeles Times*, April 2, A1.

Zimbardo, P. G. (1994). *Transforming California's prisons into expensive old age homes for felons: Enormous hidden costs and consequences for California's taxpayers*. San Francisco, CA: Center on Juvenile and Criminal Justice.

# CHAPTER 5

## Saving Our State:
## Demonizing the Immigrants

Without immigrant janitors in the offices and business parks of Century City, without farm workers in California fields, with no electronics workers in the sweatshops of Santa Ana and Silicon Valley, without immigrant dishwashers and room cleaners in the luxury hotels of Newport Beach, and with no garment workers in downtown L.A. or San Francisco's Chinatown, the economy would crumble. . . . Immigrants, especially undocumented immigrants, are indispensable to the economy of those areas where the cry for exclusion is strongest.

—David Bacon (1999, 162)

In 1993 California Governor Pete Wilson faced a major dilemma in planning his reelection campaign. How was he to garner support during a period in which the state had experienced four years of economic recession, lost several hundred thousand jobs, and encountered budgetary and fiscal accountability problems? Wilson needed a silver bullet that would deflect attention away from the real problems of the state, one that was emotionally charged enough to engender support and reelect him to California's highest state office. In a dramatic attempt to capture the attention of the nation, Governor Wilson wrote an open letter to President Clinton in July 1993, demanding that the federal government reimburse California for the high cost of public services to illegal immigrants (Smith & Tarallo, 1995). Placed as a full-page ad in national newspapers like the *Los Angeles Times*, the *New York Times*, and the *Washington Post*, the letter's goal was to politicize the immigration issue for the American electorate. Wilson went on to redefine himself, through the Proposition 187 campaign, as a fiscal neoconservative, attempting to save California taxpayers the estimated $3 billion in annual costs spent on health, education, and social services for undocumented immigrants (Schrag, 1998).

Prior to this sudden transformation, Pete Wilson, as mayor of San Diego, was considered a moderate Republican who had advocated guest worker programs and affirmative action. In his tenure as a California senator in the 1980s, Pete Wilson had welcomed immigrant farm laborers through the "Bracero Program" when the capitalist interests of agribusiness were served by relaxing border patrols and restrictions on immigration in California and the Southwestern states (Rodriguez, 1997).

In 1994 Pete Wilson rallied behind Proposition 187 in a successful attempt to defeat Democratic gubernatorial candidate Kathleen Brown, who pursued a family legacy of leadership in the state governor's office. At one point in the preelection polls, Wilson trailed Brown by twenty points, but he ultimately emerged as the winner with a 55 to 40 percent victory margin (Schrag, 1998). Wilson's victory was largely credited to his ability to empathize with the concerns of California's white, middle-class Republican voters who consistently turn out at the polls at higher rates than their proportion of the population. In recent years, these voters have increasingly expressed fears associated with the increasing diversity of the state and supported measures that presumably would insulate them from potential contact with these "minorities," "third world immigrants,"and "undocumented aliens" (Maharidge, 1996; Perea, 1997).

## CITIZENS VERSUS ALIENS: BACKGROUND OF PROPOSITION 187

On November 9, 1994, 59 percent of California voters approved Proposition 187, the so-called "Save Our State" (SOS) initiative, which banned the delivery of health, education, and social services to undocumented immigrants (Smith & Tarallo, 1995). Section 1 of the proposed law explains that the people of California have "suffered and are suffering economic hardship caused by the presence of illegal *aliens* in the state. They have suffered and are suffering personal injury and damage caused by the criminal conduct of illegal *aliens*. They have a right to the protection of their government from any person or persons entering this country unlawfully" (California Secretary of State's Office, 1995). Thus Proposition 187 was designed to offer protection and alleviate any perceived suffering experienced by the state's native-born and naturalized citizens as a consequence of illegal alien behaviors.

This legislation prohibited all publically supported social service agencies from delivering services other than emergency medical care to undocumented immigrants. The initiative also required that all public schools, health care facilities, and public welfare agencies report suspected illegal immigrants to the State Attorney General and the federal Immigration and Naturalization Service (INS), yet it did not offer guidelines for validating these suspicions, thereby placing all people who were perceived to be Hispanic under a veil of suspicion and potential harassment. Additionally, Proposition 187 made it a felony to create, sell, or otherwise distribute documents that could be used to falsely verify U.S. citizenship or residence (California Secretary of State's Office, 1995).

## Opposing Views of the Legislation

Critics pointed out that Proposition 187 creates a two-tier system through which social services would be allocated. By prohibiting undocumented residents from access to such services, Proposition 187 forced them to seek underground, substandard services and denied their children educational opportunities, thus creating a form of second-class residency status. Without access to these essential services, these children would be unlikely to achieve economic mobility or parity with native-born residents by the end of their lifetimes (McCarthy & Vernez, 1998).

Opponents of the initiative enumerated many additional criticisms of its provisions, cautioning that undocumented immigrants would delay seeking medical attention, thereby increasing the incidence of chronic and life-threatening illnesses in their communities and resulting in further strain and financial burden on already overburdened emergency facilities (Schockman, 1998). If children were kept out of school, critics warned that it would contribute to increased delinquency and the spread of teenage gangs among Latino youth. Many large farmers, hotel associations, service industries, and labor unions opposed Proposition 187 because of its potential to disrupt significant sectors of the state's profitable economy, while civil rights groups opposed it because it infringed on the basic human rights of these workers and their families (Bacon, 1999). Joining the chorus of opposition to Proposition 187 were educators, health professionals, social workers, and lawyers, who challenged the legal foundation and the ethical implications of legislation that would require them to report any child or adult suspected of being undocumented (Schrag, 1998). All of these objections of the opposing forces would play out during the months leading up to the election in a very ethnically divisive and demonizing campaign.

The current legislation actually does nothing to halt or obstruct the illegal immigration process. It does however attack, disrupt, and significantly undermine equitable life chances for illegal immigrants residing in California, denying federally guaranteed access to education for children, and compromising the public health of all Californians by refusing to immunize its most vulnerable residents against communicable diseases.

## HISTORICAL PERSPECTIVE ON CALIFORNIA IMMIGRANTS: AN UNEASY ALLIANCE

The history of Mexicans in the United States since 1890 can be characterized as over 100 years of labor exploitation, social discrimination, cultural marginalization, and political disenfranchisement. From the earliest example of special regulations established in 1917 by the U.S. Immigration Service to permit Mexican farm workers into the United States, there has been a love/hate relationship between American politicians and the Mexican government over the conflicting priorities of the need for border control and the need for agricultural labor in the United States (Carrasco, 1997). These issues have played themselves out against a backdrop of war and peace, economic boom and depression, inclusion and exclusion, assimilation and discrimination.

U.S. immigration policies have frequently responded to political pressures and economic cycles in California, from the repatriation of hundreds of thousands of Mexican workers after the depression to the establishment of the "Bracero Program" to supply agricultural workers during World War II. From 1942 through 1947, this program recruited over 167,000 Mexican workers for American farmers; before the program was officially terminated in 1964, many thousands more came and set up permanent households, particularly in California and the Southwestern states (Carrasco, 1997; Rodriguez, 1997; Zavella, 1997). However, from 1954 to 1959, during the postwar recession and deindustrialization of the defense industries, the federal government sponsored "Operation Wetback," forcibly deporting over 3.7 million Mexicans, many of whom were legal immigrants or native-born citizens (Carrasco, 1997; Johnson, 1997).

A third wave of Mexican immigrants arrived in the late 1960s and 1970s. Influenced by the "Chicano" movement, they were mobilized by Cesar Chavez and other community leaders to launch a successful strike against the California grape growers, ultimately resulting in the formation of a farm workers' union that improved wages and working conditions for most of the migratory laborers in the state (Gutierrez, 1996; Zavella, 1997).

After the passage of the Immigration Reform and Control Act (IRCA) in 1986, the U.S. government again instituted a more limited bracero program, known as the Seasonal Agricultural Worker program (SAWS) (Schrag, 1998). One of its chief sponsors was California's Senator Pete Wilson, an avowed friend of agribusiness and a self-described moderate Republican. Undocumented Mexican immigrants were once again welcome in California's fields and canneries, as long as native-born workers were neither willing nor available to fill those jobs.

It was neither an accident nor a coincidence that Governor Pete Wilson selected illegal immigrants as the prime target of his divisive gubernatorial campaign. A pragmatic politician, Governor Wilson was keenly aware that immigrant-bashing had a long and successful history in the annals of California's politics, particularly toward immigrants of color (MacDonald & Cain, 1998; Perea, 1997).

### Population Explosion of Immigrants in California

The current anti-immigration movement in California and the rest of the nation coincides with the dramatic demographic shift in the immigrant population. In 1910, during the first major wave of immigration, nearly nine of every ten immigrants were white Europeans, but by 1980 about four out of five immigrants came from Asia and Latin America (Perea, 1997). As these people of color from "third-world" developing nations changed the complexion of California, they were visible and vulnerable scapegoats for the conservative nativist organizations and the ambitious politicians who courted their support.

In the three-decade period from about 1970 and ending in the late 1990s, California's racial and ethnic composition substantially diversified, as the United States immigrant population grew from 1.3 million in 1960 to 8 million in 1995, attracting one-third of the entire nation's immigrant population to California. The immigrant population is now 22 percent of all California residents.

The Immigration Reform and Control Act (IRCA) of 1986 disrupted the informal relationships between Mexican immigrants and their California employers by setting up severe sanctions for the undocumented workers and the employers who hired them (Palerm, 1999). Although the law established three special programs that allowed for seasonal farm workers, the overall impact of the IRCA legislation made it more difficult and dangerous for immigrants to cross the border. Senator Pete Wilson lobbied hard for a seasonal agricultural worker provision (SAWS), one of the three special programs that subsequently legalized over one million undocumented workers. Ironically, this program actually established a mechanism for continued illegal immigration and fostered the development of settled immigrant enclaves that, in turn, served as magnets for families and friends from the "sending" communities in Mexico (Schrag, 1998; Smith & Tarallo, 1995).

## DEMOGRAPHIC CHARACTERISTICS OF CALIFORNIA IMMIGRANTS

In the 1970s, 1.8 million immigrants came to California, followed in the 1980s by 3.5 million more immigrants, both legal and illegal. Throughout the 1990s the rate of immigration to California remained substantial, accounting for 25 percent of the state's labor force and 50 percent of its growth in labor and population (McCarthy & Vernez, 1998).

In 1994 there were an estimated 1.3 million undocumented immigrants in California, nearly one-half from Mexico and Central America, and one-third from Asia (Schockman, 1998). Most had arrived by crossing the border by car or on foot through well-traversed routes, often with the aid of unscrupulous guides called "coyotes," many quite traumatized by long and dangerous journeys to reach "El Norte."

A socioeconomic profile of Latino immigrants in California reveals a group characterized by low education, high rates of poverty, limited English proficiency, and an unskilled labor pool (Honer, 1999; Zavella, 1997). Latino immigrants are twice as likely as native-born Americans to be poor and to participate in some type of welfare program; they have the lowest educational levels of the state's major ethnic groups; about half lack adequate English language proficiency to function effectively as citizens; the majority lack health insurance, contributing to a high incidence of undetected chronic medical conditions (Honer, 1999).

In contrast to California where they constitute 22 percent of the population, immigrants make up less than 3 percent of the population in most other states. When compared to those other immigrants, California's immigrants are, on average, younger, more recent arrivals, less educated, and more likely to be people of color (Mexican, Asian, or Central American) rather than of European ancestry (McCarthy & Vernez, 1998). California's non-European immigrants are also more likely to have larger families than natives, and lower levels of education than immigrants in other states (McCarthy & Vernez, 1998).

### Costs and Benefits of California Immigrants

In their 1998 publication, *Immigration in a Changing Economy: California's Experience—Questions and Answers*, McCarthy and Vernez suggest that California is a test case for national immigration policy. These authors illustrate how the immigrant workforce has contributed to the expansion and growth of the California economy with the state benefitting at substantial cost to immigrant workers.

The trade-off between the benefits that immigrants contribute to society and the costs incurred by that society is a perpetual debate in California, where experts have provided ammunition for both sides of the controversy (Schrag, 1998). Although the National Research Council Report concluded that California taxpayers provide net benefits for immigrants in excess of the taxes they pay, the authors also caution that the long-term balance between immigrant taxes and the costs of public services they utilize will depend on a number of complex factors such as their educational and income levels (Smith & Edmonston, 1997). By contrast, reports from the Rand Institute and the Urban Institute both suggest that the benefits of immigrant labor may outweigh the cost of services because of the increased profits to businesses due to lower labor costs and the ineligibility of undocumented immigrants for many services that their taxes support (Smith & Edmonston, 1997; Vernez & McCarthy, 1995). Many analysts would argue that the average wage of a low-wage unskilled labor pool has indirectly increased the wealth of the middle-class Californians who depend on them for minimum-wage service and domestic jobs (Schockman, 1998; Schrag, 1998).

Immigrant workers have supported the rapid expansion of the technology industry in Northern California, in the garment, factory, and aerospace industries in Southern California, and the agribusiness industry in the Central Valley and coastal areas. The impact of the developing global economy over the last twenty years has fiercely increased competition in the marketplace, further driving down wages for unskilled and semi-skilled immigrants (McCarthy & Vernez, 1998).

Although immigrants are accused of overcrowding the schools and overutilizing social services, in actuality immigrant students have boosted previously declining public school enrollment and immigrants are no more likely to utilize public social services than natives who are demographically matched across income and education variables (McCarthy & Vernez, 1998). Only refugees and elderly immigrants have a greater likelihood of using the Medicaid program and Supplemental Security Income (SSI), primarily due to medical and age-related conditions. Immigrant school-aged children are projected to increase the state's high school graduation rates by about 35 percent over the next ten years (McCarthy & Vernez, 1998). Latinos and Asians will represent about 75 percent of this increase and many of these youth will attend college. Education is a mediating factor in improving the economic status of these immigrants, helping to level the playing field through expanded employment opportunities.

The Wilson Administration argued that California's taxpayers disproportionately carry the burden of immigrant overutilization of health, education, and social welfare services. In fact, California taxpayers do pay about five times more than those in other states for these services due largely to the disproportionate settlement of *legal* immigrants in this state (National Research Council, 1997). However, these costs are offset by the substantial benefits to the state of lower wage employees who disproportionately contribute to the social security fund and state and federal taxes. In fact, undocumented immigrants rank lowest in their receipt of public assistance (Zavella, 1997). For example, in 1992 undocumented immigrants in San Diego County paid over $60 million in taxes and vehicle registration fees, yet they only utilized $27 million in health care costs (Serb, 1995).

## Illegal Alien Myths and Other Xenophobic Fears

The socially constructed myth of the "illegal alien" brings forth images of foreign beings from unknown, uncharted lands. The persistent and pervasive labeling of undocumented immigrants as "illegal aliens" reinforces widespread fears among white California residents of being invaded, taken over, or otherwise overwhelmed by the bourgeoning numbers of non-English-speaking people of color.

The demographic projection that California will become the country's first minority-majority state by the year 2010 has raised considerable anxiety among native-born whites. Racial tensions have also increased as a shift toward higher skill level jobs, particularly in the technology field, expanded opportunities for white, high skilled, and educated workers (McCarthy & Vernez, 1998).

There is also an apparent inconsistency, perhaps even some hypocrisy, in the bipartisan support for legislation to import thousands of well-educated engineers and technicians to fill the rapidly expanding jobs in the high technology industries of Silicon Valley and other areas of high growth in California. In March 2000, some of the same Republican politicians who supported Proposition 187 (or did not strongly oppose it) went on record authorizing an increase in H-1B work visas for engineers and computer experts from India, Taiwan, and other developing nations. President Clinton requested an 85 percent increase in the number of skilled foreign workers, proposing 600,000 visas over a three-year period until 2003 (Pear, 2000).

Politicians can justify this request under the 1990 Immigration Bill, which established "needed skills" as the major criterion for admission to the United States. This policy clearly distinguishes between those immigrants who are desirable because of such extrinsic characteristics as education, occupation, and income and those who are undesirable because of their lack of these middle-class attributes. The danger of this dichotomy is the development of a two-tiered community of immigrants that will replicate the social class division already pervasive in American society, in which people are valued for the degrees they hold and the jobs they perform rather than for any intrinsic attributes of character, personality, or potential (Johnson, 1997).

Governor Wilson had shown his own hypocrisy earlier over undocumented immigrants when, as a senator from California, he had sponsored a bill to reinstate the "Bracero Program," a government-sponsored program of importing Mexican agricultural laborers for seasonal work in the California agribusiness industry (Rodriguez, 1997). Since these workers are brought in under temporary contracts, they are at the mercy of their employers and, if they do not accept the wages and living conditions as stipulated in the contract, they can be shipped back to Mexico without ceremony. The "Bracero Program" has been described as a form of indentured servitude, depriving workers of any right to bargain or negotiate with their employers, and granting to employers nearly absolute control over the labor and lives of these workers (Rodriguez, 1997).

White immigrants from the United Kingdom and the British Commonwealth have also illegally entered California, mainly from Canada, Ireland, and England. One author estimated that over 10,000 illegal Irish immigrants live and work in a developed underground network located in the San Francisco Bay Area, but these people are easily assimilated into the dominant Anglo-American culture and are less likely to be targeted for discrimination based upon their immigration status (Roemer, 1989).

## THE CAMPAIGN FOR FINANCING PROPOSITION 187

Contributions to the campaign against Proposition 187 actually outstripped the contributions supporting it by a ratio of 3.74 to 1, yet the measure still passed by a wide margin. The report on *Financing California's Statewide Ballot Measures, 1994 Primary and General Elections* (California Secretary of State's Office, 1995) indicates that $860,432 were received in support of the Proposition 187 effort and $3,214,255 were received from its opponents. With so much financial support funding the opposition to the "Save Our State" (SOS) initiative, how and why did it pass?

One explanation is found in the timing of contributions to the opposition, which was too little in the beginning and too late at the end of the campaign. As of June 30, 1994 only $2,400 of opposition contributions were recorded for the SOS initiative; however, by this same date over $350,000 was received for support of Proposition 187. By June 30, 1994, the "Yes on Proposition 187" campaign had incurred $540,595 in expenditures compared with zero dollars spent by the opposition (California Secretary of State's Office, 1995). Even though the "No on Proposition 187" forces raised almost four times as much money as Proposition 187 supporters by election time, five months prior to the elections little more than $2,000 had been donated and none had been spent on an opposition campaign. Thus the opponents of the initiative were not as well-organized as its proponents, nor did they mount an effective campaign to generate support and mobilize their constituents in a timely manner.

The six top contributors to the pro-Proposition 187 effort were the California Republican Party, for $400,286; Mountjoy for Assembly 1994 Committee, $45,538; Rogers for State Senate Committee, $25,000; Ron Price, $22,000; Barbara Coe, and the Container Supply Company, each for $15,000 (California Secretary of State's Office, 1995). Among the organizations supporting the initiative with contributions under $25,000 were the Americans for Illegal Immigration, the campaign committee of State Senator Jim Brulte, and the American Tax Reduction Movement. Brulte, Mountjoy, and Roberts were all campaigning for office in conservative districts, representing the views of their constituents who were more likely to be sympathetic to anti-immigration arguments. However, it was noted that there were no significant direct contributions from the agribusiness, service, construction, or manufacturing industries, all of which depend on immigrants (documented and undocumented) for much of their unskilled and semi-skilled labor.

### Financing the Opposition Campaign

The largest contributions to the anti-Proposition 187 campaign were filed by the California Teachers Association for $660,581; David Gelbaum, $405,000; California State Council of Services Employees, $349,853; Univision Television Group, Inc., $300,000; John Moores, $100,000; and Pace California School Employees, $90,371 (California Secretary of State's Office, 1995). Among the organizations opposing the initiative with contributions over $25,000 were the American Federation of State, County, and Municipal Employees (AFSCME) of the AFL-CIO, the Association of California School Administrators, the California Federation of Teachers (CFT), the California Trial Lawyers, the California Hospitals Committee on Issues, the California Latino PAC, the St. Joseph Health System, and the United Food and Commercial Workers Union. In fact, a number of labor unions, teachers' unions, health care professionals, and lawyers had sponsored an umbrella organization called "Taxpayers Against 187" in order to demonstrate their opposition to this discriminatory and exclusionary legislation. These groups represented many of the workers who supply the unskilled labor and workers in California's agricultural and service industries, as well as many of the professionals who understood the potentially devastating impact of the legislation on the schools, hospitals, and criminal justice system (Schrag, 1998; Smith & Tarallo, 1995).

In contrast to the Republican Party's generous financial and enthusiastic political support of Proposition 187, the California Democratic Party was noticeably absent in opposing the initiative, perhaps for fear of alienating independents and liberal Republicans who might vote for Democrats like Senator Diane Feinstein and gubernatorial candidate Kathleen Brown (Schrag, 1998). Although President Clinton had expressed lukewarm objection to Proposition 187 toward the end of the campaign, very few prominent California Democratic political leaders and office holders had shown the courage to oppose an initiative that would have a disparate and negative impact on some of their primary constituencies—labor, minorities, and the disadvantaged.

The late, though valiant, effort of the Proposition 187 opposition was slow to organize, thus unable to sway the opinions of likely voters after they had already made decisions to support the proposition. Additionally, the opponents of Proposition 187 failed because they targeted unlikely voters and people who were not registered to vote at a time in the election process that was too late for targeted groups to register. Many of these residents are low-income legal immigrants and people of color marginalized in society due to their unequal access to institutions of power and influence.

## THE CAMPAIGN FOR PROPOSITION 187—PRINCIPLE OR PLATFORM?

Pete Wilson's gubernatorial campaign in the 1994 election was based on a platform of fear for public safety and fear of outsiders. His passionate support of the Proposition 184 "Three Strikes" initiative and, concurrently, the so-called "Save Our State" (SOS) Proposition 187 initiative appealed to white, suburban, middle-class workers who were anxious about their safety and economic viability in a state that was then viewed as too lenient on crime and "illegal aliens." This demonization of racial groups of color in California has a long legacy that was revived with the SOS initiative and manipulated by Pete Wilson to advance his conservative agenda through legislation that spoke directly to the pockets and pocketbooks of his conservative and right-wing constituents.

The proponents of Proposition 187 described undocumented immigrants as a threat to organized labor and their unions because they accepted lower wages and more dangerous working conditions than legal resident workers (Armbruster, Geron, & Bonacich, 1995). Undocumented laborers were also falsely accused of not paying taxes and taking a free ride on the education, health care, and public social service bandwagon. Finally, proponents argued that illegal immigrants possessed traditional cultural characteristics that middle-class, white Americans found unappealing; for example, they married too young, had multiple children, didn't achieve enough academically, had too many social problems, and spoke English imperfectly. For all the above reasons, Governor Pete Wilson convinced many supporters that they should cast their votes for Proposition 187, but several authors suggested that the major goal of this initiative was to deflect attention away from California's faltering economy (Maharidge, 1996; Schrag, 1998).

### The Polls and the Campaign for Proposition 187

Eighteen months prior to the November election, the issue of illegal immigration was ranked next to last in statewide polls of California likely voters, but by election day exit polls revealed that this topic was one of the four major concerns of the actual voters (Schockman, 1998). During that eighteen months, support for the proposition had gradually increased among non-Hispanic white voters as the politicians and the media had publicized the initiative and polarized the public. Although in the two months preceding the election, overall support had appeared to decline to a slim majority of the voters (52 percent), support among Republicans had remained stable at 66 percent (Field Institute, 1994). Only two weeks before the election, supporters were confident that Proposition 187 would win and would sweep Pete Wilson to a second term as governor (Schockman, 1998).

### The Advocates for Proposition 187

The campaign for Proposition 187 was characterized by anti-immigration rhetoric, racist stereotypes, and xenophobic charges, reflecting the irrational fears and the nativistic attitudes of the major supporters of the initiative. The Republican Party and Governor Wilson's Campaign Committee identified the "Save Our State" initiative early on as a significant wedge issue that they could exploit and manipulate quite effectively throughout the campaign (Schockman, 1998; Schrag, 1998). Wilson and his supporters stayed on message relentlessly, coordinating their assault on illegal immigrants through campaign literature, media advertising, talk shows, and political speeches.

What were the major components of this message? Capitalizing on the stated rationale for the initiative, the advocates of Proposition 187 argued that the state would save at least $5 billion expended on the costs of education, welfare, and health care for illegal immigrants. Second, it would create more job opportunities for legal residents, who could not compete with the undocumented workers for low-wage jobs. Third, it would discourage further waves of illegal immigrants who were attracted to the United States for benefits and for bearing children in California who would be entitled to citizenship. Fourth, the supporters of Proposition 187 intended to "send a message" to the Clinton Administration that the costs of illegal immigrants should be borne by the federal government by reimbursing the state. This message was reinforced by an appeal to the Clinton Administration to police its border with Mexico more aggressively to deter illegal immigration (Schockman, 1998; Schrag, 1998). One of their most effective television ads featured a realistic photo of dark, shadowy figures, furtively running across the border at night, while the unseen announcer solemnly repeats, "They keep coming. They just keep coming" (Schrag, 1998).

Many Republican candidates for state offices proselytized this message, aided and abetted by several state and national anti-immigration organizations and conservative political action committees. Just as most of the state's agribusiness and other major industries did not make major contributions to finance the campaign for Proposition 187, so too were they conspicuously absent from the campaign debate and public advocacy for the initiative (Schrag, 1998). Although many leaders of these industries may have personally contributed to the Republican Party's general coffers, they

seemed reluctant to associate themselves with the anti-immigration movement that impacted on so much of their labor pool.

In late October 1994, William Bennett and Jack Kemp, two prominent
conservative Republicans and cofounders of "Empower America,"
authored an op-ed piece in the *Wall Street Journal* in which they urged Republicans to vote against Proposition 187 on the grounds that it reflected
badly on the Republican Party as a "protectionist, and isolated, and xenophobic" party (Smith & Tarallo, 1995, 675).

### The Opponents of Proposition 187

Despite their superior fundraising efforts, the opponents of Proposition
187 were less successful at coordinating their statewide campaign and dis-
seminating a consistent message (Armbruster, Geron, & Bonacich, 1995;
Schrag, 1998). Civil rights groups focused on the provisions of the initiative
that clearly violated the constitutional rights of immigrants, as had been established in previous Supreme Court decisions, such as the 1982 *Plyer v. Doe*
case which guaranteed access to public education for the children of illegal
immigrants (Schockman, 1998). Educators warned that excluding over
400,000 immigrant children from schools would inevitably increase juvenile delinquency and adolescent antisocial behaviors in communities with
well-organized street gangs. Teachers' organizations joined ranks with
health care professionals, social workers, and lawyers to protest the legislation requiring them to report suspected undocumented persons, virtually
turning them into informers and violating their professional ethics of confi-
dentiality in services to clients as protected under the Family Education
and Privacy Act (Smith & Tarallo, 1995).

Liberal politicians and social scientists challenged the cost savings of
Proposition 187, pointing out that the potential loss of federal funds and the
cost of verifying the legal status of suspected undocumented immigrants
could cost the state as much as $15 billion annually, thus offsetting the ex-
pected $5 billion in savings (Schockman, 1998).

Finally, public health officials expressed grave concern over the danger
of epidemics of infectious diseases and other health risks that might escalate because uninsured immigrants would lack access to medical services,
their children would not be inoculated, and emergency services would be
overwhelmed (Honer, 1999).

Although these themes were repeatedly stressed throughout the campaign by opponents of Proposition 187, advocacy groups, religious organizations, and editorial writers in the state's leading newspapers, the
underlying message—that undocumented immigrants were a valuable resource in California society, an essential segment of the labor force, and a
group entitled to basic human and civil rights—was never made explicit in

a cohesive, coordinated strategy to win the hearts and minds of California voters (Schrag, 1998).

The largest political rally ever organized by Latinos in Los Angeles occurred on October 16, 1994 as an anti-Proposition 187 protest march (Armbruster, Geron, & Bonacich, 1995). A record number of over 100,000 protestors participated, but there was sharp disagreement about what image the march should project. Should it be a Mexican American, Chicano, Latino, multi-ethnic, or multi-racial event?

The march ultimately projected a predominant image of a Latino-Mexican protest movement, with Latinos from Mexico and Central America carrying their national flags, wearing the colors of the Mexican flag, carrying banners and signs with Spanish slogans, and singing and chanting in Spanish, "Si, se puede" (Yes, we can!), the motto of Cesar Chavez's farm laborers' movement. Widely publicized in the media, the marchers sent a powerful signal to the voters of California that Latino people were resisting oppression and that Latino power was on the ascendancy. The march backfired, however, as white voters and undecided voters from other ethnic groups perceived these marchers as unpatriotic foreigners, defiant and disrespectful of American laws, and ungrateful for their opportunities in the United States (Maharidge, 1996). In the final analysis, this massive demonstration of Latino solidarity probably alienated many undecided voters and contributed to the victory of Proposition 187 at the polls.

### The Voters Speak

Analysis of the voting patterns on Proposition 187 revealed some surprising results. Although Latinos comprised 15 percent of the state's registered voters, they accounted for only 8 percent of the total vote on Proposition 187, indicating that nearly half of the Latinos had not even bothered to vote. Although some polls had predicted that one-third of Latino voters would support the initiative, fewer than one-fourth (23 perent) voted for Proposition 187 and over three-fourths (77 percent) voted against it. While white voters were expected to support the initiative, 63 percent voted for it and 37 percent voted against it, thus over one-third of the whites did not succumb to the hysteria of the anti-immigration rhetoric. Contrary to most predictions, African American and Asian American voters were clearly divided in their opinions about Proposition 187, with nearly half (47 percent) of both groups supporting it and a slim majority of both groups (53 percent) opposing it. In response to the unexpectedly light turnout of Latino voters, several of their community critics complained of the lack of political mobilization at the local level, the lack of information about the initiative by Spanish-language media, and the problems of motivating voters with low education, poor literacy, and fear of political involvement (Smith & Tarallo, 1995).

## EVALUATION OF POTENTIAL IMPACT OF
## PROPOSITION 187

The so-called "Save Our State" initiative would cost the State of California much more than it would gain in benefits. An independent legislative analyst estimated that, while the annual savings to California from Proposition 187 would be about $200 million in health, education, and social services, about $100 million of that saving would be spent enforcing the law in its first year alone. These costs would be primarily associated with verification of citizenship and reporting of all suspected undocumented immigrants to the State Attorney General and the INS. Additionally, passage of the SOS initiative in 1994 placed the state at risk for loss of several billion dollars of federal funding as the bill's provisions were in direct opposition to federal laws. Federal funds could have been lost in subsidies to education, health care, and social services.

If the goal of Proposition 187 was to take back the state while reducing funding for illegal immigrants, this initiative would not accomplish that task but actually would have increased both the misuse of state revenues and the risk for loss of federal funding.

### Social Costs of Proposition 187

If we don't immunize undocumented children, we will increase the incidence of measles, whooping cough, mumps, rubella, diphtheria, and hepatitis B in all children, not just the undocumented.

Brian D. Johnston (1994, B7)

The relationship between social costs and fiscal savings must be analyzed to understand the true short-term consequences and long-term implications of Proposition 187. Proposition 187 has resulted in greater polarization between whites and people of color, fueling an atmosphere in which all phenotypically non-white Americans are thought to be undocumented and are thus treated as unwelcome and unworthy outsiders (Schrag, 1998).

A study evaluating the impact of Proposition 187 on health care costs at Children's Hospital of San Diego found that the short-term cost savings of not treating undocumented immigrants is far outweighed by the substantial long-term costs for treating this population (Serb, 1995). This is because emergency care, which is exempted under Proposition 187, costs more per patient than preventive care.

Even before Proposition 187 was presented to California voters, failure to immunize preschool-aged immigrant children had resulted in several outbreaks of communicable diseases, such as a measles epidemic largely impacting low-income Latino communities in central and southern California (Dales et al., 1993). This epidemic resulted in 16,400 reported cases and seventy-five deaths and cost over $30 million to control from 1988 to 1990.

Restructuring health care, social services, and education will not stop illegal immigration, but it will act to further marginalize disenfranchised groups. Such marginalization will play into the partisan pulse of Californians who are hostile to the recent population explosion and changing demographics of the first state in the contiguous union to have a majority of ethnic minority group members. Conflict with immigrants in California is not new but it is experiencing a resurgence in reaction to demographic changes and economic interests. Since it is clear that the architects of Proposition 187 were not primarily concerned with the interests of the majority of Californians, whose interests were served by the passage of this initiative?

The short-term consequences of Proposition 187 were predicted to be:

1. English-speaking and non-English-speaking immigrants alike would become suspect of illegal immigrant status,
2. denial of access to health care would result in increased public health concerns, and
3. undocumented immigrants would avoid above-board employment that reduces their payment of payroll, sales, and income taxes.

Long-term implications of 187 were predicted to include:

1. increases in expenses to treat chronic diseases that might be preventable if detected early,
2. a greater reduction in the availability of educated citizens to enter into the legitimate labor market,
3. development of a second-class social service system designed to circumvent the legal system and provide much needed community social services, and
4. approval of an anti-immigrant agenda setting the stage for expanded racially divisive legislation.

If the Proposition 187 debate were rational and reasonable, fiscal, public health, and humanitarian arguments might be effective in persuading Proposition 187 supporters to consider alternatives to full implementation of the proposition. However, because Proposition 187 supporters and opponents approached the issue with such passion, there was little effective persuasion on either side.

## THE CONTINUING SAGA OF PROPOSITION 187:
## IMPLICATIONS FOR THE FUTURE

If the 1990s are any indication, the coming years are likely to bring great volatility and rancor in the public debate about immigration. Indeed, race, ethnicity, and immigration status, and the intersection of these increasingly
overlapping characteristics, may prove to be the social dividing lines in the
United States for the foreseeable future.

Kevin R. Johnson (1997, 166)

The passage of Proposition 187 in California elevated the anti-immigration movement to a national crusade. Shortly after the November election,
anti-immigration groups in New York, Florida, and Washington state
contacted Ronald Prince, the Orange County businessman who had helped
to write Proposition 187. The National Republican Party was jubilant,
confident that they had latched on to an issue that would resonate with
voters all over the country and would assure victory at the polls for the 1996
presidential and congressional elections.

In fact, the Democrats also took notice of Proposition 187 and convinced
President Clinton and their congressional leaders to launch a preemptive
strike by proposing some severe measures against legal immigrants as well
as undocumented immigrants. The Democrats were instrumental in passing provisions to reduce food stamps and Supplemental Security Income
(SSI) to poor, elderly, and disabled legal immigrants as part of the 1996 Welfare Reform Act. These measures were uniformly criticized by civil rights
and immigrant advocacy groups, as well as by nearly all the major newspapers in the United States.

After nearly a year of these draconian measures, the U.S. Congress restored SSI benefits for virtually all legal immigrants in September 1997. By
July 1998, food stamp benefits were also restored to 250,000 immigrants.
Political gamesmanship had been replaced finally by political reality—these legal immigrants are voters and they are not as easily intimi-
dated or victimized as undocumented immigrants, who are without a
voice or a vote.

Although Proposition 187 passed with almost 60 percent of the voters'
support, its constitutionality has been aggressively challenged in state and
federal courts for the past six years. Since the passage of Proposition 187,
much has changed in California politics. Like most of the nation today, California is in the midst of a booming economy. In January 1999 the governor's mansion was occupied by Gray Davis, a Democrat who targeted
Latino voters and openly campaigned voicing opposition to Proposition
187, indicating that he would have difficulty implementing the legislation
(Gunnison, 1999).

In 1995 Judge Mariana R. Pfaelzer of the U.S. District Court in Los Angeles ruled that most provisions of Proposition 187 were unconstitutional,

angering former Governor Pete Wilson and prompting him to later file a formal appeal to this decision (Schrag, 1998). In March of 1999 Governor Gray Davis was faced with one of the most important and controversial decisions of his new administration, whether or not to continue Wilson's appeal or drop it and accept the judge's decision (Nieves, 1999). Davis's actions were monitored closely to see if he would fulfill his campaign promises to his Latino constituency or if he would follow the lead of the former governor to appeal the court's unfavorable ruling on Proposition 187. Davis opted for neither of these choices and requested federal court mediation of the issues with the state represented by the governor's office and the anti-Proposition 187 coalition by the Mexican American Legal Defense Fund on opposite sides of the controversy (Purdum, 1999).

This decision brought strain to the governor's relationship with his Lieutenant Governor Cruz Bustamante, a Latino male, who has been openly opposed to Proposition 187. Although Bustamante defied the governor by filing a brief to halt the governor's mediation plan, the lieutenant. governor's efforts were not successful (Nieves, 1999). Following a mediation period, which proponents of Proposition 187 say they were barred from attending, the governor and opponents of Proposition 187 reached a satisfactory settlement. Most of the measures covered in Proposition 187 were later included in a 1996 federal immigration law that restricted health care, education, and welfare services for illegal immigrants around the nation. However, the educational restrictions targeted higher education and not primary schooling (Smith, 1999).

On September 13, 1999, Judge Pfaelzer approved an agreement between the state of California and civil rights groups to drop their appeals to her earlier ruling, effectively terminating the Proposition 187 appeals process (Associated Press, 1999). Since much of the state's legislation was more appropriately covered by a subsequent federal immigration law, only a few of the initiative's original sections were upheld. With this final judicial decision, it became a criminal act to manufacture, sell, or use false documents to determine citizenship or to aid the immigration process. The state also acknowledged compliance with all current federal immigration laws essentially conceding that California had no legal authority to establish its own immigration policies.

After release of this news, proponents of Proposition 187 began an unsuccessful campaign to recall Governor Davis, complaining bitterly that the will of the people has been overturned by the governor's actions (McDermott, 1999). In actuality it seemed that the will of the voters of California is at odds with the constitution of this nation. California politics in the post-Proposition 187 era has found Latino voters in touch with their ever-increasing political strength. In a clear backlash to the immigrant bashing and deceptive manipulation of Proposition 187 issues, Latino voters are steadily flowing into Democratic party ranks, with over 500,000 voters switching sides in the aftermath of the passage of the ill-fated Proposition 187 (McDermott, 1999).

This was the first initiative that specifically targeted immigrants of color, but the unintended consequence of this assault would ultimately change the balance of California's political parties and challenge the enduring power of the state's ruling elite. A precedent for anti-immigrant, nativist, political activism was established in the SOS campaign that provided the groundwork for the anti-affirmative action and anti-bilingual education initiatives soon to follow as ballot measures in the statewide elections of 1996 and 1998.

## REFERENCES

Almaguer, T. (1994). *Racial fault lines: The historical origins of white supremacy in California*. Berkeley, CA: University of California Press.

Armbruster, R., Geron, K., & Bonacich, E. (1995). The assault on California's Latino immigrants: The politics of Proposition 187. *International Journal of Urban and Regional Research, 19*(4), 655–663.

Associated Press. (1999). Federal judge approves deal ending battle over Prop. 187. *San Francisco Chronicle*, September 14, A26.

Bacon, D. (1999). For an immigration policy based on human rights. In S. Jonas & S. Dod Thomas (Eds.), *Immigration: A civil rights issue for the Americas* (pp. 157–173). Wilmington, DE: Scholarly Resources.

California Secretary of State's Office. (1995). *Financing California statewide ballot measures: 1994 primary and general elections*. Sacramento, CA: Political Reform Division.

Carrasco, G. P. (1997). Latinos in the United States: Invitation and exile. In J. F. Perea (Ed.), *Immigrants out! The new nativism and the anti-immigrant impulse in the United States* (pp. 190–204). New York: New York University Press.

Chavez, L. R. (1997). Immigration reform and nativism: The nationalist response to the transnational challenges. In J. F. Perea (Ed.), *Immigrants out! The new nativism and the anti-immigrant impulse in the United States* (pp. 61–77). New York: New York University Press.

Dales, L. G., Kizer, K. W., Rutherford, G. W., Pertowski, C. A., Waterman, S. H., & Woodford, G. (1993). Measles epidemic from failure to immunize. *Western Journal of Medicine, 159*, 455–464.

Field Institute. (1994). *The field poll*. No. 1734, October 27.

Gunnison, R. B. (1999). Davis plans low-key defense of Prop. 187. *San Francisco Chronicle*, A17.

Gutierrez, D. G. (1996). Sin fronteras? Chicanos, Mexican Americans, and the emergence of the contemporary Mexican immigration debate. In D. G. Gutierrez (Ed.), *Between two worlds: Mexican immigrants in the United States* (pp. 175–209). Wilmington, DE: Scholarly Resources.

Honer, B. (1999). *Report on the status of Latino immigrants in California*. Sacramento, CA: Catholic Social Service.

Johnson, K. R. (1997). The new nativism: Something old, something new, something borrowed, something blue. In J. F. Perea (Ed.), *Immigrants out! The new nativism and the anti-immigrant impulse in the United States* (pp. 165–189). New York: New York University Press.

Johnston, B. D. (1994). Can we deny aid to the poor? *Los Angeles Times*, October 27, B7.

MacDonald, K., & Cain, B. E. (1998). Nativism, partisanship and immigration: An analysis of Prop. 187. In M. B. Preston, B. E. Cain, & S. Bass (Eds.), *Racial and ethnic politics in California* (pp. 277–304). Berkeley: Institute of Governmental Studies Press, University of California, Berkeley.

Maharidge, D. (1996). *The coming white minority: California, multiculturalism and America's future*. New York: Vintage Books.

Martinez, G. (1994). Leader of Proposition 187 files for bankruptcy. *Los Angeles Times*, November 18, B1.

McCarthy, K. F., & Vernez, G. (1998). *Immigration in a changing economy: California's experience—Questions and Answers*. Santa Monica, CA: RAND, National Defense Research Institute.

McDermott, T. (1999). Some embittered by fate of Proposition 187. *Los Angeles Times*, August 2, p. 3.

Morain, D. (1994). California elections, the propositions: Funds fuel Proposition 187 fight. *Los Angeles Times*, October 29, A23.

National Research Council. (1997). *The new Americans: Economic, demographic, and fiscal effects of immigration*. Washington, DC: National Academy Press.

Nieves, E. (1999). California calls off effort to carry out immigrant measure. *New York Times*, July 30, A12.

Palerm, J. V. (1999). The expansion of California agriculture and the rise of peasant-worker communities. In S. Jonas & S. Dod Thomas (Eds.), *Immigration: A civil rights issue for the Americas*. Wilmington, DE: Scholarly Resources.

Pear, R. (2000). Clinton asks Congress to raise the limit on visas for skilled workers. *New York Times*, May 12, A14.

Perea, J. F. (Ed.). (1997). *Immigrants out! The new nativism and the anti-immigrant impulse in the United States*. New York: New York University Press.

Purdum, T. S. (1999). Governor seeks compromises on aid to illegal immigrants. *New York Times*, April 16, A14.

Rodriguez, N. P. (1997). The social construction of the U.S.-Mexico border. In J. F. Perea (Ed.), *Immigrants out! The new nativism and the anti-immigrant impulse in the United States* (pp. 223–243). New York: New York University Press.

Roemer, J. (1989). The shadow world of the new Irish. *San Francisco Magazine*, March, pp. 31–85.

Sanchez, R. (1999). California's divisive proposition 187 is voided. *Washington Post*, July 30, A3.

Schockman, H. E. (1998). California's ethnic experiment and the unsolvable immigration issue: Proposition 187 and beyond. In M. B. Preston, B. E. Cain, & S. Bass (Eds.), *Racial and ethnic politics in California* (pp. 233–276). Berkeley, CA: Institute of Governmental Studies Press, University of California, Berkeley.

Schrag, P. (1998). *Paradise lost: California's experience, America's future*. Berkeley: University of California Press.

Serb, C. (1995). Dollars and sense behind Prop. 187. *Hospitals & Health Networks*, 69(18), 63.

Smith, D. (1999). Davis, foes of Proposition 187 reach pact: US law's restrictions will be used. *Sacramento Bee*, July 29, p. 1.

Smith, J. P., & Edmonston, B. (Eds.). (1997). *The new Americans: Economic, demographic and fiscal effects of immigration*. Washington, DC: National Academy Press.

Smith, M. P., & Tarallo, B. (1995). Proposition 187: Global trend or local narrative? Explaining anti-immigrant politics in California, Arizona, and Texas. *International Journal of Urban & Regional Research, 19*(4), 664–676.

Stefancic, J. (1997). Funding the nativist agenda. In J. F. Perea (Ed.), *Immigrants out! The new nativism and the anti-immigrant impulse in the United States* (pp. 119–135). New York: New York University Press.

Vernez, G., & McCarthy, K. F. (1995). *The fiscal costs of immigration*. Santa Monica, CA: RAND, National Defense Research Institute.

Zavella, P. (1997). The tables are turned: Immigration, poverty and social conflict in California communities. In J. F. Perea (Ed.), *Immigrants out! The new nativism and the anti-immigrant impulse in the United States* (pp. 136–161). New York: New York University Press.

# CHAPTER 6

# Affirmative Action: Resisting Change, Reclaiming Privilege

As the United States grows steadily more diverse, we believe . . . that the country must continue to make determined efforts to include blacks in the institutional framework that constitutes America's economic, political, educational and social life. This goal of greater inclusiveness is important for reasons, both moral and practical, that offer all Americans the prospect of living in a society marked by more equality and racial harmony than one might otherwise anticipate.

> —William G. Bowen and Derek Bok (1998, 285)

The successful passage of Proposition 187 both encouraged and emboldened those individuals and groups who were mounting an assault against affirmative action in California's state government and institutions of higher education. In celebrating the adoption of this anti-immigration legislation, conservative politicians clearly recognized the underlying xenophobic and exclusionary sentiments that were ripe for massaging and manipulation in the service of eliminating affirmative action.

Thomas Wood and Glynn Custred, two obscure college instructors in Hayward, California, seized this opportunity to link their incipient campaign against affirmative action to the groundswell of support for Proposition 187. A campaign that had seemed mired in anonymity and ineptitude suddenly took on new life, attracted new supporters, and captured media attention.

After two years of an intensely bitter and divisive campaign, these two unlikely warriors managed to engineer a major victory in the November 1996 election when the California electorate overwhelmingly voted for Proposition 209, the California Civil Rights Initiative (CCRI), by a margin of 55 percent to 45 percent (Chavez, 1998).

The proposition is deceptively simple, as its language specifically:

> Prohibits the state, local governments, districts, public universities, colleges, and schools, and other government instrumentalities from discriminating against or giving preferential treatment to any individual or group in public employment, public education, or public contracting on the basis of race, sex, color, ethnicity, or national origin. (California Secretary of State's Office, 1996a, 44)

When Proposition 209 was passed, its advocates hailed the elimination of racial preferences and quotas, while its opponents decried the dismantling of equal opportunity and goals. In their heated campaign rhetoric to woo voters, the pro-Proposition 209 forces had equated affirmative action with reverse racism, goals had been redefined as quotas, and equal opportunity had been morphed into racial preferences. Propaganda became fact, minorities became the enemy, and the battle could only have one conceivable outcome in a state where the battle lines had been clearly drawn.

In order to understand the surprising success of the Proposition 209 campaign, it is useful to trace the strands of issues, the multiple actors, and their diverse agendas, all of which eventually coalesced to generate a coherent message, a coordinated strategy, and a committed bloc of voters to support the anti-affirmative action movement in California.

## BUILDING MOMENTUM FOR PROPOSITION 209: BACKGROUND ISSUES

The California Civil Rights Initiative, which ultimately appeared on the ballot as Proposition 209 in the November 1996 statewide elections, was the brain child of two academics in the Bay Area, both of whom had personal axes to grind about affirmative action (Chavez, 1998). Since the late 1980s, Glynn Custred, a fifty-five–year-old professor of anthropology at California State University at Hayward, had become disenchanted with his administration's efforts to mount an aggressive campaign to recruit women and minority faculty members and to increase the admissions of minority students at the four-year college located southeast of Oakland. Custred founded the California chapter of the National Association of Scholars, an organization of conservative professors who envisioned themselves as a Maginot Line defending the academy against assault from the radical left and the militant minority groups who threatened to contaminate the traditional canons and lower intellectual standards with such revolutionary ideas as women's studies, ethnic studies, gay and lesbian studies, and multiculturalism.

In 1991 Custred opposed a bill in the California State Assembly that proposed that the entering freshman classes at the state's public colleges and universities ought to reflect the ethnic diversity of the state's public high schools in order to achieve educational equity. Encouraged by the governor's subsequent veto of this bill, Custred decided to tackle a much larger target—dismantling the entire apparatus of affirmative action in California state-supported programs (Chavez, 1998; Schrag, 1998).

Custred found an eager confidant in Thomas E. Wood, a forty-four-year-old part-time researcher who had failed to find an academic position despite his doctorate in the philosophy of religion from UC Berkeley. Frustrated with his own lack of professional success and embittered by his belief that his race and sex handicapped him competitively, Wood also joined the California Association of Scholars in 1991 and, from 1992 to 1994, Wood collaborated with Custred on developing an anti-affirmative action initiative, planning it as a nonpartisan measure to place on the state ballot. Through researching civil rights statutes and using polling data, they made an important decision to focus on the language of "race-based preferences" rather than on "affirmative action programs," which were actually supported by a majority of the state's voters (Chavez, 1998).

Following a series of media articles on the potential divisiveness of affirmation action, Custred and Wood met Ward Connerly, a member of the Board of Regents at the University of California, who joined them in support of Assembly Bill 47, at the hearings held by the Judiciary Committee in August 1994. This bill, proposing to outlaw the use of race and gender as selection criteria in state employment, contracting, and education, was a forerunner to the California Civil Rights Initiative in both its language and its intent, but the bill didn't make it out of committee. However, Custred and Wood had established an important contact with Connerly, who was to become their major ally and advocate (Chavez, 1998).

Ward Connerly, then a fifty-five-year-old African American businessman, was a self-made man from humble Southern roots. Early in his career as a government civil servant, he had befriended Pete Wilson, an ambitious state legislator who later became governor of California in 1990. To repay Connerly for his years of political support and generous contributions, Wilson appointed him to the University of California Board of Regents in 1993 as a trade-off to gain approval of a controversial nomination of a conservative white male businessman to the board by balancing him with a moderate black businessman (Chavez, 1998). Although Connerly has vociferously denied that his private consulting business had benefited substantially from the state's affirmative action policies toward awarding minority firms a certain percentage of consulting contracts, he has publicly acknowledged that his race played a role in his appointment to the Board of Regents, one of the most prestigious and long-term appointments in the governor's political patronage treasure chest.

By the summer of 1994 Connerly was leading the charge against affirmative action on the Board of Regents, serving as the stalking horse for Governor Pete Wilson who was then playing up the hot-button issue of illegal immigration to revive his sagging poll ratings in his second California gubernatorial election. Wilson's anti-immigrant campaign demagoguery succeeded in derailing Democrat Kathleen Brown's cautious campaign, gaining him momentum in the last few weeks of the race and coasting him to victory with a 55 percent margin in the November election. Proposition 187 won by an even greater margin of 58.9 percent. The Republicans had demonstrated once again that scapegoating immigrants and people of color was a winning strategy, so Custred and Wood were not the only ones who could see the similarities between the CCRI and Proposition 187, both of which appealed to the latent racism and xenophobia of so many Californians.

## PLANNING THE CAMPAIGN FOR PROPOSITION 209

By late December of 1994 Custred and Wood had formed a campaign team of conservative Republican operatives to help them plan an overall strategy and raise funds to place the initiative on the state ballot in 1996. After recognizing the potential of affirmative action as a wedge issue to spark his campaign for the Republican presidential nomination, Pete Wilson abandoned his long-term support for it and made a calculated decision in the spring of 1995 to support the CCRI.

As journalist Lydia Chavez chronicles in her book *The Color Bind* (1998), a detailed account of the campaign for the CCRI, Ward Connerly and Pete Wilson moved in tandem to achieve their mutual goals of eliminating affirmative action in all state-supported educational institutions, employment, and contracting, while exploiting this issue to promote Wilson's presidential aspirations and political agenda. In July 1995, after nearly two years of high-profile lobbying, Connerly pressured the Board of Regents to vote on his proposal to eliminate race and ethnicity as criteria for admissions or employment at the University of California's nine campuses. Despite unanimous opposition from the chancellors of all nine campuses, spirited student demonstrations on several campuses, and a direct emotional appeal from the Reverend Jesse Jackson at the meeting, the regents voted to abolish affirmative action at the University of California, with separate votes affirming the ban on hiring and promotion of faculty and staff (15–10) and the ban on race as a factor in student admissions (14–10). The board's vote clearly revealed a major split between the conservative white males, mainly Republican appointees, and the liberal women, minority, and Democratic members, a split that was to foreshadow the vote on Proposition 209.

After this historical retreat from affirmative action by the governing board of America's premier public university, Ward Connerly and Pete Wilson were catapulted into the national media limelight, hailed as heroes by the Republican party leaders, and lionized by right wing conservative groups for "defending the rights of the majority" and "rejecting reverse racism" (Chavez, 1998, 188).

### Leadership and Fund-Raising Issues

Custred and Wood, also emboldened by the regents' vote to end affirmative action at the University of California, refiled their CCRI initiative with the state attorney general's office. They were also encouraged by an infusion of funds to the campaign by the state Republican Party, which contributed $464,859, and by Darrell Issa, an electronics executive, who gave $50,000, enabling them to hire a professional signature-gathering firm to field workers throughout the state for the 600,000 signatures needed to place an initiative on the California election ballot. In the fall of 1995, their campaign staff sent out appeals to Governor Wilson and the Republican Party for additional funds.

Meanwhile, Pete Wilson's campaign for the Republican presidential nomination was derailed by a number of factors, including his untimely throat surgery and the threat of General Colin Powell, military hero and national icon, who was being courted by the Republican king- makers as their ideal candidate. As Wilson's candidacy faltered and failed to generate excitement from state or national Republican leaders, he apparently decided that he could still be useful to the CCRI campaign. His friend Ward Connerly was reluctantly recruited to chair the campaign in November of 1995, one year before the initiative would be placed on the California ballot.

## LAUNCHING THE CAMPAIGN FOR PROPOSITION 209

The campaign for the California Civil Rights Initiative, intended by its coauthors to be nonpartisan, veered sharply to the right soon after Ward Connerly assumed the helm. In order to raise funds to finance the campaign, Connerly and Wilson appealed to the Republican Party and its conservative contributors. Among the early contributors to support the CCRI were Howard Ahmanson, the conservative founder of Home Savings of America ($50,000); Ron Unz, the Silicon Valley entrepreneur ($23,000); Patricia Hume, a wealthy donor ($25,000); and Theodore J. Forstmann, a New York Republican philanthropist ($10,000) (California Secretary of State's Office, 1996b). But donations were slow to arrive and funds from traditional sources such as corporations and political action committees were negligible. Although the early polls registered strong support for the CCRI among white voters, contributors seemed reluctant to associate themselves with the volatile issue of dismantling affirmative action programs in the state of California.

In the previous campaigns for Propositions 184 and 187, Republican state and national leaders had openly and enthusiastically manipulated the wedge issues of race and immigration to energize white voters, particularly the "angry white males," who were particularly vulnerable to arguments that scapegoated minorities and immigrants for economic and social anxieties of working-class and middle-class white voters in California. Pat Buchanan had successfully wooed white working-class voters in his campaigns for the Republican presidential nomination in 1992 and 1996, but the CCRI campaign staff was initially reluctant to use such blatant appeals to white racism, preferring the more subtle approach of attacking "quotas" and "set-asides."

Connerly and Wilson persuaded Senator Robert Dole, the presumptive Republican presidential candidate, to endorse the CCRI in an op-ed piece in the *Los Angeles Times* on November 19, 1995. Although Dole, like Wilson, represented the moderate wing of the Republican Party and had consistently supported affirmative action programs in the U.S. Senate, his political advisers recognized the CCRI as a powerful wedge issue that could vault him to victory in the upcoming California presidential primary (Schrag, 1998). However, Dole's lukewarm endorsement of the CCRI at a March 1996 rally in Orange County reflected his growing concern that it would alienate moderate swing voters and women, two groups he needed to woo aggressively in order to win the California primary (Chavez, 1998).

### Mixed Messages About the CCRI

In the spring of 1996, two more prominent Republicans expressed their opposition to the CCRI—retired General Colin Powell, then still a leading contender for the Republican presidential nomination, and Richard Riordan, the recently elected mayor of Los Angeles, causing great consternation among state and national Republican leaders. Nonetheless, when the Republicans held their national convention in San Diego in July 1996, Newt Gingrich, the feisty Speaker of the House of Representatives, and the party leadership were united in their support for the CCRI, assuring the convention's overwhelming endorsement of Proposition 209. Colin Powell, the keynote speaker at the convention, was the only prominent Republican to reaffirm his commitment to affirmative action (Chavez, 1998).

But the campaign consultants had not anticipated the growing opposition of the corporate sector to the CCRI. The members of the influential California Business Round Table announced their opposition to Proposition 209, defending affirmative action programs as both economically effective and morally defensible in a state where the majority of working-age adults would soon be people of color. According to Chavez (1998), Governor Wilson brought pressures to bear on a number of corporate executives whose companies were subject to state regulatory commissions, cautioning them not to contribute any funds to the opponents of Proposition 209.

The advocates for Proposition 209 approached election day with one major advantage, that is, the ballot's summary did not even mention that this initiative would have any adverse impact on affirmative action programs in California. Prepared by the Republican Attorney General Dan Lungren's office, the summary was factual but misleading. Although challenged in court by opponents of the CCRI, Lungren's ballot language was ultimately upheld by the 3rd District Court of Appeals. This was a major setback for the opponents because the CCRI's own campaign polls in April had indicated that 72 percent of potential voters would support the initiative if it ended "racial preferences," but only 45 percent would support it if it ended "affirmative action," thus the language of the initiative was a crucial factor in its appeal and acceptability to the voters (Chavez, 1998).

### Financing the Campaign for Proposition 209

By the last weeks of the campaign, just in time to launch a media blitz, contributions of $3 million began to flood in from supporters who believed that the CCRI had the potential of generating support for the faltering candidacy of Bob Dole and Jack Kemp at the top of the Republican ticket. Major donations to the California Republican Party included: $750,000 from international media mogul Rupert Murdoch; $500,000 from George Joseph, the C.E.O. of Mercury Casualty Insurance Company in Los Angeles; $100,000 from Cypress Semi-Conductor Company in San Jose, some of which funds were diverted to congressional races and the "Yes on 209" campaign (California Secretary of State's Office, 1996b). Individuals and groups also contributed directly to the Proposition 209 campaign, including $10,000 from Thomas L. Rhodes, the president of the National Review Magazine; $100,000 from John Uhlmann, Kansas City businessman; $10,250 from W. Glenn Campbell, former director of the Hoover Institute at Stanford University; $10,000 from Edward Allred, a physician from Long Beach, CA; $125,000 from Virginia and Richard Gilder, New York investors; $100,000 from Richard Mellon Scaife, conservative Pittsburgh philanthropist; $25,000 from the Project for the Republican Future; $20,000 from W. Alan Dayton, retired Palm Beach, FL, investor; and $25,000 from Carole Coggan of Aiken, SC. In fact, the five pro-Proposition 209 organizations raised $5,239,287, more than $3 million of which represented single donations of $10,000 and more. Banker Howard Ahmanson donated an additional $300,000 from his Fieldstead & Company, based in Irvine, CA (Coleman, 1998). These pro-Proposition 209 forces raised more than twice as much as their opponents, whose total fund-raising efforts generated just $2,180,491, both too little and too late to defeat Proposition 209.

These contributors supporting the Proposition 209 campaign also shared a number of political, financial, and organizational connections. Thomas L. Rhodes was a founder and director of the Project for the Republican Future and a fellow trustee with Virginia Gilder of both the Empire Foundation for Policy Research and Change New York, conservative organizations advocating lower taxes and limited government. Rhodes was also a trustee of the Heritage Foundation, an ultra-conservative think tank that was one of Richard Mellon Scaife's major beneficiaries in the late 1990s.

Richard Mellon Scaife was also a major financial contributor to the Hoover Institution, a conservative think tank at Stanford University whose Director Emeritus, W. Glenn Campbell, was a supporter of Proposition 209. Scaife was also registered as a generous contributor to the American Enterprise Institute and the Cato Institute, both conservative think tanks with long records of opposition to affirmative action.

## THE CAMPAIGN AGAINST PROPOSITION 209

The campaign against the California Civil Rights Initiative was befuddled and bedeviled from the very beginning: it got off to a late start, it had too many strong leaders, it had multiple agendas, and it never developed a clear, compelling, or consistent message. Hoping to learn from their losing battle to defeat Proposition 187, the anti-immigration initiative, a loose coalition of groups including liberal Democratic activists, civil rights veterans, women's groups, labor leaders, and civil liberties groups held a series of meetings early in 1995 to discuss strategies to defeat the CCRI at the polls long before it became known as Proposition 209. Unfortunately, this same coalition had not been successful in reversing the tide favoring Proposition 187, so many of its members were dispirited and their energies depleted from the bruising battle (Chavez, 1998)

Moreover, an early split developed between the north and south in terms of planning a grassroots campaign, raising funds, and developing a clear message that would appeal to a broader constituency. The Northern California campaign was led by a veteran civil rights leader and a pragmatic labor organizer, while the Southern California leaders from the NAACP Legal Defense Fund and the Feminist Majority were more ideological and concerned about mobilizing the women's organizations. Both groups worked with representatives from the Mexican American Legal Defense and Educational Fund, the Asian Pacific Legal Center, labor leaders, and the National Organization for Women (NOW) (Chavez, 1998).

The pragmatists in Northern California, led by Eva Patterson of the Northern California Lawyers Committee, labored over the summer of 1995 to create an alternative initiative giving voters a clear choice to modify but not to abolish affirmative action, the "mend-it-don't-end-it" approach advocated by President Clinton in a nationally televised speech on affirmative action in July 1995. But their efforts to craft language that would appeal to moderate voters failed and by the end of December 1995, the Northern California Coalition had abandoned its alternative game plan (Chavez, 1998).

### Fund-Raising and Strategy Issues

In January 1996 the leaders of two major women's groups, Eleanor Smeal, president of the Feminist Majority, and Patricia Ireland, president of the National Organization for Women (NOW), decided to launch an ad campaign aimed at women, both to educate them about the issues at stake and to get out the vote against Proposition 209. Fund-raising was a chronic problem and a constant struggle for the anti-Proposition 209 coalition, particularly because they lacked the support of the major democratic donors and the wealthy liberal white women in Southern California who were giving generously to the Clinton-Gore campaign but ignoring pleas to fund the coalition to defeat Proposition 209. Among the early contributions to the coalition were: $467,072 from the California Teachers Association (the largest single donation); $50,000 from the AFL-CIO; $20,000 each from Don King Productions, Inc. (the boxing promoter's company); $25,000 from Molly Munger; and Boyz II Men, Inc. (the singing group) (California Secretary of State's Office, 1996b). Celebrities like Johnnie L. Cochran and Bruce Springsteen each gave $10,000 to groups opposing Proposition 209. About $100,000 was raised from corporate donors but most of the large California corporations did not contribute to the campaign even though many were opposed to Proposition 209 in principle, but perhaps unwilling to alienate Governor Wilson and the Republican legislators in Sacramento (Chavez, 1998).

The leaders of the California Democratic Party wanted to steer clear of Proposition 209 altogether because they feared that the party's candidates for statewide and congressional offices would be dragged down to defeat if Proposition 209 passed. When the California Democratic Party held its state convention in Sacramento in April 1996, the delegates defied the party leaders and voted overwhelmingly to oppose the CCRI as a "misguided attempt to repeal affirmative action progress in this nation" (Chavez, 1998, 19). After the state convention, the Democratic National Committee donated $100,000 to the campaign, but the Democratic Party in California only contributed $275,169 to defeat the initiative, much less than the Republicans gave to support Ward Connerly's campaign of "Yes on 209."

In August 1996, the leaders of the Feminist Majority withdrew from the statewide Coalition Against Proposition 209 dividing the opposition into two camps (Chavez, 1998). Now there were two major groups lobbying against Proposition 209: the "Stop Prop 209" camp and the "Campaign to Defeat 209," searching for a powerful message and an effective strategy to defeat the CCRI. The fragmentation and infighting within the opponents' camps substantially sabotaged their efforts to defeat the initiative.

The campaign heated up after Labor Day, organizing women's groups, college students, and civil rights organizations for the final push. In the media advertising competition, the Connerly campaign's soft-edged appeal to "fair play" and "equal opportunity without quotas" trumped the Southern California Coalition's hard-edged ad linking the pro-Proposition 209 campaign supporters to David Duke and the Ku Klux Klan. Critics claimed that this ad backfired by alienating the moderate swing voters and the "undecideds."

The media campaign was symbolic of the ineffective strategies of the assorted groups and organizations that were opposed to Proposition 209. Had these groups been better organized and financed, they might have mounted an effective campaign to defeat Proposition 209.

## THE VOTERS SPEAK

On election day, November 5, 1996, the California voters turned out to express their preferences for the president and the propositions. They voted resoundingly to reelect Democrat Bill Clinton to the presidency by a margin of 51 percent to 38 percent for Republican Bob Dole. But the ten-point margin of victory for Proposition 209, 55 percent to 45 percent, was ample cause for celebration by Pete Wilson, Ward Connerly, and the Republican Party in California. They had out-strategized, out-smarted, and out-spent the opponents of the CCRI and had propelled California into the vanguard of the anti-affirmative action movement that was building around the nation.

An analysis of voting patterns showed that the voters were split along racial and gender lines, with Proposition 209 supported by 63 percent of whites and opposed by 74 percent of African Americans, 76 percent of Latinos, and 61 percent of Asians. Despite their attempts to confuse the voters by the language of the initiative and by their misleading media ads, the campaign for Proposition 209 was unable to convince the majority of minority voters that the CCRI was in their best interests. Although nearly two out of five Asian Americans voted for Proposition 209, the majority responded to appeals from prominent Asian educators and civil rights leaders that Proposition 209 would increase employment discrimination against them in occupations where they were victims of the "glass ceiling" effect. Latino voters, angry and energized by the passage of Proposition 187 in 1994, showed the highest level of opposition to Proposition 209 and signaled to the state's politicians that they were becoming a force to be reckoned with in future elections.

Males favored Proposition 209 over females by a margin of 61 percent to 48 percent. Although a bare majority (52 percent) of all women voters opposed Proposition 209, 58 percent of white women favored it. The arguments of the Feminist Majority had failed to convince white women that their fate was linked to the passage of the CCRI, partly because the supporters of Proposition 209 played up the racial issue and gained the sympathy of white women concerned about economic security for their husbands, fathers, and sons. Race was a more powerful rallying symbol than sex in this campaign and the Connerly forces played the "race card" very subtly and very effectively. The opponents of Proposition 209 had failed to develop a clear and compelling theme for women, minorities, workers, and moderates to find common ground. Without a convincing message, without a coordinated statewide strategy, and without adequate funding, the campaign to defeat Proposition 209 never targeted its audience or mobilized its troops for an effective battle plan, so their defeat was predictable and inevitable.

## AFTERMATH OF VICTORY: THE MEDIA RESPONSE TO PROPOSITION 209

The media, which had waxed and waned in their coverage of the CCRI, went into overdrive in the weeks following the passage of Proposition 209. Conservative pundits like Pat Buchanan and Rush Limbaugh, who had agitated for elimination of affirmative action programs, praised the precocity of the California electorate and predicted the demise of all state and federal affirmative action measures. Liberal journalists such as Frank Rich and Cynthia Tucker decried the retreat from affirmative action and foresaw dire consequences for California's minorities in higher education and state employment. Editorials in papers such as *The New York Times, The Washington Post*, the *Los Angeles Times*, and the *San Francisco Chronicle* offered more measured analyses of the vote, yet revealed an undercurrent of pessimism about its immediate consequences.

Within the first year following the passage of Proposition 209, Ward Connerly was both lionized and demonized in the media for his pivotal role in guiding the initiative to victory. Described by his supporters as brilliant, charismatic, and articulate, he was depicted by his critics as amoral, opportunistic, and manipulative. The African American community, in particular, vilified him as an "Uncle Tom," compared him to Supreme Court Justice Clarence Thomas, and portrayed him in their media as a puppet figure manipulated by wealthy white conservatives (Coleman, 1998). His success in California catapulted him to national fame, landing him on the cover of *Time* magazine, providing him invitations to participate in nationally televised debates about affirmative action, and awarding him treatment as a celebrity on the conservative fund-raising circuit. President

Clinton even invited him to the White House to present his views on the President's initiative on race relations. This successful black entrepreneur, whose race was a major factor in his appointment to the University of California Board of Regents, had succeeded in changing the rules and blocking access to the university for future generations of African Americans.

Meanwhile, the media slowly began to recognize the negative synergistic impact of Proposition 209 with the 1995 decision of the University of California Board of Regents to eliminate race as a factor in college admissions. Reports began to surface that applications from minority students to the University of California were down from previous years, that recruiters were encountering frustrated students in inner-city communities, and that University of California administrators were anticipating severe reductions in the numbers of minority students in the entering class of 1998.

### Legal Challenges to Proposition 209

Hardly had the vote on Proposition 209 been certified before a loose coalition of civil rights and liberal advocacy groups and groups opposed to the initiative filed suit in the U.S. District Court of Northern California to challenge its constitutionality. In November 1996, Judge Thelton B. Henderson, the first African American to hold the post as Chief Judge of the Court, blocked the implementation of Proposition 209 on the grounds that its constitutionality was in doubt because it barred minorities from seeking preferences that other groups were allowed to seek based on factors such as age, disability, and military service (Chavez, 1998). Judge Henderson, ironically one of two blacks in his 1962 graduating class from UC Berkeley's Boalt Hall School of Law, was subject to months of vilification, hate mail, and protest demonstrations outside the federal courthouse in San Francisco. Stunned by the criticism of his ruling and the racially offensive threats against him, Judge Henderson noted in an interview that his decision was based on "a sound bit of legal reasoning—the case in its legal analysis had nothing to do with affirmative action or my views. It had to do with the constitutionality of (Prop) 209" (Chiang, 1997, A16).

However, the U.S. Court of Appeals for the 9th Circuit, also located in San Francisco, disagreed with Henderson's legal thinking and reversed his decision in April 1997, allowing state and local governments to begin to implement the measure (Chavez, 1998). The anti-Proposition 209 litigants appealed to the U.S. Supreme Court, unwilling to believe that the Supreme Court, even with its conservative majority, would really permit the state of California to adopt such a sweeping elimination of affirmative action remedies in education and employment.

In November 1997, after a year of legal challenges, the U.S. Supreme Court declined to hear an appeal of the Court of Appeals decision, thus allowing Proposition 209 to become law by rejecting the challenge to its constitutionality (Chavez, 1998). Affirmative action had been dealt a knock-out, if not terminal, blow by the very legal system that had legitimated and enforced it for nearly twenty-five years.

## IMPACT OF PROPOSITION 209 ON HIGHER EDUCATION IN CALIFORNIA

Shortly after the Board of Regents of the University of California voted in July 1995 to eliminate affirmative action in admissions criteria, they reached a compromise with the campus chancellors that their new policy would be gradually phased in over two years, allowing the admissions officers of each campus ample time to develop plans and procedures to implement it. Thus, the change would affect only admissions to the graduate schools for the incoming fall class of 1997 and the undergraduate departments for the fall of 1998. Connerly, flush with victory, had at first resisted any delay of the new policy, but ultimately was persuaded that a two-year timetable would result in a smoother transition and create fewer administrative problems.

In the spring of 1997, Boalt Hall School of Law at UC Berkeley announced that there would be only one African American in the first-year class in the fall. Although fourteen black students had been admitted (compared to seventy-five in 1995), they had all declined to enroll, and the lone black student in the incoming class had actually been admitted the previous year and had postponed his entry for a year. In 1997 Latino student admissions to Boalt had dropped from seventy-eight in 1995 to thirty-nine, of whom only fourteen students decided to enroll in the first-year class. Faculty and students at Berkeley's Law School were vocal in their criticism of the regents' action, arguing that it would deprive them of a diverse student body, one of the major assets of a legal education in a multicultural society.

In focusing on the drama at Berkeley, the media missed the larger story of significant declines in the overall enrollments in the three law schools in the University of California system (Berkeley, Davis, and Los Angeles), where the total number of first-year African American students declined by 63 percent in 1997 (from forty-three in 1996 to sixteen) and Latino students declined by 34 percent (from eighty-nine to fifty-nine). For the five medical schools in the UC system, the enrollment of "underrepresented minorities" (blacks and Latinos) dropped by only 3 percent between 1996 and 1997, following a precipitous 24 percent decline in the previous year. An editorial in the *San Francisco Chronicle* concluded:

> The first results of the affirmative action ban are extremely dismaying to those who believe in promoting diversity in all societal institutions. The regents have a responsibility to mitigate the deleterious effects of their decision to end affirmative action. (Reaping, 1997, B8)

Educators and civil rights advocates predicted grave consequences for diversity in the professional schools throughout the UC system, which trains the majority of California's lawyers and doctors for a state that is rapidly transitioning into a majority-minority population (Coleman, 1998). Spokespersons for the San Francisco Bar complained that the decline of minority students in the university's law schools would inevitably impact on the ability of major law firms in San Francisco to recruit a diverse group of new associates to serve their increasingly heterogeneous clients (Nakao, 1997).

In the months following the passage of Proposition 209, proponents of affirmative action publicized reports from follow-up studies of lawyers and doctors, showing that the professional achievements and career paths for whites and African Americans were not significantly different. Opponents of affirmative action offered less optimistic interpretations of the studies, pointing out that the studies only compared those white and minority students who actually survived until graduation, thus ignoring the higher rates of attrition and failure of those minority students who did not successfully complete their professional training programs.

Although the top administrators at UC Berkeley had opposed the regents' SP-1 ruling and Proposition 209, there was a core of conservative faculty members who publicly supported the elimination of affirmative action in university admissions and faculty recruitment and hiring. Belying Berkeley's vaunted liberalism, these prominent professors from departments such as the Law School, political science, and public policy represented a reactionary minority who perceived any major policy change as a threat to academic excellence and/or faculty governance.

Hardly had the furor over the steep decline in graduate admissions abated than the university announced the results of implementing the new policy in undergraduate admissions for the incoming freshman class in the fall of 1998. The statistics showed a dramatic decline of African American and Latino students at Berkeley and UCLA, the two flagship campuses with the most selective admissions criteria, but an uneven distribution of minority students at the other six undergraduate campuses (UCSF does not have an undergraduate program). At Berkeley, the proportion of "underrepresented" minority students admitted to the freshman class dropped from 20 percent in 1997 to 11.3 percent in 1998, a decline of 54.7 percent. The number of admitted African American students dropped from 562 in 1997 to 191 in 1998, while Latinos/Chicanos dropped from 1,266 to 600. American Indians, only a small fraction (0.3 percent) of the undergraduate student body, saw their numbers decline from 69 in 1997 to 27 in 1998, a 58.9 percent decrease. While the proportion of white and Asian students did not increase significantly from 1997 to 1998, there was a major increase in the number of students who omitted race/ethnicity on their application forms, perhaps as a form of protest or as a way of subverting the Board of Regents ruling, a form of "Don't ask, don't tell."

Similar, but less drastic, declines were registered between 1997 and 1998 in admissions of minority freshmen to UCLA (43 percent for African Americans and 33 percent for Latinos/Chicanos) and four other campuses at San Diego, Santa Barbara, and Irvine. The only two UC campuses to report an overall increase in admissions of underrepresented minority students in 1998 were at Riverside and Santa Cruz, but Riverside was the only campus that increased its number of African American freshmen admitted for the incoming fall 1999 class.

Predictably, the debate heated up again, with the pundits pontificating about the pros and cons of the policy, and the students raising their voices in protest marches and rallies on the campuses. Some university administrators and policy analysts surmised that minority students had been discouraged from even applying to a UC campus because of the passage of Proposition 209, a more recent and more divisive initiative than the earlier Regents policy change. In their view, the controversy over Proposition 209 had compounded the exclusionary message of the Regents' ruling to send shock waves through minority communities, where parents, counselors, and teachers responded with anger, anxiety, and apprehension about the lowered expectations and heightened qualifications for their children. It took only a few months for the latent message of both these rulings to spread throughout these communities, communicating to these students of color that they didn't have "the right stuff" to make it at the University of California, and undermining their aspirations, their self-esteem, and their motivation to compete for slots at the state's premier public university.

## PROTESTS AND PUBLIC BACKLASH TO PROPOSITION 209

On August 28, 1997, the first day that Proposition 209 was finally enforceable, Jesse Jackson, the ubiquitous civil rights leader and erstwhile presidential candidate, led thousands of demonstrators across the Golden Gate Bridge to protest the death of affirmative action in California (Moore, 1997). A multiracial and multigenerational crowd, marching to "Save the Dream," listened to a series of speakers denounce Proposition 209 and its primary sponsors, Ward Connerly and Governor Pete Wilson, for torpedoing equal opportunity for future generations of Californians, the majority of whom will be people of color. Hari Dillon, cochair of the march and a veteran of the 1968 student strikes at San Francisco State University, was outraged:

> This is tragic: Pete Wilson and Ward Connerly have launched a blinding assault on people of color. Boalt Hall is lily-white. There's nothing color-blind about that. (Moore, 1997, A19).

Jesse Jackson noted that August 28 was the thirty-fourth anniversary of Martin Luther King, Jr.'s, "I Have a Dream" speech at the 1963 Civil Rights March on Washington, then thundered,

> It is poetic injustice that on this day, 34 years from the day that the dream of hope and inclusion was projected, that Proposition 209 has been unleashed like a Scud missile, with the effect of bludgeoning the dreams of this generation. (Moore, 1997, A19–20)

Ward Connerly, ensconced in his Sacramento office, reiterated his support for Proposition 209 and his determination to monitor its implementation.

> It's only going to happen with vigilance from us and others who will make sure that every city and county, state colleges, and University of California, community colleges, mosquito abatement people, all of them, that they will be held accountable to bring their policies into compliance with Proposition 209. (Moore, 1997, A19)

## UNANTICIPATED CONSEQUENCES OF PROPOSITION 209

By the fall of 1998, two years after the passage of Proposition 209, the impact on minority enrollment at the state colleges and universities began to sink in throughout the educational system. The number of African American and Latino students had plummeted at the two most competitive campuses (UC Berkeley and UCLA), making them virtually invisible as significant segments of the student body. Although there were slight increases in the number of African American and Latino undergraduates at a few of the other six University of California undergraduate campuses, it seemed inevitable that the campuses would quickly revert to student bodies that were predominantly white and Asian, creating a two-tier system and betraying the mandate of the California master plan to provide educational opportunities for all the students who reflect the diversity of the state's population.

While conservative politicians and policy analysts praised the new system of meritocratic admissions, civil rights organizations and enlightened educators decried the narrow interpretation of grades and SAT scores as criteria for "merit" (Bowen & Bok, 1999; Coleman, 1998). It was noted with some irony that Ward Connerly and several of his fellow regents had been exposed in 1995 for lobbying the admissions staff at Berkeley and UCLA to admit the children of their wealthy friends and political associates who were not eligible for admission under the standard criteria. Somehow, those regents were able to rationalize their efforts to influence admissions decisions for unqualified white students, while railing against "preferential treatment" of minority students. Moreover, opponents of Proposition 209 pointed out that universities, including the University of California, traditionally granted preferences to various categories of students, such as children of alumni, children of donors, outstanding athletes, and gifted musicians and artists, believing that a heterogeneous student body enhanced the learning environment (not to mention its impact on increasing alumni contributions and generating income from athletic events). Critics of Proposition 209 asked why would the admission of a small percentage of minority students, who met the basic criteria for admission, create so much controversy and division when the public did not seem at all perturbed by favorable treatment given to other groups of "preferred students"?

Morale plummeted among the minority faculty at the university, a small but not insignificant group of accomplished scholars who had organized too little and too late to mount an effective challenge to Proposition 209. But faculty morale was also low because many of these minority faculty members viewed themselves and their children as beneficiaries of affirmative action. Many were veterans of the Civil Rights Movement in the 1960s and had formed the vanguard of integrating the student bodies and the faculties of the predominantly white major universities and colleges. Now middle-aged and tenured, they had proven themselves qualified and competent, produced prodigious scholarship in myriad fields, enhanced the stature of their departments and university campuses, and served as role models and mentors to two generations of students. Yet, now they could see the system returning to its old ways, excluding the next generation of students of color, and replicating the privilege and power of the dominant majority.

Campus reputation is a fragile and mysterious quality, built as much from a series of historical events, colorful characters, and memorable incidents as from the excellence of its faculty, the volumes in its libraries, and the contributions of its alumni. It took only a few months for the educational community, parents, and potential students to understand the severe impact that Proposition 209, combined with the regents' ruling, would have on racial and ethnic diversity throughout the state college and university systems. The elimination of affirmative action sent a signal to minority students that they would have to prove that they were equally prepared and competitive for admission despite their often inferior schools and resource-poor environments; it sent a signal to parents that equal opportunity was no longer an operative goal in California's higher education system; and it sent a message to high school counselors that they no longer had to make special efforts to identify potential minority candidates to apply to the university system. With the predictability of a self-fulfilling cycle, applications from minority students declined, further shrinking the pool of actual students eligible for admission to the university.

Similarly, appointments of African American and Latino faculty members declined at most of the university campuses. In the fall of 1998 there were no new black and only five Latino faculty members appointed at the

Berkeley campus, a dramatic decline from the pattern of the previous decade. Just as the campus would become increasingly dichotomized with a predominantly white and Asian student body, so too would the faculty reflect a declining number of people of color who were deemed "underrepresented minorities."

University administrators had been quietly planning other strategies to increase the recruitment of minority students, primarily through outreach programs to high schools in inner-city areas and partnerships with elementary and secondary schools to strengthen their curricula and upgrade teachers' skills. Even these plans were attacked by Ward Connerly as preferential treatment for minorities, but the other regents were reluctant to join his call for elimination of all efforts to improve the chances of minority students to meet the criteria for admission to the University of California.

## REMEDIES AND POLICY OPTIONS: GETTING AROUND PROPOSITION 209

Soon after Proposition 209 passed, a number of remedies and alternative policies were advanced by educators, moderate politicians, civil rights leaders, and editorial writers. These options ran the gamut from challenging the use of SAT scores in undergraduate admissions to invoking moral arguments about social justice and legal arguments about educational equity (Applebome, 1997; Price, 1998). One early proposal, first floated by University of California President Richard Atkinson, to admit the top 4 percent of all California public high school graduates, was initially greeted with enthusiasm but gradually waned in its appeal. By the time the UC Academic Council endorsed the proposal in December 1998, the critics pointed out that high-achieving minority students in academically rigorous high schools would be less likely to be admitted than good students from mediocre high schools (Guthrie, 1999). As the *San Francisco Chronicle* (Good Intentions, 1998) pointed out in an editorial,

> despite the good intentions, the plan is flawed . . . the 4 percent admissions plan lacks an incentive for bad and mediocre schools to get better. . . . This blanket attempt at increasing the number of minorities lacks quality control. (22)

Proponents of Proposition 209 were quick to respond that this proposal would discriminate against many white and Asian students who had excellent qualifications and deserved to be admitted on their merits.

The only glimmer of hope for the opponents of Proposition 209 was the reassurance by Richard Atkinson, the president of the University of California, that the university, as a federal contractor, was still bound to maintain compliance with federal affirmative action programs for hiring of minorities and women and was still obliged to "best fulfill our responsibilities as a public university in the nation's most ethnically and culturally diverse state" (Atkinson, 1996).

Soon after Gray Davis, a Democrat, was inaugurated as governor of California on January 4, 1999, he reintroduced the idea of the "4 percent plan" for admission to the University of California system, and it was adopted by the State Board of Regents on March 19, 1999. Although critics still dismissed the plan as ill-conceived and inadequate to address the lack of underrepresented minority students, the Regents' vote was viewed as a minor victory by the opponents of Proposition 209 and a sign of retreat by its supporters.

By sending a signal that high-achieving students from all high schools would be eligible for admission to the university or at least one of its campuses, the Davis administration and the regents had reframed the debate and rekindled the hopes and aspirations of thousands of students of color. By April 2000, the University of California system had admitted 7,336 minorities to the entering freshman class for fall 2000, a slight increase from the number admitted in 1997, the last year when affirmative action measures were implemented. However, the numbers of minority students admitted to the two most competitive campuses at Berkeley and UCLA was still lower than their cohorts in 1997, even though they had steadily risen in the three years since Proposition 209 was passed.

After three years of intensive outreach efforts targeting low-income and minority students, African American and Latino students applied to the University of California at Berkeley in record numbers for the freshman class entering in fall semester of 2000 (Schevitz, 2000). However, the numbers of African Americans (3.9%) and Hispanics (9.1%) who actually enrolled in August 2000 were still considerably lower than their representation in the entering class of 1997, prior to the elimination of affirmative action (University of California, 2000). This pattern reinforced the views of those critics who had predicted that a two-tier system would result from the elimination of affirmative action, with white and Asian students predominating at Berkeley and UCLA, and African American, American Indian, and Latino students segregated on less selective campuses at Irvine and Riverside.

After four years of struggling to overcome the adverse publicity of the regents' edict to terminate affirmative action in the graduate and professional schools at the University of California, the Boalt Hall School of Law at UC Berkeley managed to enroll seven African American students, fewer than one-tenth of the total number of blacks admitted to the fall of 1996 entering class. Four years later, minority students accounted for 29 percent of the first-year law class, still below the 37 percent of the first-year class enrolled in 1996 before the policy changed.

### The Business Sector Responds

While most of the public's attention and concern had been focused on Proposition 209's impact on educational opportunity and diversity in higher education, many large corporations and businesses were quietly continuing their efforts to diversify their workforce. Leaders of companies such as Pacific Bell, Pacific Gas & Electric, IBM, and the Bank of America understood the urgent need to recruit and train workers who are representative of the state's diversity and will be the key to economic productivity and prosperity in the twenty-first century (Reid, 1998).

Just over two years after the passage of Proposition 209 on November 30, 1998, the California Superior Court upheld three of five crucial affirmative action state laws that had been challenged by Governor Wilson and Ward Connerly as illegal under Proposition 209. These three laws set general hiring goals for state civil service workers and community college employees, as well as goals for awarding contracts by the state lottery to businesses owned by minorities and women. However, the court struck down two other major affirmative action laws that mandated specific quotas for awarding state contracts and Treasury bonds to minority-owned companies. The Pacific Legal Foundation, a conservative organization representing Governor Wilson in the lawsuit, announced immediately after the decision that it would appeal the judge's ruling.

According to Michael Reid, a corporate diversity consultant, large corporations have come to understand that diversity is profitable:

> Diversity's benefits have been widely accepted: a diverse work force responds better to diverse consumers and entry-level workers; the global marketplace demands an understanding of other cultures, and diverse task forces routinely outperform homogeneous ones in creative problem-solving. (1998, W42)

Although the private sector actually accounts for a much larger share of the California economy than the government sector, in the short run, businesses cannot replace the stable civil service jobs and the state contracts that have contributed so greatly to building a middle class among African Americans in this state. Yet it is a hopeful sign that the members of the Business Roundtable, seventy-three of the state's most influential business leaders and entrepreneurs, strongly opposed Proposition 209 and did not contribute any significant funds to its campaign.

While the liberals were debating short-term strategies and discussing the long-term consequences of Proposition 209, the conservatives were gearing up for another assault on the rights and the privileges of immigrants and people of color in California. They had found a winning formula in Proposition 187 to contain and control the flood of undocumented immigrants from Mexico and Central America, so they were now ready to take away their children's right to be educated in their own language in the American public school system. Bilingual education became the next target to attack and the next domino to fall in their game plan to restore the status quo and reassert the power of the dominant, but rapidly shrinking, Anglo-American population.

## IMPLICATIONS FOR THE FUTURE

> Given the coded and formal messages of Propositions 187 and 209, many Latino youth were made to feel . . . that the society at large wanted to exclude them from membership in the California community. With these propositions, the largest single ethnic group in the state has been told that it must work extra hard to be accepted and that its path to full political incorporation will be made particularly difficult.
>
> Andres E. Jiménez (1997, 4P)

The passage of Proposition 209 will continue to impact California's educational system and its economy for decades to come. As many educators and business leaders have warned, the failure to educate significant numbers of ethnic minority students deprives the state's economy of a well-educated and well-trained workforce. In turn, the state's high technology industries will find themselves without competent workers, reducing their productivity and impairing their global competitiveness. Additionally, Proposition 209 has widened the gap between whites and people of color, exacerbated racial and ethnic tensions, and contributed to a growing sense of resentment, anger, and alienation of communities of color toward the dominant majority.

Finally, Proposition 209 has aroused the political consciousness of the large Latino community, many of whom were first angered by the passage of Proposition 187. With Proposition 209 they are confronted with one more piece of evidence that they are not viewed as first-class citizens and that their children are still barred from equal opportunity. It is only a matter of time before the Latinos understand that they must unleash the potential of their numbers to have their voices heard and their presence felt in the corridors of power in the state of California.

## REFERENCES

Academic Senate, Office of Public Information. (1998). *Notice.* University of California, Berkeley, 22(6), April, p. 1.

Almaguer, T. (1994). *Racial faultlines: The historical origins of white supremacy in California.* Berkeley: University of California Press.

Applebome, P. (1997). Seeking new approaches to diversity. *New York Times*, April 23, A19.

Atkinson, R. (1996). *Letter to University of California faculty and staff*. Berkeley: Office of the President, University of California, November 6.

Bowen, W. G., & Bok, D. (1998). *The shape of the river: Long-term consequences of considering race in college and university admissions*. Princeton, NJ: Princeton University Press.

Bowen, W. G., & Bok, D. (1999). Affirmative action in admissions—It works. *Focus*, February, pp. 3-8. Washington, DC: Joint Center for Political and Economic Studies.

Borjas, G. J. (1990). *Friends or strangers: The impact of immigrants on the U.S. economy*. New York: Basic Books.

Brackman, H., & Erie, S. P. (1998). At rainbow's end: Empowerment prospects for Latinos and Asian Pacific Americans in Los Angeles. In M. B. Preston, B. E. Cain, & S. Bass (Eds.), *Racial and ethnic politics in California. Vol. II* (pp. 73–107). Berkeley: Institute of Governmental Studies Press, University of California, Berkeley.

Brimelow, A. (1995). *Alien nation: Commonsense about America's immigrant disaster*. New York: Random House.

Cain, B. E. (1998). The politicization of race and ethnicity in the nineties. In M. B. Preston, B. E. Cain, & S. Bass (Eds.), *Racial and ethnic politics in California. Vol. II* (pp. 457–468). Berkeley: Institute of Governmental Studies Press, University of California, Berkeley.

California Secretary of State's Office. (1996a). *California voter information guide: General election, November 1996*. Author.

California Secretary of State's Office. (1996b). *Financing California's statewide ballot measure: 1996 primary and general elections*. Sacramento, CA: Political Reform Division.

Chavez, L. (1998). *The color bind: California's battle to end affirmative action*. Berkeley: University of California Press.

Chiang, H. (1997). The man behind infamous ruling. *San Francisco Chronicle*, August 28, A1.

Cho, S. K. (1993). Korean Americans vs African Americans: Conflict and construction. In R. Gooding-Williams (Ed.), *Reading Rodney King/Reading urban uprising* (pp. 196–211). London: Routledge.

Christopher Commission. (1991). *Report of the Independent Commission on the Los Angeles Police Department*. Los Angeles: Office of the Mayor.

Coleman, J. W. (1998). Affirmative action wars. *Emerge*, March, pp. 30–37.

Davis, C., Estes, R., & Schiraldi, V. (1996). *"Three strikes": The new apartheid*. San Francisco: Center on Juvenile and Criminal Justice.

Davis, M. (1992). *City of quartz: Excavating the future in Los Angeles*. New York: Vintage Books.

Edley, C., Jr. (1996). *Not all black and white: Affirmative action and American values*. New York: Hill and Wang.

Fenton, S. (1999). *Ethnicity, racism, and class and culture*. Lanham, MD: Rowman & Littlefield.

Gewertz, K. (2000). Student organized conference to focus on "mixed race experience." *Harvard University Gazette*, April 13, p. 8.

Gibbs, J. T. (1996). *Race and justice: Rodney King and O. J. Simpson in a house divided*. San Francisco: Jossey-Bass.

Gibbs, J. T., & Huang, L N. (1998). *Children of color: Psychological interventions with culturally diverse youth.* San Francisco: Jossey-Bass.

Glasgow, D. (1981). *The black underclass.* New York: Vintage Books.

Good intentions, bad policy. (1998). *San Francisco Chronicle,* December 14, p. A22.

Gooding-Williams, R. (Ed.). (1993). *Reading Rodney King/Reading urban uprising.* London: Routledge.

Guerra, F. (1998). Latino politics in California: The necessary conditions for success. In M. B. Preston, B. E. Cain, & S. Bass (Eds.), *Racial and ethnic politics in California. Vol. II* (pp. 439–453). Berkeley: Institute of Governmental Studies Press, University of California, Berkeley.

Guthrie, J. (1999). UC plan seen as no help to ethnic students. *San Francisco Examiner,* January 17, C1.

Hahn, H. (1996). Los Angeles and the future: Uprisings, identity, and new institutions. In M. J. Dear, H. E. Schockman, & G. Hise (Eds.), *Rethinking Los Angeles* (pp. 77–95). Thousand Oaks, CA: Sage Publications.

Hollinger, D. (1995). *Post ethnic America.* New York: Basic Books.

Horne, G. (1995). *Fire this time: The Watts uprising and the 1960's.* Charlottesville: University Press of Virginia.

Horton, J. (1999). Chinese suburban immigration and political diversity in Monterey Park, California. In S. Jonas & S. D. Thomas (Eds.), *Immigration: A civil rights issue for the Americas* (pp. 119–129). Wilmington, DE: Scholarly Resources.

Jaynes, G. D., & Williams, R. M. (Eds.). (1989). *A common destiny: Blacks and American society.* Washington, DC: National Academy Press.

Jiménez, A. E. (1997). California's racial divide. *San Jose Mercury News,* September 21, 4P.

Kymlicka, W. (1995). *Multicultural citizenship.* New York: Oxford University Press, Inc.

Lipsitz, G. (1998). *The possessive investment in whiteness: How white people profit from identity politics.* Philadelphia: Temple University Press.

Lynch, M. W. (1999). Davis' 4 percent plan no path to diversity. *San Francisco Chronicle,* February 15, A21.

MacDonald, K., & Cain, B. E. (1998). Nativism, partisanship, and immigration: An analysis of Prop. 187. In M. B. Preston, B. E. Cain, & S. Bass (Eds.), *Racial and ethnic politics in California. Vol. II* (pp. 277–304). Berkeley: Institute of Governmental Studies Press, University of California, Berkeley.

Maharidge, D. (1996). *The coming white minority: California, multiculturalism, and America's future.* New York: Vintage Books.

McCarthy, K. F., & Vernez, G. (1998). *Immigration in a changing economy: California's experience—Questions and answers.* Santa Monica, CA: RAND, National Defense Research Institute.

Mindel, C.H., & Habenstein, R. W. (1981). *Ethnic families in America: Patterns and variations.* (2d ed.) New York: Elsevier.

Moore, T. (1997). Jackson calls law banning preferences "poetic injustice." *San Francisco Chronicle,* August 29, A1.

Nakanishi, D. T. (1998). When numbers do not add up: Asian Pacific Americans and California politics. In M. B. Preston, B. E. Cain, & S. Bass (Eds.), *Racial and ethnic politics in California. Vol. II* (pp. 3–43). Berkeley: Institute of Governmental Studies Press, University of California, Berkeley.

Nakao, A. (1997). Big minority dip at Boalt rattles S.F. law firms. *San Francisco Examiner*, July 6, A1.

Navarro, C., & Acuna, R. (1990). In search of community: A comparative essay on Mexicans in Los Angeles and San Antonio. In N. M. Klein & M. J. Schiesl (Eds.), *20th century Los Angeles: Power, promotion, and social conflict* (pp. 195–226). Claremont, CA: Regina Books.

Pachon, H. P. (1998). Latino politics in the Golden State: Ready for the 21st century? In M. B. Preston, B. E. Cain, & S. Bass (Eds.), *Racial and ethnic politics in California. Vol. II* (pp. 411–438). Berkeley: Institute of Governmental Studies Press, University of California, Berkeley.

Pettigrew, T. E., & Alston, D. A. (1988). *Tom Bradley's campaigns for Governor: The dilemmas of race and political strategies.* Washington, DC: Joint Center for Political Studies.

Preston, M. B., Cain, B. E., & Bass, S. (Eds.). (1998). *Racial and ethnic politics in California. Vol. II.* Berkeley: Institute of Governmental Studies Press, University of California, Berkeley.

Preston, M. B., & Lai, J. S. (1998). The symbolic politics of affirmative action. In M. B. Preston, B. E. Cain, & S. Bass (Eds.), *Racial and ethnic politics in California. Vol. II* (pp. 161–198). Berkeley: Institute of Governmental Studies Press, University of California, Berkeley.

Price, H. B. (1998). Just open up the door. Press release. New York: National Urban League, April 13.

Reaping what UC sowed on affirmative action. (1997). *San Francisco Sunday Examiner and Chronicle*, June 1, B8.

Reid, M. J. (1998). Profit motivates corporate diversity effort. *San Francisco Sunday Examiner and Chronicle*, March 15, W42.

Rieff, D. (1991). *Los Angeles: Capital of the third world.* New York: Simon & Schuster.

Rodriguez, N. (1999). U.S. immigration and intergroup relations in the late 20th century: African Americans and Latinos. In S. Jonas & S. D. Thomas (Eds.), *Immigration: A civil rights issue for the Americas* (pp. 131–144). Wilmington, DE: Scholarly Resources.

Root, M. P. (Ed.). (1992). *Racially mixed people in America.* Newbury Park, CA: Sage Publications.

Root, M. P. (Ed.). (1996). *The multiracial experience: Racial borders as the new frontier.* Thousand Oaks, CA: Sage Publications.

Saito, L. T. (1998). Beyond numbers: Asian American and Latino politics in Los Angeles' San Gabriel Valley. In M. B. Preston, B. E. Cain, & S. Bass (Eds.), *Racial and ethnic politics in California. Vol. II* (pp. 45–72). Berkeley: Institute of Governmental Studies Press, University of California, Berkeley.

Schevitz, T. (2000). Minorities reconsider U.C. Berkeley. *San Francisco Chronicle*, January 27, A22.

Schlesinger, A., Jr. (1992). *The disuniting of America: Reflections on a multicultural society.* New York: W. W. Norton.

Schockman, H. E. (1998). California's ethnic experiment and the unsolvable immigration issue: Proposition 187 and beyond. In M. B. Preston, B. E. Cain, & S. Bass (Eds.), *Racial and ethnic politics in California. Vol. II* (pp. 233–276). Berkeley: Institute of Governmental Studies Press, University of California, Berkeley.

Schrag, P. (1998). *Paradise lost: California's experience, America's future.* Berkeley: University of California Press.

Sonenshein, R. (1993). *Politics in Black and white: Race and power in Los Angeles.* Princeton, NJ: Princeton University Press.

Sonenshein, R. (1998). Jewish participation in California politics: A revisit in the 1990s. In M. B. Preston, B. E. Cain, & S. Bass (Eds.), *Racial and ethnic politics in California. Vol. II* (pp. 109–136). Berkeley: Institute of Governmental Studies Press, University of California, Berkeley.

Sowell, T. (1981). *Ethnic America.* New York: Basic Books.

Streisand, B. (1997). Is it "hasta la vista" for bilingual ed? *U.S. News and World Report, 123,* 36–38.

Takaki, R. (Ed.). (1994). *From different shores: Perspectives on race and ethnicity in America.* 2d ed. Boston: Little, Brown, and Company.

University of California. (2000). Class of 2004 begins arriving for new school year at U.C. Berkeley. Press release, Office of Public Affairs.

Wildmon, S. (Ed.). (1996). *Privilege revealed: How invisible preference undermines America.* New York: New York University Press.

Zavella, P. (1997). The tables are turned: Immigration, poverty, and social conflict in California communities. In J. F. Perea (Ed.), *Immigrants out! The new nativism and the anti-immigration impulse in the United States* (pp. 136–161). New York: New York University Press.

# CHAPTER 7

## Bilingual Education: Language, Culture, and Identity

Languages are suppressed, defended or promoted, precisely because people sense that a language is an item of culture which symbolizes the value accorded to a whole population who have some sense of shared fate.... The education system thus becomes the battleground of contested national and ethnic identities.

—Steve Fenton (1999, 176)

Language is one of the identifying characteristics of an ethnic group, a shared form of communication that symbolizes a group's uniqueness, and its ways of perceiving and categorizing its common environment and experiences (DeVos, 1995; Fenton, 1999). For many of the world's peoples, the spoken language has been the principal vehicle for transmitting the ethnic group's oral history: for preserving its cultural store of folklore, myths, and traditions, and for reinforcing its cultural identity in the face of social change, political upheavals, and forced relocations (DeVos, 1995). According to anthropologists, an individual's primary language is an essential component of his or her personal identity, establishing one's place in a social system and shaping the parameters of one's social boundaries, cultural worldview, and psychological processes (Galindo, 1997; DeVos, 1995).

Throughout history, there are countless examples of groups who, despite colonization, military defeat, and ethnic cleansing, have maintained their language in defiance of brutal oppression, brainwashing, cultural misappropriation, and forced acculturation (Fenton, 1999). Colonial governments have often established their language as the official language of their colonized societies, but indigenous languages have not only been highly resistant to extinction but they have flourished as a symbol of cultural resilience and survival, as in India and Africa. Misguided attempts of latter-day twentieth-century authoritarian governments to impose the language of the ruling classes in educating the subjugated ethnic or tribal groups have provoked fierce political opposition, sometimes escalating into armed conflicts as in the use of Afrikaans in South Africa, Chinese languages in Malaysia, and Albanian in Kosovo (Fenton, 1999).

These intense conflicts over language attest to its deep meaning as a symbol of a group's ethnic and social identity. An assault on a group's language or an attempt to deny its right to use its primary language is perceived as an attack against the group's identity, a threat to its sense of community, and a strategy to undermine its political power.

In order to comprehend and assess the furor over Proposition 227, which challenged the very foundation of bilingual education, it is essential to appreciate the significance of the Spanish language as a symbol of the growing visibility of Latinos in California society. This perspective provides the lens through which advocates and opponents viewed the controversy over the proposal to eliminate virtually all of the bilingual programs in California's public schools.

Proposition 227, known as "English for the Children," called for the termination of the current state-supported and designed bilingual programs to be replaced by an "English immersion" program for the nearly 1,400,000 "limited English proficient" (LEP) children in the public schools. These LEP children would be allowed only one year of a bilingual program before they would have to transfer to a regular classroom with no language assistance. The initiative also had a number of other features that mandated English immersion classes for all LEP students, without taking into account individual differences, linguistic fluency or ability, parental preferences, or teachers' recommendations. The initiative also severely limited parental choice by making it extremely difficult to obtain a waiver for a child to remain in a bilingual program by requiring a minimum class of twenty in a particular school. The initiative further threatened teachers and administrators with legal penalties if they circumvented the law by helping any student in a foreign language. By restricting foreign-language instruction for all students, the initiative also limited the rights of native English speakers to learn a foreign language, apparently to equalize foreign language *illiteracy* for all students. Further, it proposed the appropriation of $15 million a year to teach adults English so they could tutor children in community-based programs.

Finally, the initiative later to be placed on the ballot as Proposition 227 would require a two-thirds vote for amendments to the English-only provision, thus making a repeal or modification highly unlikely. After a contentious campaign of nearly two years, involving charges of political opportunism, anti-immigrant xenophobia, and racism, the California electorate passed Proposition 227 by a margin of 61 to 39 percent at the June 1998 primary election.

## LANGUAGE AND POLITICS: BACKGROUND ISSUES

In an unusual convergence of social, political, and cultural factors, the foundation was laid for the campaign to promote Proposition 227, a ballot initiative that would essentially dismantle or severely damage bilingual education in California public schools. First, the conservatives had discovered that Proposition 187, the proposition targeting undocumented immigrants, had proven to be an effective "wedge" issue, particularly for Republican candidates in the 1994 statewide elections. Anti-immigrant and anti-Mexican sentiments had been stirred up by months of negative slogans and xenophobic rhetoric in the mass media, right wing talk shows, and political rallies. Moreover, the organizations and individuals who spearheaded the campaign for Proposition 187 were still committed, eager to expand their all-American agenda to exclude more and more non-white Americans. Thus, the organizational and logistical support for a related ballot initiative was in place, waiting to be motivated and activated.

Politically, the climate was very receptive to finding a scapegoat to blame for the state's economic slowdown, the sorry state of its educational system, and the deterioration of its infrastructure of overcrowded freeways, unplanned urban growth, and lack of affordable housing. Who better to blame than the recent Asian and Latino immigrants, people whose skin was darker, whose cultures were alien, and whose languages were incomprehensible. Ron Unz, a self-made Silicon Valley millionaire and a candidate for the Republican gubernatorial nomination, seized upon the language issue as a "hot button" wedge issue that might propel him into the governor's office. Unz became the major sponsor of the "English for the Children" ballot initiative and spent over $1 million of his own funds to get it on the state ballot.

In 1996, only two years after the passage of Proposition 187, the anti-immigrant initiative, the conservative forces rallied behind another movement to eliminate or eviscerate bilingual education in the state of California. Although Ron Unz had no background in education, he used his considerable financial resources and political contacts to gather support for completely overhauling the system of bilingual education that had evolved in California since 1967 when Governor Ronald Reagan signed a bill to repeal the state's ninety-five-year-old mandate requiring all instruction in the English language.

With Reagan's support, a bipartisan bill was passed to authorize bilingual instruction in the public schools after convincing data showed that English-only instruction had caused irreparable damage to Asian, Latino, and Native American students (Lyons, 1997). In 1960, half of the state's 1.4 million Hispanic residents had dropped out of school before completing eighth grade and, three decades later, one-third of the Latino students dropped out of high school (Lyons, 1997). Although numerous reasons have been cited for the persistently high Latino dropout rate, there is a consensus among educators and researchers that language and literacy problems account for some of these drop outs, but the majority of Latino dropouts are American born and speak English fluently (August & Hakuta, 1998; Headden, 1997).

In 1974, the U.S. Supreme Court mandated in the landmark *Lau v. Nichols* case, initiated by a Chinese family in San Francisco, that the public schools must take "affirmative steps" to provide equal educational opportunities for children with limited proficiency in English, establishing the rationale for bilingual education programs (Ed Source, 1998).

In 1976, the California State Legislature passed the Chacon-Moscone Bilingual-Bicultural Act, which expired in 1987 and was never replaced by any other legislation to set state standards or guidelines for the teaching of English to nonnative speakers in the public schools. By fiscal year 1997–1998 over $836 million in federal funds to California were targeted for special programs for educationally and economically disadvantaged students, including funds for bilingual education programs (Ed Source, 1998). Finally, in April of 1998, in response to the increasing volume of complaints about the quality of bilingual programs, the lack of qualified teachers, and the lack of resource materials, the California State Board of Education adopted a policy that allowed school districts great flexibility in developing their own bilingual programs as long as they met federal guidelines, with the caveat that the programs must be based on "a sound educational theory and legitimate educational strategy" (Ed Source, 1998, 2).

### The Proponents' Arguments

The supporters of the "English for the Children" initiative charged that bilingual education programs had failed non-English-speaking students in the California public schools, pointing to the high dropout rates and low achievement scores of Latino students. Noting that the high costs of these programs, estimated at $319 million per year for LEP students, did not justify the poor results, the advocates of this initiative proposed that alternative uses of these funds would yield better educational outcomes for these students (One Nation/One California, 1997). Proponents were opposed to bilingual education on the grounds that it reinforces the child's native language and retards the acquisition of English, making it more difficult for these immigrant children to adjust to school and to become acculturated to American society. Supporters of this initiative also criticized the teaching methods and assumptions of bilingual education programs, claiming that these methods did not challenge the children and did not enable them to perform well in subject classes other than English (Porter, 1997). Even more important to many advocates of English as the only language of instruction is its function as a common language unifying the nation. They charged that bilingual education programs segregate immigrant children with the effect of discriminating against them by denying them the right to learn English (U.S. English, 1998).

Proponents attributed the low test scores and the high dropout rates of Latino students as evidence that bilingual programs have failed, claiming that "many thousands of students pass through the schools without learning to read and write in English at even a minimal level" (Fitzgerald, 1998, 47). According to these advocates, a one-year sheltered immersion English-language program was sufficient to prepare these LEP children for regular classrooms, citing research to support their claim that this method was the most effective way to teach nonnative English speakers and the most appropriate strategy to facilitate their assimilation into American society (One Nation/One California, 1998a).

### The Opponents' Arguments

According to James J. Lyons, the executive director of the National Association for Bilingual Education (NABE), the "English for the Children" initiative campaign was based on "deception . . . the denial of fundamental rights . . . (and) debases democracy" (Lyons, 1997, 1). The NABE prepared several position papers criticizing the Unz initiative and marshalling opposition to its provisions.

The initiative proposed a "one-size-fits-all" approach to teaching all LEP students, without accounting for differences in student ability levels, teacher's skills, or school resources. The dilemma of gearing instruction to the native English speakers or to the LEP students would have deleterious effects on one group or the other (Crawford, 1999; Lyons, 1997).

Opponents also claimed that the initiative would deny LEP students equal educational opportunity under the 1964 Civil Rights Act in several ways: students would be mixed by age and grade in English-only immersion programs; language assistance was only available for one year, no matter what the child's needs; the English-only curriculum had no evaluation built in to determine its effectiveness; there were no assessment and accountability mechanisms for monitoring students' progress in English fluency; and there were no professional standards or training mandated for teachers of LEP students (Crawford, 1999).

The Unz initiative deprived parents of their right to choose an appropriate language program for their child by denying parental waivers of the English-only program for nearly all LEP students in grades K through four, with exceptions only for children with special needs or disabilities. Ironically, the initiative also prohibited students under the age of ten to enroll in foreign-language classes, with very limited exceptions, thus creating the unintended effect of eliminating most foreign language instruction from elementary schools at a developmental period which empirical evidence suggests is optimal for the acquisition of a second language (Crawford, 1995; Fitzgerald, 1998).

The Unz initiative was also opposed on the grounds that it would cause irreparable damage to the public schools by lowering achievement, violating the principle of local control, and demoralizing teachers (Lyons, 1997; Crawford, 1999).

## THE DEBATE OVER BILINGUAL EDUCATION

In her provocative article on the ideological dimensions of the bilingual education debate, Galindo (1997) analyzes the competing public discourses that shape the positions supporting or opposing bilingual education. She notes that: "The attitudes, values, and beliefs that come into play in debates over bilingual education are those that relate language to broader social issues, such as nationalism, cultural identity, the aims of education, and more broadly, the roles of languages in society"(167).

Ruiz (1984), in proposing a framework for analyzing language planning and policy issues, proposed that societies have three orientations toward minority languages, that is, as a problem, a right, or a resource. In the United States, he asserts that there are primarily two opposing views of bilingualism and bilingual education: language-as-right versus language-as-problem. Those who view bilingual education in Spanish as a problem have a tendency to link it with social problems associated with the Latino population, thereby devaluing the language, the Hispanic people, and their culture.

In the United States, as of 1998, there were over six million school-aged children whose parents spoke English as a second language. Nearly half (45 percent) of these children were classified as limited English proficient (LEP), making them eligible for some type of special program to improve their proficiency in English. California, one of five states that account for 40 percent of these LEP students, classified nearly 25 percent of its public school students in this category in 1997–1998, with three out of four LEP students from Spanish-speaking households (August & Hakuta, 1998).

Thus, what is a barely visible problem in most of the nation's school districts has mushroomed into an educational crisis in California.

In California there are over 100 languages and dialects spoken in the schools and 40 percent of the students in the Los Angeles County school district have limited English-speaking skills. The state's educational system has been overwhelmed in recent years with the challenges of providing quality education to students in classrooms that are linguistically, culturally, and socioeconomically diverse (Ed Source, 1998). Since the Chacon-Moscone Bilingual-Bicultural Act of 1976 expired in 1987, in their well-intentioned attempts to meet the needs of this increasingly heterogeneous student population, the state's educational bureaucracy has allowed local school districts to adopt a range of strategies to improve the English-language skills of the students from non-English-speaking families.

These educational strategies have included five major approaches: English as a second language (ESL) classes, structured immersion in English (also called sheltered instruction), transitional bilingual education (TBE), maintenance bilingual education, and two-way bilingual programs (August & Hakuta, 1998). Innovative teachers have sometimes combined these approaches or modified an approach for a particular group of students, but in many cases teachers have not been adequately trained in any of these methods and have simply ignored the language problems of these students or failed to address them in any consistent manner. For example, California is one of several states where teachers are allowed to teach in bilingual programs with temporary credentials, because the demand for these teachers is much greater than the supply. However, the controversy surrounding the use of uncredentialed teachers seems to be driven as much by political factors as by educational standards, particularly since the state of California does not have a comprehensive strategy for teaching bilingual education or for evaluating the progress of LEP students.

Inevitably, after years of crowded classrooms, lack of credentialed teachers, and lack of ancillary resources for these LEP students, parents have become frustrated with their progress, educators have become defensive, and politicians have discovered another wedge issue to anger and to divide the voters. This combination of factors laid the groundwork for dissatisfaction over bilingual education, but the controversy over the remedy was fueled by a few traditional educators and conservative politicians who seized on this issue as a natural follow-up to the anti-immigrant sentiment that had been harnessed and exploited in the campaign to adopt Proposition 187, the so-called "Save Our State" ballot initiative in 1994.

These politicians who wanted to exploit the controversy over bilingual education joined forces with a few frustrated teachers and dissatisfied parents to launch a movement for sweeping changes in teaching English to non-English-speaking students (Galindo, 1997; Griswold, 1998). They enlisted educators to provide "expert" testimony, to support their claim that the current bilingual programs were ineffective and failed to produce English language proficiency in these students. While this position generated most of the publicity and created a very negative impression of bilingual education, its advocates also distorted the findings of extensive research on these programs and frequently misrepresented the conclusions of these studies.

Professor Kenji Hakuta,[1] a linguistics expert from Stanford University, who served as an expert witness in a 1998 court hearing on bilingual education programs, submitted a deposition with a stinging rebuke of several self-proclaimed experts who had misrepresented and distorted the results of evaluation studies of various methods of teaching in bilingual programs. Hakuta makes a clear distinction between the research findings and the politicization of these findings and concludes that the "total immersion" method of teaching English to non-English-speaking children is not as effective as other forms of bilingual programs because it takes at least five years before the average child from a non-English-speaking home can master English in terms of language proficiency and academic content. In other words, non-English-speaking students who enter first grade will not become fluent English speakers until around the end of fifth grade if they are enrolled in structured immersion programs, according to Dr. Hakuta's analysis of a large study of the Westminster School District in Orange County, California.

As Hakuta so aptly points out, Proposition 227 targeted the symptoms rather than the underlying causes of the less than optimal results present in the current bilingual program models. These programs were severely handicapped by the lack of a standardized curriculum across the state, well-trained bilingual teachers, integration into the broader curriculum, and adequate evaluation measures. Additionally, Hakuta and other linguistic experts have noted that the debate over the teaching of bilingual students obscures the more important issues of helping them to master academic content and teacher accountability for student achievement (García & Gonzales, 1995; Hakuta, 1984).

In its briefing paper on *English Only*, the American Civil Liberties Union (1998) concluded that "the latest studies show that bilingual education definitely enhances a child's ability to acquire the second language. Some studies even show that the more extensive the native language instruction, the better students perform all around, and that the bilingual method engenders a positive self-image and self-respect by validating the child's native language and culture" (4).

In the final analysis, the debate over bilingual teaching strategies reflects a "smoke and mirrors" approach in which the critics of traditional bilingual programs have manipulated the facts to suit their ideological purposes and the advocates of these programs have defended a system that is badly in need of a major overhaul. In 1998, California was ranked forty-sixth out of the fifty states in terms of per-pupil spending and several other standard-ized criteria, so it is self-evident that the public schools are failing the major-ity of the state's students, whether they are native or nonnative speakers of English. This controversy over bilingual education needs to be viewed in the broader context of setting academic standards, recruiting better-trained teachers, developing more multiculturally diverse curricular materials, and improving schools for all students (Crawford, 1995).

Moreover, the debate about bilingual education is, on the surface, a de-bate about mastering English, but it is, at a much deeper level, a debate about cultural identity and minority power (Galindo, 1997; Tollefson, 1995). For a Mexican American child, his or her language reflects his or her ethnic origins, cultural traditions, and worldview. If the student's family is forced to enroll him or her in an immersion program without adequate bi-lingual transitional support, the message is conveyed to them that their na-tive language (Spanish) is somehow inferior and their culture is not as valued as Anglo-American culture. In turn, the Mexican American child is likely to feel ashamed of his or her language, ambivalent about his or her ethnicity, and anxious about adjusting to the English-speaking classroom, all of which are factors that may foster negative attitudes toward school and inhibit learning.

Asian children account for approximately 14 percent of the LEP stu-dents, speaking a total of eight different languages (Ed Source, 1998). The number of bilingual teachers for Asian students is much lower proportion-ately than the ratio for Spanish-speaking students, thus leading to more complaints and greater dissatisfaction with the schools among Asian par-ents (Slater, 1997).

## IMPACT OF THE "ENGLISH-ONLY" MOVEMENT

Proposition 227 is a stepchild of the "English Only" movement that has been a persistent theme of nativists and anti-immigration activists since the first major waves of immigration in the early twentieth century. By then, most English-speaking Americans had forgotten that the U.S. Constitution had been initially printed in English and German, that merchants in New York had conducted business in Dutch, English, and German in the early nineteenth century, and that many of the early settlers in California, New Mexico, and Texas had been fluent in English and Spanish (ACLU, 1998). Before World War II, linguistic diversity had always been tolerated in America, as successive waves of Europeans, Asians, South Americans, Caribbeans, and Africans came to California searching for a better life, po-litical freedom, and economic mobility.

Advocates of "English Only" frequently compare the contemporary im-migrants from developing countries with the earlier waves of European immigrants, claiming that the latter group adapted to America more easily, mastered English in the schools more quickly, and assimilated to the mainstream society more successfully. Unfortunately, this claim reflects more nostalgia than historical accuracy. In reality, past European immigrants were left to "sink or swim" and the majority dropped out before completing elementary school. In 1911, the U.S. immigration service reported that "77 percent of Italian, 60 percent of Russian, and 51 percent of German immigrant children were one or more grade levels behind in school compared to 28% of American-born white children" (ACLU, 1998, 4). According to recent data, "today's Asian and Latino immigrants are acquiring English proficiency and assimilating as fast as did earlier generations of Italian, Russian, and German immigrants" (ACLU, 1998, 4).

After World War II, a number of factors converged to create a push for conformity and homogeneity in American life. The growth of the Levittown suburbs with standardized low-cost housing, the GI Bill that subsidized higher education and training and moved millions of working-class veterans into the middle-class, the promotion and marketing of the "American way of life" in everything from consumer goods to community celebrations—all of these developments reaffirmed and reinforced the preference for English as the national common language and, by contrast, the rejection of things that were foreign, different, and unfamiliar. After all, wasn't that why American soldiers had defeated the forces of Fascism and Nazism—"to make the world safe for Democracy" and, particularly, to preserve the "American way of life"?

Despite the antipathy expressed toward the newer immigrants from Asia, the Middle East, Africa, and Central America, by 1980 only three states had passed laws to establish English as their official language (Hawaii, Illinois, and Nebraska). The pace picked up in the 1980s and ten more states in the Midwest and the South passed statutes designating English as an official language between 1981 and 1990 (Tatlovich, 1997). By 1998, a total of twenty-three states had proclaimed English as an official state language either by statute or a constitutional amendment, although only twenty state laws were still in effect at the end of 1999 (English First, 1999).

Bucking the trend toward English-language exclusivity, three states (New Mexico, Oregon, and Washington) passed "English Plus" laws promoted multilingualism and language diversity as an official policy (Tatlovich, 1997). However, in 1993, Republican Congressman William Emerson of Missouri introduced H.R. 123, a bill designating English as the official language of the nation, but it failed to win a majority in the U.S. Congress.

It is interesting to note that even in most of those twenty-three states with "English Only" laws, bilingual education programs had not been outlawed or discouraged. The laws seem to be largely symbolic and reflect the efforts of a small cadre of conservative politicians in these states. For example, one study found that the majority of the supporters of these laws were state legislators who were predominantly white, male, and Republican (Tatlovich, 1997). In most cases, these laws were passed by overwhelming majorities in these state legislatures that were predominantly white, male, and Republican (Tatlovich, 1997). And, in most cases, these laws were also passed without much public debate or protest, yet in the Southern states of Alabama, Mississippi, North Carolina, and Tennessee, the majority of African American legislators voted against these laws. As Tatlovich points out, most of the states with "English Only" laws had populations with fewer than 2 percent Latinos, so the motivation for adopting these laws is unclear because there was no apparent threat of English being superseded by Spanish or any other language.

By contrast, in states where "English Only" initiatives were adopted by ballot referenda (Arizona, California, Colorado, and Florida), their populations have a high proportion of Spanish speakers. The high levels of public support for these initiatives suggests that Anglo-American voters feel threatened by the increasing number of immigrants who speak languages other than English.

Although these "English-Only" initiatives were opposed by civil rights organizations, religious groups, and bilingual educators, they apparently struck an empathic chord among voters who want to preserve the status quo of English as the preferred language. In California, 73 percent of voters supported the 1986 "official English" referendum on Proposition 63, which had been strongly endorsed by Republican Governor Pete Wilson. Exit polls showed that Proposition 63 received its major support from whites, conservatives, and less-educated voters. Its strongest opponents were Hispanics, Asians, liberals, and highly educated voters (Tatlovich, 1997).

In 1995 the Republican majority in the U.S. House of Representatives introduced H.R. 123, the "Language of Government Act of 1995"; about 60 percent of the sponsors of this bill represented states with existing official English laws. In the presidential campaign of 1996, the Republican candidate Senator Dole expressed support for official English legislation and commented negatively on its relationship to bilingual education and multiculturalism. His opponent, President Bill Clinton, who had earlier supported an official English bill as governor of Arkansas, did not support this federal initiative.

In the 1990s, more and more Americans were expressing negative attitudes toward the newer immigrants of color in national polls, endorsing nativist statements such as "immigrants are a threat to American culture" and a tax burden for American society. Language had become a synonym for ethnicity and it was no longer viewed as an asset for an American child to be fluent in another language.

Conservative organizations such as U.S. English, Federation for American Immigration Reform (FAIR), and Population Environment Balance lobbied aggressively for the passage of these "English Only" laws and ballot initiatives. Reflecting the culturally conservative views of the far right wing of the Republican Party, these organizations promote a nativistic, ethnocentric, and xenophobic agenda for America. They envision an ideal society that excludes non-European immigrants, exploits people of color, and suppresses liberal ideological notions of freedom, equal opportunity, and equal justice for all citizens. Their rhetoric is racially offensive, their goals are antidemocratic, and their strategies are politically divisive.

Although these rightwing groups form the nucleus of the "English Only" movement, experts have noted that "the movement attracts support from all along the ideological spectrum" (Tatlovich, 1997, 89). These are the Americans who, eschewing their own immigrant past, have come to see themselves as entitled to special status and special privileges for superficial characteristics such as skin color, social class, or Western European heritage. These are the Americans who believe they are superior because they are white, middle-class, and native speakers of English. These are the Americans who have walled themselves off from the poor and people of color in their gated communities, have opposed affirmative action for minorities, and have turned deaf ears against the legitimate aspirations of immigrants for a better life in "the land of the free and the home of the brave."

## FINANCING THE CAMPAIGN: PRO AND CON

Through a combination of shrewd political alliances with "English Only" advocacy groups, an effective media campaign, and appeals to wealthy conservatives, Ron Unz was able to raise millions of dollars to rally support for his "English for the Children" initiative. Unz contributed $752,738 in direct funds, plus an estimated $250,000 in indirect contributions to the campaign. By November 15, 1997 the progressive political consulting firm he had hired had successfully gathered over 700,000 signatures, well over the number needed to qualify the initiative for the June 1998 statewide ballot (Curran, 1998).

Among the major organizations that contributed over $10,000 to support the initiative were the California English Campaign, One Nation/One California, the California Republican Party, the Lincoln Club of Orange County (a longtime supporter of Ronald Reagan), and Fieldstead and Company, a real estate company controlled by the family of Howard Ahmanson (also a close associate of Ronald Reagan) (California Secretary of State's Office, 1998; One Nation/One California, 1998c).

Well-known conservatives from California and around the nation also contributed generously to the pro-initiative campaign, including William A. Dunn, a financier from Florida and an ally of Newt Gingrich; Lawrence E. Golub, an investment banker and Republican fundraiser from New York; and Richard Gilder, a prominent New York Republican (Curran, 1998; California Secretary of State's Office, 1998).

The major organizations contributing funds to oppose the initiative were the California Association for Bilingual Education, the California Teachers Association Issues PAC, the California Federation of Teachers, the American Federation of Labor Congress (AF of L), the California State Council of Service Employers PAC, LA County Federation of Labor, and the David L. Gould Company. Teachers' unions combined their forces to raise about $800,000 to defeat Proposition 227.

Contributions from individual donors to defeat the initiative came from some unexpected sources such as Jerrold Perenchio, the CEO of Univision, the nation's largest Spanish-language television network aimed at a global Latino audience, but most of the individual contributions were under $10,000 and were "bundled" into the advocacy committees (California Secretary of State's Office, 1998).

By the time the Unz initiative was placed on the ballot in November 1997 as Proposition 227, the battle was joined between the conservative "English Only" supporters of the initiative and the liberal opponents of the measure, who faced the daunting challenge of convincing the moderates and the pragmatists that their position was the preferred choice for the state's non-English-speaking students. The polls would play a significant role in creating the perception of a public consensus about support for Proposition 227.

### Polling the Public

In California, a state of great distances and great diversity, polls not only function to reflect the public's opinions, but they also shape political and social attitudes. In lieu of informed intellectual debate and impartial expert analysis, voters in California are very vulnerable to the muckraking traditions of the Hearst newspapers and the histrionic hyperbole of the Hollywood media industry, a combination used very effectively by conservative politicians such as Ronald Reagan, Richard Nixon, and Pete Wilson to launch their political careers (Schrag, 1998a). Polls are the perfect medium that can be manipulated by creative political and media consultants to sway public opinion toward specific public policy outcomes.

The early polls showing high Latino support for Proposition 227 probably reflected the response to simplistic questions such as "Do you want your child to learn English?" (Curran, 1998). In fact, the results of the California Field Poll, conducted in late November 1997, indicated strong support for the initiative across the political spectrum and among all ethnic groups (Field Institute, 1997). This poll showed that two-thirds of Latino voters and 55 percent of Asian voters supported the language of the initiative, but 71 percent of whites and African Americans supported it.

The support of Latino and Asian voters for Proposition 227 fluctuated, depending on the wording of the questions, the size of the sample, and the methodology used, but a majority of Latino voters continued to express approval of the initiative in several polls conducted by the Field Poll, the Los Angeles Times Poll, and the Public Policy Institute of California, from October 1997 through April 1998 (One Nation/One California, 1998b). However, a close reading of those polls indicated that support among Latino and black voters was beginning to decline by spring of 1998 from its highest levels in the fall of 1997, while support among whites had remained fairly stable and support among Asians had actually increased.

As the June election approached, the polls still suggested that the majority of the Latino community supported Proposition 227 and would use their electoral clout to pass it. But the polls probably suffered from the "Dewey" effect (in the 1948 presidential election, New York's Governor Thomas Dewey, the Republican candidate, was predicted to beat incumbent Democratic President Harry Truman on the basis of a sample of middle-class voters with telephones). A cross section of low-income Latinos and those with limited English had not been adequately sampled in any of the polls, so the results reflected the attitudes of upwardly mobile, more acculturated Latinos who tend to be more ambivalent about bilingual education (Field Institute, 1997).

## PROS AND CONS: THE CAMPAIGN FOR PROPOSITION 227

When the California Republican Party endorsed the "English for the Children" initiative at their annual convention in September of 1997, Mike Schroeder, the party chairman, warned the delegates that their support of the Unz initiative would further alienate Latino voters, who had already "abandoned the party in record numbers" after the passage of Propositions 187 and 209 (Trounstine, 1997, 1).

The Democratic Party leaders charged that this initiative was a blatant attempt to exploit the anti-immigrant sentiments of California voters, but they predicted that it would backfire as a wedge issue in the forthcoming elections. But by the time the Unz supporters had collected the 600,000 signatures needed to qualify the initiative for the June 1998 ballot, they had also orchestrated a successful campaign of distortions and misinformation about bilingual education programs in California public schools.

Political leaders in both parties recognized the potential and the pitfalls of using Proposition 227 as another wedge issue to pit native-born citizens against immigrants, particularly since nearly 80 percent of the LEP students enrolled in bilingual programs were Latino, so the issue could easily be labeled as an appeal to racism. In fact, Dan Lungren, the California attorney general and a candidate for the Republican gubernatorial nomination, had declared his opposition to Proposition 227, clearly calculating the damage Proposition 209 had inflicted on Pete Wilson's presidential ambitions and Bob Dole's doomed presidential campaign in 1996. Art Torres, the chairman of the California state Democratic Party, had been very vocal in his opposition to Proposition 227, declaring that "It's another attack on the Latino community. Bilingual education has never been given a chance to work in California" (Trounstine, 1997, 1).

Torres's criticism was frequently repeated during the months preceding the election by teachers, parents, and advocacy groups. Among their pieces of evidence to support this charge were the facts that there was an acute shortage of certified bilingual teachers, the programs lacked adequate resources and curricular materials, and there was too much flexibility and too little monitoring of standards in the programs throughout the state (Martin, 1997; Slater, 1997). Supporters insisted that the programs were in need of resources and redesign, but not deserving of elimination.

Latino political leaders, civil rights organizations, labor unions, and professional associations were united in their opposition to Proposition 227 (Citizens for an Educated America, 1998). Latino advocacy groups opposing the Unz initiative reflected the breadth of the political spectrum from the more conservative League of United Latin American Citizens (LULAC) to the more radical National Council of La Raza. They enlisted the support of hundreds of Latino educators, religious leaders, and entrepreneurs to mobilize their colleagues and constituencies to protest against the initiative. Working in tandem with the influential Spanish-language print and broadcast media, such as the state's leading Spanish newspaper, *La Opinion*, and the television network Univision, the opponents of Proposition 227 waged a multipronged and vigorous attack to defeat it.

By contrast, from the inception of the "English for the Children" initiative, it was apparent that many African Americans and Asian Americans either supported it or were ambivalent about its provisions. In a statewide survey completed in November 1997, only three weeks after the initiative qualified for the June ballot, the Field Poll reported that 71 percent of all African American and 55 percent of all Asian American voters said they would vote for the measure (Field Institute, 1997). From January to the end of May, statewide polls consistently showed a pattern of higher support among African Americans and Asian Americans than among Latinos for Proposition 227. It was also surprising that, as support for the initiative declined among blacks, it increased among Asians. By the end of April, 74 percent of Asian American voters and 66 percent of African American voters expressed support for the initiative; whites and Asians registered nearly equal levels of support for it (One Nation/One California, 1998b).

These surprising results probably reflected the ambivalence of African Americans toward Latinos whom they perceived as taking away their jobs, taking over their neighborhoods, and depressing their wages (Gibbs, 1996; Ratnesar, 1997; Schrag, 1998a). Both African Americans and Asian Americans had also registered complaints about their children being placed in bilingual classes, either against their will (in the case of black parents) or against their children's best interests (in the case of Asian parents) (Martin, 1997; Slater, 1997). Cases had been documented of black and Asian children being marginalized in Spanish-English bilingual classes, unable to progress in either language. Moreover, some black educators and parents in Oakland had complained bitterly that their children weren't eligible for ESL instruction in "black English," and Asian parents had objected that the language needs of their children were neglected due to the lack of trained teachers and materials (Slater, 1997). As the earlier votes on Proposition 187 and 209 had demonstrated, the state's three major ethnic minority groups each had their own agendas that sometimes united and sometimes divided them. Right up until the election on June 2, pundits could not accurately predict whether or not African Americans and Asian Americans would join Latinos in a united effort to reject Proposition 227 or if their schisms and interethnic conflicts would prevail and contribute to the dismantling of bilingual education programs in California.

In the months of debate surrounding the initiative, Unz and his supporters appealed to the same conservative voters whose nativist attitudes and xenophobic fears had resulted in the successful campaigns to adopt Propositions 184, 187, and 209. Their media campaign blatantly appealed to the "English First" and "English Only" advocates who strongly believe that the use of any language other than English undermines the Anglo-American heritage and culture of the nation (Curran, 1998; Fitzgerald, 1998).

The poll results could not measure the impact of other factors that had influenced Latino and Asian voters in the last six months of the campaign, that is, the grass-roots voter education efforts of Latino and Asian civil rights advocacy organizations, who were all opposed to Proposition 227; the anti-Proposition 227 advertising campaign that targeted voters in their own languages; and the opposition of numerous high-profile politicians, community leaders, professional organizations, labor unions, and celebrities, including President Bill Clinton, the state superintendent of public instruction, the California League of Women Voters, the Los Angeles City Council, the San Francisco Board of Supervisors, and the American Civil Liberties Union, as well as hundreds of mayors, school boards, and religious organizations throughout the state (Citizens for an Educated America, 1998).

Linda Chavez, the president of the Center for Equal Opportunity and a well-known conservative Latina activist, concurs with this view, claiming that bilingual programs balkanize American society by assigning non-English students to "special programs that try to maintain native languages rather than teach English" (Center for Equal Opportunity, 1999, 1).

In his media blitz to shape public opinion in favor of the initiative, Ron Unz claimed the high ground in an op-ed column in the *Los Angeles Times* in October 1997: "Only by ending our failed system of bilingual education can we foster the true growth of bilingualism and the unity and prosperity of our multi-ethnic society" (cited in Curran, 1998, 20). But the meta-message underlying these statements of concern about the failure of bilingual students is that English-only instruction is the only route to success and mobility in American society, a message that inherently contradicts the ideal vision of a multicultural society.

The National Association for Bilingual Education emphasized that there was no scientific research to support the initiative's claim that an English immersion program would produce better educational results for immigrant children than bilingual programs. Moreover, such an abrupt termination of the current system would "disrupt the learning environment for all students," as both the students and teachers were unprepared for the change (Crawford, 1999, 1). In addition, opponents predicted that California schools would lose federal funding earmarked for bilingual education, would waste $500 million on an untested program to train tutors for LEP children, and would probably engage in years of costly litigation (Crawford, 1999).

Finally, the Unz initiative alienated many thoughtful people because it was another political time bomb to polarize the state's voters along ethnic lines, to deprive immigrant children of their valuable native languages in a global economy, and to endanger the long-term educational outcomes of these youth by phasing out bilingual programs.

The debate became increasingly more vituperative and divisive as the election neared, with Mauro E. Mujica, the chairman of U.S. English and a Chilean immigrant, lashing out at the Clinton administration's support of Proposition 227 by stating: "Bureaucrats and teachers unions are the only ones who benefit from bilingual education. By siding with them, President Clinton is abandoning the thousands of immigrant families who are begging that bilingual education be reformed" (U.S. English, 1998, 1).

Mujica and his like-minded colleagues must have celebrated when the California electorate passed Proposition 227 by a margin of 61 to 39 percent on June 2, 1998, but the opponents of the initiative could take some comfort from the pollsters' misreading of the Latino voters who voted against Proposition 227 by a majority of 60 percent (Asimov, 1998a).

## AFTERMATH OF PROPOSITION 227

Within days after the passage of Proposition 227, the pundits were analyzing the unexpectedly strong opposition of Latino voters, the public advocacy groups were filing legal challenges against it, and the politicians were trying to placate the angry Latino supporters of bilingual education.

The California public school educators had varied reactions, but over 1,500 teachers involved in bilingual education vowed to defy the new law by continuing to participate in bilingual programs (Asimov, 1998c). They warned that Latino dropout rates would rise as these students fell further behind, failed their courses, and fulfilled the negative expectations of society.

Some bilingual teachers pointed to the results of the newly-adopted statewide Standardized Testing and Reporting (STAR) examinations which were published just one month after Proposition 227 was adopted (Asimov, 1998b). In the San Francisco and San Jose school districts, students in the third and fourth grades who had completed bilingual education programs actually obtained higher everage scores than their native-English speaking classmates. Although bilingual high school students generally scored lower than their native-English speaking peers, their overall scores compared favorably with the national average of 50 points on the STAR examination. Unfortunately, these results were too late to influence the outcome of Proposition 227, but they provided a psychological boost to the proponents of bilingual education.

Parents of children in these programs reflected the opposing camps of the debate, with some claiming victory over their elimination and others complaining about their demise. School board members in communities with large LEP student populations expressed serious concern about the logistics of phasing out the current bilingual programs for an untested plan of a noneducator. Moreover, they expressed doubts about developing a curriculum for a one-year transitional program, about retraining teachers for the new approach, and for negotiating with parents over the appropriate plan for each child. The proponents of Proposition 227 had obviously not carefully anticipated all the bureaucratic challenges and curricular implications of their revolutionary plan.

Editorial responses to Proposition 227 in the state's major newspapers were also varied, mirroring the biases of their editorial boards on the issue of bilingual education. Those papers that had opposed it before the election were consistent in their criticisms after the election, while those favoring its passage were smugly self-congratulatory in their praise ("Latinos," 1998; Sehrag, 1998b; Shultz, 1998).

The successful campaign for Proposition 227 was another signal that the Anglo-American voters harbored anger and resentment against the Asians and Latinos who had immigrated to their state, transformed their neighborhoods, crowded their schools, and creolized their culture. With this decisive victory, the Anglo-American nativist forces had reasserted their supremacy, preserved the hegemony of the English language, and protected their cultural heritage from further foreign incursions.

In July 1998, Judge Charles Legge of the U.S. District Court denied an appeal to block the implementation of Proposition 227. Mujica praised the judge's decision (U.S. English, 1998).

### Implications for Multicultural California

Proposition 227, "English for the Children," was the final piece in the package of 1990s initiatives to limit the rights and opportunities of people of color in California. In only four years, the majority of white voters in California had enthusiastically endorsed Proposition 184 that would have a disproportionate impact on African American and Latino offenders in the criminal justice system; had overwhelmingly supported Proposition 187 that denied immigrants' basic rights to education, employment, and social services; had unabashedly adopted Proposition 209 that outlawed affirmative action in publically financed education, employment, and contracting; and had unapologetically passed Proposition 227 as the logical last brick in the wall to separate whites from people of color, native-born from immigrants, English speakers from non-English speakers.

Premature implementation of Proposition 227 was predicted to create chaos in school districts with a substantial number of LEP students because of the lack of adequate time to prepare for the transition to a one-year program, the lack of trained teachers, the lack of resources to cope with the inevitable problems of children who would still need intensive language assistance, and the lack of communication with parents who had difficulty comprehending the ramifications of the initiative.

Among the parents and children involved in the bilingual programs throughout the state, the passage of Proposition 227 was experienced as a major assault on their cultural identity, denigrating their language and denying their children the right to learn in the familiar language of their family and community. This political repudiation of linguistic diversity in the public schools certainly has the potential danger of increasing the immigrants' feelings of social and cultural marginalization from the dominant society, as well as the possible risk of increasing their anger and alienation from the educational system.

Both of those outcomes could be problematic for future public policy options in California and the nation. On the positive side, the passage of Proposition 227 finally angered Latino voters enough to "awaken the sleeping giant" and energized them to register and vote in significant numbers in the 1998 gubernatorial elections. They voted overwhelmingly for the Democratic ticket, resulting in the election of a moderate governor, a Latino lieutenant governor, and twenty-three Latino state legislators (Salladay, 1998). However, while this loyalty to the Democratic Party may have short-term benefits for Latinos to overturn the discriminatory initiatives against people of color, it may have long-term negative consequences for the vitality and viability of the two-party system in California (Pachon, 1998; Schrag, 1998b). With Latinos projected to be the largest ethnic group in California by 2020, they have the obvious capability of dominating the political system and creating a tyranny of a brown-skinned majority to replace the current white majority.

By the end of the decade, much of the conservative right wing agenda in California had been achieved at the expense of people of color, the poor, and the powerless. This agenda would ratify the continued dominance of the status quo in California politics, educational institutions, government contracting, and civil service. It would result in the incarceration of thousands of minority offenders who had become ensnared in the criminal justice system with one or two previous non-violent drug offenses and inadequate resources to defend themselves. It would deny equal educational and employment opportunities to the majority of the states' public high school graduates. It would strip essential benefits from undocumented immigrants and cause undue harassment to legal immigrants of color. Moreover, it would deny immigrant children their linguistic rights to an equal education, deprive them of their cultural identity, and increase their alienation from the public schools.

If Proposition 227 is not overturned, many Latino students will probably continue to have poor educational outcomes and high dropout rates, a combination that will create negative consequences for the system of higher education in California, and ultimately impact on the labor force. Since Latinos constitute over 30 percent of students in public schools currently, projected to increase sharply over the next twenty years, their educational preparation and eligibility for higher education will affect the supply for the state's colleges and universities for the foreseeable future. If they do not complete college because of inadequate educational backgrounds and language skills, California will not be able to produce enough highly educated workers to fill the state's expanding high tech and information economy (Crawford, 1999; Schrag, 1998a).

In a recent statewide survey ranking all the public schools in California, there was a striking positive correlation between the school's rank and the ethnicity and income of its students (Bazely, 1998). Highest-ranking schools were located in upper-middle-class, predominantly white neighborhoods while lowest-ranking schools were located in neighborhoods with high concentrations of poverty and people of color. These survey results clearly confirm the findings of a study by the Public Policy Institute of California that found "startling inequities between schools serving the state's poor students and those serving the affluent," including major disparities in class size, teaching experience, and availability of advanced placement classes in high school (cited in Asimov, 2000, A12). Although this association between low economic status, school resources, and school achievement has been well documented in the literature, it takes on a special significance in California, the home of the high technology industries, the media and entertainment industries, and the telecommunications industry, all of which require well-educated, highly skilled workers.

Thus, the education of Latino and other immigrant youth is closely linked to the future growth of the California economy and its competitiveness in the global economy. The voters in California may have been extremely shortsighted and parochial in supporting Proposition 227. It is time for California's political leaders, corporate executives, and public opinion makers to educate the electorate about the long-term implications of this and other racially divisive initiatives. In the California of the twenty-first century, immigration status and ethnicity will be increasingly irrelevant, but education and employability will be essential for the survival of the state.

## NOTE

1. Professor Hakuta chaired the Committee on the Education of Limited English Proficient and Political Students of the National Research Council, which issued a 1997 report called "Improving Schooling for Language Minority Children: A Research Agenda."

## REFERENCES

American Civil Liberties Union. (1998). *English only. ACLU Briefing Paper #6.* New York. Available online: http://www.aclu.org/library/pbp.html

Asimov, N. (1998a). Big victory for measure to end bilingual education. *San Francisco Chronicle*, February 25, A12.

Asimov, N. (1998b). Bilingual surprise in state testing. *San Francisco Chronicle*, July 7, A1.

Asimov, N. (1998c). Schools try to resist bilingual law. *San Francisco Chronicle*, June 6, A1.

Asimov, N. (2000). Study finds unequal education in California. *San Francisco Chronicle*, February 25, A12.

August, D. E., & Hakuta, K. (Eds.). (1998). *Educating language minority children.* Washington, DC: National Academy Press.

Bazely, M. (1998). Critics hit Ron Unz measure initiative: Some conservatives rethink "English for the Children" support. *San Jose Mercury News*, May 27, p. 1.

California Secretary of State's Office. (1998). *Financing California's statewide ballot measure: Campaign receipts and expenditures.* Sacramento, CA: Political Reform Division.

Cardinale, K., Carnoy, M., & Stein, S. (1998). *Bilingual education: How do local interests and resources shape pedagogical practices.* Report Series 98.1. Berkeley, CA: PACE.

Center for Equal Opportunity. (1999). *Home Page.* Available online: http://www.ceousa.org/ceousa.html

Citizens for an Educated America. (1998). *Talking points against Proposition 227.* Available online: http://www.noonunz.org/points/points.html

Crawford, J. (1995). *Bilingual education: History, politics, theory and practice.* Los Angeles: Bilingual Education Services.

Crawford, J. (1999). *The Unz initiative: Extreme, irresponsible, and hazardous to California's future.* Washington, DC: National Association for Bilingual Education.

Curran, R. (1998). Xenophobia 101. *San Francisco Bay Guardian*, May 13, pp. 19–20.

DeVos, G. A. (1995). Ethnic pluralism: Conflict and accommodation. In L. Romanucci-Ross & G. A. DeVos (Eds.), *Ethnic identity: Creation, conflict, and accommodation*. 3d ed. (pp. 15–47). Walnut Creek, CA: Alta Mira Press.

Ed Source, Inc. (1998). *Bilingual education in California*. Palo Alto, CA: Ed Source.

English First. (1999). *Official home page of English First*. Available online: http://www.Englishfirst.org/

Fenton, S. (1999). *Ethnicity: Racism, class and culture*. Lanham, MD: Rowman & Littlefield.

Field Institute. (1997). *The Field Poll* (Release #1860). San Francisco: author.

Fitzgerald, M. J. (1998). The making of an initiative. *California Lawyer*, May, pp. 44–87.

Galindo, R. (1997). Language wars: The ideological dimensions of the debates on bilingual education. *Bilingual Research Journal, 21*, 163–201.

García, E., & Gonzales, R. (1995). Issues in systemic reform for culturally and linguistically diverse students. *Teachers College Record, 96(3), 418–431.*

Gibbs, J. T. (1996). *Race and justice: Rodney King and O. J. Simpson in a house divided*. San Francisco: Jossey-Bass.

Griswold, B. (1998). The language lie. *San Francisco Bay Guardian*, May 13, pp. 19–20.

Guthrie, J. (1997). 21st century test for schools: Millions of students with limited English. *San Francisco Examiner*, May 15, p.1.

Hakuta, K. (1984). *The mirror of language: The debate on bilingualism*. New York: Basic Books.

Headden, S. (1997). The Hispanic dropout mystery. In *U.S. News Online*. Available online: http://www.usnews.com/usnews/issue/971020/20.hisp.htm

Latinos trail other groups in education. (1998). *San Francisco Chronicle*, July 22, A3.

Lipsitz, G. (1998). *The possessive investment in whiteness: How white people profit from identity politics*. Philadelphia: Temple University Press.

Lyons, J. J. (1997). Democracy, deception and denial: The 1998 California "English for the Children Initiative." *N.A.B.E. News*, 21(1), 1–4.

Martin, H. G. (1997). Rewarded for failure: California's bilingual education system. *California Political Review*, March/April, 19–20.

National Education Association. (1996). *The debate over English only*. Available online: http://www.nea/org/society/engonly.html

One Nation/One California. (1997). *Proposed fiscal analysis of the "English for the Children Initiative."* Available online: http://www.onenation. org/fiscalan. html

One Nation/One California. (1998a). *Falsehoods and facts about "English for the Children."* Available online: http://www.onenation.org/0298/0298facts. html

One Nation/One California. (1998b). *Polls, polls, polls on Proposition 227*. http://www.onenation.org/0598/051298on2.html

One Nation/One California. (1998c). *Review of Prop. 227 campaign spending*. Available online: http://www.onenation.org/finan.html

Pachon, H. P. (1998). Latino politics in the Golden State: Ready for the 21st century? In M. B. Preston, B. E. Cain, & S. Bass (Eds.), *Racial and ethnic politics in California. Vol. II* (pp. 411–438). Berkeley: Institute of Governmental Studies Press, University of California, Berkeley.

Porter, R. P. (1997). The politics of bilingual education. *Society, 34*, 31–39.

Ratnesar, R. (1997). The next big divide? *Time Magazine*, December 1, p. 52.

Rieff, D. (1991). *Los Angeles: Capital of the third world*. New York: Simon & Schuster.

Romanucci-Ross, L., & DeVos, G. A. (Eds.). (1995). *Ethnic identity: Creation, conflict, and accommodation*, 3d ed. Walnut Creek, CA: Alta Mira Press.

Ruiz, R. (1984). Orientations in language planning. *National Association for Bilingual Education Journal, 8*, 15–34.

Salladay, R. (1998). Changing faces in the state capitol. *San Francisco Examiner*, December 6, C1.

Schrag, P. (1998a). *Paradise lost: California's experience, America's future*. Berkeley: University of California Press.

Schrag, P. (1998b). Wilson: The lame duck adds to his legacy. *The Sacramento Bee*, May 12, B7.

Shultz, J. (1998). Lessons of 227. *San Jose Mercury News*, June 5, 6B.

Slater, D. (1997). Does Oakland have the time to make its bilingual program work? *East Bay Express*, September 26, pp. 3–4.

Streisand, B. (1997). Is it "hasta la vista" for bilingual ed? In *U.S. News Online*. Available online: http://www.usnews.com/usnews/news/english.htm

Tatlovich, R. (1997). Official English as nativist backlash. In J. Perea (Ed.), *Immigrants out! The new nativism and the anti-immigration impulse in the United States* (pp. 78–102). New York: New York University Press.

Tollefson, J. (Ed.). (1995). *Power and inequality in language education*. New York: Cambridge University Press.

Trounstine, P. J. (1997). State GOP back measure to end bilingual classes. *San Jose Mercury News*, September 29, p. 1.

U.S. English. (1998). U.S. English chairman denounces Clinton Administration's opposition to California's English for the Children initiative. Available online: http://www.us-english.org/press/Clinton227.htm

Virtual campaign comes to a close. *San Francisco Chronicle*, June 1, A28.

# CHAPTER 8

## Culture Wars at Home and Abroad: National and International Trends

In California in the 1990s, an electorate that is still predominantly white and Anglo, aware that demographic trends will soon make them the new minority group, passed the initiatives heavily promoted by the ambitious Governor Wilson, denying education and nonemergency health and social service benefits to illegal aliens and ending race-based affirmative action programs in the universities and government agencies.

—David Broder (2000, 219)

California has been the pace setter in the nation's ambivalence toward immigrants and people of color, so it is in the vanguard of a national backlash to their growing visibility and their increasingly assertive demands for equal rights and equal opportunities (Maharidge, 1996; Preston, Cain, & Bass, 1998; Schrag, 1998). The American public, which has been extraordinarily receptive to the conservative political ideologies of California-bred politicians from Ronald Reagan in the 1970s to Pete Wilson in the 1990s, has followed California's lead in turning back the tide of minority progress.

In this chapter, we first discuss the impact of the initiative process itself on creating public policies through direct democracy; next, we examine the influence of California's conservative initiatives in criminal justice, immigrants' rights, affirmative action, and bilingual education on trends in other states dealing with similar issues. Third, we compare these national trends to similar developments in other multiethnic Western industrialized countries such as Canada and Great Britain, countries that are most similar to the United States in their Anglo-Saxon heritage, language, and culture.

## THE INITIATIVE CAMPAIGNS: DIRECT DEMOCRACY OR MAJORITY TYRANNY?

In his recent critical book about the initiative process, David Broder (2000), political columnist for the *Washington Post*, closely followed several initiative campaigns in California and Oregon to assess their impact on our constitutional system of representative democracy. He describes the initiative campaigns as a "lucrative industry," providing employment for scores of signature-gathering firms, political consultants, lawyers, campaign managers, and advertising agencies in California and the twenty-three other states where initiatives are legal. According to Broder, the initiative process, introduced to California by Governor Hiram Johnson's Progressive Party in 1911, has expanded exponentially until it has seriously challenged and nearly usurped the role of state legislatures to create legislation and public policy. Campaign consultants estimate that it costs about $1 million just to qualify an initiative for the ballot, then hundreds of thousands more for a media and direct-mail campaign to rally voter support for it. Broder discusses a number of serious flaws in the initiative process, for example, wealthy individuals or organizations can promote their specific agendas through direct access to the ballot—there are no checks and balances to assure that the ballot measure would be good public policy; the supporters and opponents of an initiative often mislead the voters with half-truths and misinformation; and the majority can pass initiatives that infringe on the rights of minorities, as in the cases of Propositions 187, 209, and 227, or adversely impact their life chances, as does Proposition 184.

After weighing both the advantages and disadvantages of ballot initiatives, Broder (2000) concludes that "wealthy individuals and special interests . . . have learned all too well how to subvert the process to their own purposes" and it is a "system that promises laws without government" (243).

Broder's critique is clearly applicable to the launching, financing, and campaign strategizing for the four propositions discussed in this book. By following the money trail, we have documented not only the large sums of money contributed by a few conservative organizations and wealthy donors for each of these propositions, but we have also shown some of the links between these donors and organizations.

Many of the out-of-state contributors to these four initiatives have ties to ultraconservative advocacy organizations and think tanks in New York and Washington, DC. Several contributors have successful careers in in-

vestment banking, financial institutions, and real estate. One can legiti-
mately question their interest in supporting these issues, which are
patently intended to slow the political progress of minorities, to limit their
access to professional and executive jobs, to deprive them of equal opportunities and access to capital, and to limit their economic and social mobility
in American society. Are they protecting their own empires of wealth and
power or insuring the continued privilege of their class and their descendants for decades to come?

Proposition 184, "Three Strikes and You're Out," is the only one of these
initiatives that was motivated by a middle-class victim's father's personal
crusade against crime rather than by a calculated political strategy. However, once the media stoked public outrage over a similar tragedy in the
kidnap murder of Polly Klaas, the Republican Party quickly recognized its
potential to galvanize voters as a wedge issue and soon exploited its
fund-raising possibilities. Supporters of Proposition 184 spent fully
twenty-eight times more than its opponents ($1,295,791 versus $45,419), so
there was actually no contest in terms of financial resources to assure the
passage of the initiative. Two major contributors to the Proposition 184
campaign, the California Republican Party ($439,859 in direct support) and
the Container Supply Company ($10,000) also contributed generously to
the campaign to support Proposition 187, the anti-immigration initiative,
in the same election cycle.

Propositions 187 and 209 were both identified as "wedge" issues by
Governor Pete Wilson, hoping to enhance his national reputation in order
to position himself as a viable candidate for the Republican presidential
nomination in 1996. By openly targeting immigrants and minorities of
color, Wilson expanded his support beyond his natural constituency of Republican moderates to attract support from conservatives and right wing
organizations that generously financed Proposition 187 with contributions
of $1,067,529 and Proposition 209 with contributions of $5,239,287, more
than twice as much raised by the opponents of the anti-affirmative action
initiative. Ironically, the opponents of Proposition 187 actually spent more
than three times the amount spent by its supporters, but the anti-immigrant
sentiment was such a hot-button issue that voters effectively tuned out the
counterarguments. Proposition 187 is one of the rare examples of an initiative that passed in spite of being outspent by the opposition.

In 1996 the Republican Party and several Republican candidates made
large contributions (over $10,000) to the campaign for Proposition 209.
Richard Scaife, one of the heirs to the Mellon fortune, donated $100,000; he
was also involved with the Laurel Foundation and the Pioneer fund, two
organizations that supported controversial research on race intelligence
and eugenics (Stefancic, 1997). Ron Unz, a Silicon Valley entrepreneur who
contributed $23,000 to the campaign for passage of Proposition 209, would

later be the major sponsor of Proposition 227 mandating the virtual elimination of bilingual education programs.

Other major contributors to the campaign for Proposition 209 were Thomas L. Rhodes, the president of the conservative *National Review Magazine* that serves as an outlet for right wing ideology and policy agendas, and Rupert Murdoch, wealthy publisher of a network of conservative newspapers and magazines. Republican banker Howard Ahmanson donated $50,000 from Home Savings of America and $300,000 from Fieldstead & Company, two companies he founded. Richard and Virginia Gilder, New York investors and Republican Party donors, contributed $125,000 to the initiative.

Proposition 227, the anti-bilingual education initiative, was the only one of these measures financed primarily by one person, millionaire Ron Unz. Searching for an issue to enhance his political viability and conservative credibility, Unz latched on to the controversial topic of bilingual education in a state in which Latino students were failing and dropping out in hordes. Supporters of Proposition 227 spent $1,198,317, but Unz contributed $752,738 of that amount. Like Proposition 187, opponents of this "English for the Children" measure outspent the supporters more than 4 to 1 ($4,855,586), yet could not overcome the emotional salience of the language issue for the majority of non-Hispanic voters.

In addition to Ron Unz, the Republican Party was a major contributor to the Proposition 227 campaign, as was the California English campaign, another organization supported by the same persons who founded U.S. English and the Federation for American Immigration Reform (FAIR), both anti-immigration organizations. New York investors Richard and Virginia Gilder, who contributed generously to the Proposition 209 campaign, also together contributed $100,000 to Proposition 227. Howard Ahmanson was another contributor to both propositions through his Fieldstead & Company, which donated $130,000 to the "English for the Children" initiative.

It does not require an advanced degree in economics or political science to conclude that there was a small group of wealthy donors and advocacy groups who had a vested interest in supporting all four of these propositions. Many of these individuals and groups have past ties with organizations that have advocated right wing, reactionary, and racist policies such as restricting immigration from non-white countries, supporting research on eugenics and population control, opposing affirmative action and busing for school integration, and opposing bilingualism and bilingual education programs (Diamond, 1999; Stefancic, 1997). Although their actions may seem uncoordinated in terms of each proposition, if considered collectively, a credible case can be made that these individuals and groups used their considerable wealth and resources to fund a series of initiatives that would deprive people of color of their civil rights, disempower them politically, deny them equal opportunities, and strip them of their linguistic and cultural identities, all to preserve the economic and political power of the dominant majority group in the United States.

## PART I: NATIONAL TRENDS

Since the 1980s, American society has witnessed a series of demographic, economic, and political changes that have contributed to social and cultural dislocations, widened the disparities between socioeconomic groups, and heightened racial, ethnic, and class tensions. These changes include escalating income inequality between rich and poor, with the middle class losing ground; accelerated decay and dysfunction in the inner cities; continuing white flight away from the urban centers; and continuing decline of public schools, public transportation, and urban infrastructure (Hacker, 1992; Jaynes & Williams, 1989; Wilson, 1987).

The rapid transformation of the economy from a manufacturing-industrial-agricultural base to a high technology-information processing-service base has created profound economic anxieties for many families whose breadwinners do not have the education or skills to compete for jobs in the new economy (Maharidge, 1996; Schrag, 1998). These dislocated or disillusioned workers were ripe targets for the political demagogues and right wing organizations who blame "unqualified" minorities for gaining good jobs through affirmative action and "undocumented" immigrants for depressing wage rates and accepting nonunion jobs.

In order to appease angry voters, both major political parties launched an assault on entitlement programs, particularly the Aid to Families with Dependent Children (AFDC), to demonstrate their antipathy to "welfare cheats" and undeserving welfare recipients. In 1995, a Democratic administration rallied a bipartisan Congress to enact a draconian welfare reform bill with strict eligibility requirements and unrealistic time limits for benefits (Schrag, 1998).

The scapegoating of ethnic minorities and immigrants of color also fostered a resurgence of overt racism in many institutions where some progress had been made in the 1960s and 1970s such as education, housing, public accommodations, and transportation (Jaynes & Williams, 1989). Although this book focuses primarily on the four areas enumerated earlier, it is important to note the persistent and pervasive discrimination against people of color in every aspect of American life. For example, several studies have documented the hypersegregation of housing areas in American cities, the resegregation of public schools that are now more racially separate in the North than in the South, the discrimination in bank lending and housing sales, the discrimination against African Americans in some restaurant chains and hotels, the continuing disparities in health care, the unequal resources and facilities in inner-city schools, and the unequal access to public transportation for inner-city residents (Hacker, 1992; Jaynes & Williams, 1989; National Urban League, 1999; Orfield & Ashkinaze, 1991).

In addition to the daily hassles confronting people of color, especially in low-income urban communities, one of their major challenges is coping with police harassment and misconduct. In just the past decade alone, there have been a number of highly publicized cases of police misconduct or brutality in Los Angeles, Miami, New York City, Detroit, and Buffalo, but these cases have only been the tip of the iceberg of widespread abuses against ethnic minorities and immigrants, as documented in comprehensive reports about police misconduct in Los Angeles (Christopher Commission, 1991), New York (Mollen Commission, 1994), and other American cities (Amnesty International, 1998; Burris, 1999; Skolnick & Fyfe, 1993).

Relations between the police and ethnic minority communities have worsened in recent years, particularly in urban areas with large populations of African Americans and Latinos. The prevalent practice of racial profiling, often referred to as "driving while black or brown" (DWB) has created such adversarial relationships between police officers and minority drivers that, by the end of 1999, lawsuits had been filed against local police or state highway patrol officials in at least fifteen states, including California, Colorado, Connecticut, Florida, Illinois, Indiana, Maryland, New Jersey, North Carolina, Pennsylvania, Ohio, Oklahoma, Rhode Island, Texas, and Virginia (Davis, 1999). As the American Civil Liberties Union (1999) report on racial profiling concludes, "Widespread DWB practices deeply undermine the legitimacy—and therefore, the effectiveness—of the criminal justice system. Pretextual traffic stops fuel the belief that police are not only unfair and biased, but untruthful as well" (37).

Finally, the last two decades of the twentieth century witnessed a proliferation of white supremacist hate groups in the United States, spreading their propaganda nationally through the electronic advances of e-mail and the Internet. The Southern Poverty Law Center (2000) estimates that there were at least 457 organized hate groups in the United States by the end of 1999, including numerous right wing organizations, "skin-heads," the Ku Klux Klan, Neo-Nazi, and Christian Identity groups. These individual and group purveyors of racist and anti-immigrant rhetoric discovered a particularly receptive audience in younger, working-class, white males who saw themselves as victims of technological progress and affirmative action. According to Martin Lee, an expert on hate groups, "As economic globalism has accelerated, producing definite losers and winners, so too has the momentum of neofascist and right-wing extremist organizations" (Southern Poverty Law Center, 2000, i).

In 1990 and 1996 the United States Congress passed two hate-crime bills requiring law enforcement agencies to report crimes motivated by racial, ethnic, sexual orientation, or religious bias. In 1997 over 11,200 law enforcement agencies reported hate crime data to the FBI, revealing that race is the most frequent motivation for hate crimes and represents about 60 percent of all offenses. Moreover, African Americans are more likely to be the victims of violent crime than any other racial groups (U.S. Department of Justice, 1997). Hate crimes committed in California represented 23 percent of all such crimes nationwide (Congressional Information Service, 1997).

Several recent studies have documented an alarming increase in hate crimes targeting Asian Americans in California in 1996 and 1997. Although hate crimes against Asians decreased nationally between 1996 and 1997, by ten percent, they increased by twenty percent in California, particularly in the San Francisco Bay Area (Pimentel, 1998). As Victor Hwang, executive director of the Asian Law Caucus, noted, "The statistics reflect increasing anti-immigrant sentiment in politics and in communities undergoing drastic demographic shifts" (Rojas, 1997, A2).

Hate speech and hate crimes serve the same function in American society as the canary in the mine shaft; that is, they symbolize the invisible toxins in the social environment that signal a warning about the severe danger of exposure to white supremacist ideology. Unfortunately, these inflammatory ideas have influenced the political agenda of right wing conservatives, who have translated them into less threatening rhetoric and used this rhetoric of "law and order," "undocumented aliens," "reverse discrimination,"and "English for Americans" to mobilize the electorate into an effective reactionary force in order to roll back the clock to an era of unchallenged white power and privilege.

In reviewing the influence of California's four initiatives on the policies of other states in the areas of crime and punishment, immigrants' rights, affirmative action, and bilingual education, one can speculate about the role of such code words to persuade voters that these conservative policies would keep minorities in their place and maintain the status quo.

### "Three Strikes" Laws and the Criminal Justice System

Using the subliminal slogan of "law and order" to rally voters concerned about crime in support of Proposition 184, the "Three Strikes" initiative easily achieved passage in California in 1994. This law disproportionately impacted African Americans and Latinos and was implemented under the guise that it would reduce crime rates, creating safer communities by severely punishing offenders, minimizing recidivism, and deterring criminal activity.

However, previous increases in police power had contributed to the tremendous explosion in the prison population nationally, fueled largely by convictions of nonviolent drug offenders. By the beginning of 2000, the United States prison population was nearly two million inmates, most of them nonviolent (Irwin, Schiraldi, & Ziedenberg, 1999). This is larger than the combined prison population of the European Union, whose countries have nearly 100 million more citizens than the total United States population.

By 1999, at least twenty-two other states had followed California's lead in adopting some version of the "Three Strikes" law (Schiraldi & Ambrosio, 1997). It is interesting to note that nearly all of these states have a high proportion of minorities, and a disproportionate number of those minorities are incarcerated (e.g., Arkansas, Georgia, Louisiana, and South Carolina).

As a consequence of implementing these laws in jurisdictions where they are strictly enforced, the conviction rates of minority offenders have soared, resulting in the incarceration of thousands of young African American, Latino, and American Indian males, many of whom were convicted for a nonviolent drug offense as a "third strike" (Schiraldi & Ambrosio, 1997). In combination with more severe sentences for drug offenses, the "Three Strikes" laws have created a crisis in the penal system of overly harsh punishment for youthful offenders, overcrowded prison facilities, and over-burdened state budgets that cannot absorb the costs of the expanding long-term prison population without sacrificing other essential state-funded services (Gangi, Schiraldi, & Ziedenberg, 1998).

In June 2000, the Human Rights Watch issued a report that confirmed the continuing national trend of incarcerating African American males and females for drug offenses at nearly twice the rate of whites (Holmes, 2000). Although surveys report that there are five times more whites who use drugs than blacks, African Americans are still more likely to be targeted, arrested, convicted, and incarcerated for drug offenses (also see Males and Macallair, 2000).

The recent popularity of "Three Strikes" laws also reflects the public's perception that violent crime is on the rise in the United States, therefore, extreme measures are necessary to control it. According to FBI statistics, the overall national crime rate and the rate of violent crime actually declined in the 1990s, but the public perception is distorted due to the media's sensationalism of incidents of violent crime and mayhem (U.S. Department of Justice, 1997). Media crime stories disproportionately focus on minority suspects, further fueling the fear and paranoia of them.

Despite the fact that the rate of violent crime has been declining throughout the nation since 1995, politicians and conservative pundits continue to agitate for harsh penalties for juvenile delinquents, long sentences for non-violent drug offenders, and capital punishment for an extensive list of felony offenses. They do not seem to make the obvious connection between a prosperious economy, low unemployment, and falling crime rates, a connection that suggests the need for a more enlightened, more equitable, and more humane criminal justice system with an emphasis on prevention and rehabilitation.

During the 1980s, states increased spending on corrections by 95 percent, while reducing spending on education by 6 percent (Schiraldi &

Ambrosio, 1997). For example, from 1989 to 1999, New York reported a $615 million decrease in funding for its public colleges and universities and a corresponding $761.3 million increase in funding for its corrections facilities (Gangi, Schiraldi, & Ziedenberg, 1998).

The recent rise of private prisons and the increasing use of prison labor by American corporations have created considerable controversy and understandable alarm among African Americans and Latinos, who are disproportionately represented in the nation's correctional institutions (Davidson, 1997; Schlosser, 1998). Since 1984 private prisons have proliferated from 2 to 163 in 26 states by 1999, frequently located in economically depressed areas whose officials welcome inmates in exchange for jobs (Belluck, 1999). Unregulated by state and federal laws and unmonitored for basic standards and programs, these prisons have been harshly criticized for the high rates of violence, severe disciplinary problems, frequent human rights' abuses, and too many escapes.

The growing collaboration between the correctional system and large corporations, fueled by the spread of "three-strikes" laws, represents an unwelcome alliance that actually creates a demand for cheap prison labor that will reap enormous profits for participating industries (Davidson, 1997; Schlosser, 1998). With the aid of Wall Street investment banks and major insurance companies underwriting the bonds for prison construction and the high technology companies contributing their specialized security devices, the $35 billion prison-industrial economy has become one of the most profitable and most powerful forces in American society. As state legislatures enact more legislation and prioritize financing prison construction over schools, low-income housing, and urban redevelopment programs, politicians reinforce the vicious cycle of school drop-outs, unemployment, drugs, crime, and incarceration for thousands of young minority males (Davidson, 1997; Gibbs, 1988; Schlosser, 1998).

Critics of these "Three Strikes" laws have pointed out a number of negative consequences from the laws, which are fundamentally flawed in their intention, their interpretation, and their implementation (Davis, Estes, & Schiraldi, 1996). First, they are inflexible and many versions do not differentiate between violent and nonviolent offenses in counting the three strikes. Second, they discriminate against poor and uneducated defendants who are not usually able to obtain first-class legal counsel who can minimize the consequences of an arrest through plea bargaining, alternative sentencing, probation, and so on. Third, they strain the resources of the legal system and perpetuate conditions that are inhumane and punitive rather than humane and rehabilitative for incarcerated prisoners. Fourth, these laws will eventually require large tax increases or bankrupt state budgets in order to support more prison construction, more corrections staff, higher health costs for aging prisoners, and persistent rates of recidivism for prisoners who do not receive adequate counseling, education or job training, or drug treatment while incarcerated.

Finally, their major negative impact will be on young African American males, who are more likely than white youth to be unemployed, more likely to be exposed to criminal activity, more vulnerable to police arrest and misconduct, and more likely to receive differential treatment in the courts, with longer sentences imposed for similar offenses, and fewer options for treatment and training programs than youth of other racial or ethnic backgrounds (Gibbs, 1988; Mauer, 1995; Poe-Yamagata & Jones, 2000).

## IMMIGRANTS AND THE MYTH OF THE MELTING POT

Critiques of post–World War II immigration to the United States have frequently been couched in terms of a threat to America's "common culture and shared values," yet the rhetoric of these critics reveals a thinly disguised appeal to ethnocentrism, cultural hegemony, and racism (Brimelow, 1995; Borjas, 1999; Schlesinger, 1992). These critics generally subscribe to the outdated theory of American society as a "melting pot" in which ethnic groups voluntarily engaged in a process of rapid acculturation, culminating in gradual assimilation to Anglo-American mainstream society over a period of one or two generations. The myth of the melting pot has really never applied to immigrants of color, who rarely ever become completely assimilated into the mainstream (Fenton, 1999; Kymlicka, 1995).

California's passage of Proposition 187, the anti-immigrant initiative, resonated with voters in other states with large immigrant populations that have similarly altered the state's demographic profile, its cultural homogeneity, its labor force, and its social customs—changes many native-born citizens viewed as threatening the stability of the social fabric (Maharidge, 1996; Schrag, 1998).

Moreover, the anti-immigration literature is replete with negative stereotypes about immigrants of color from Asia, Africa, the Caribbean, Mexico, and South America. These immigrants are often depicted as culturally and intellectually inferior, socially deviant, and unassimilable in a predominantly white society (Borjas, 1990; Brimelow,1995). Some conservatives assume that admission of these non-European groups will disrupt the society through unrestrained birth rates, lowered educational standards, increased welfare dependency, and increased crime. Therefore, they must be excluded and denied full membership in this society. As Schlesinger (1992) asserts in his polemic against multiculturalism, "Europe was the birthplace of the United States of America, . . . European ideas and culture formed the republic, . . . the United States is an extension of European civilization and . . . nearly 80% of Americans are of European descent" (912).

States with a high influx of undocumented immigrants such as Texas, Arizona, New Mexico, and Florida have been particularly concerned about protecting their borders from an unwanted invasion of people of color (Jonas & Thomas, 1999; Perea, 1997). Legislatures in these states have proposed various measures to discourage immigration from their brown-skinned neighboring countries, ranging from barbed-wire fences and border patrols in Texas to armed customs boats along the Florida coast.

The linkage of federal welfare reform to immigration status has profound implications for the de facto implementation of immigration policy in the United States. As an Urban Institute study has cautioned, "The devolution of immigrant policy to the states is triggering a further 'pass through' devolution to counties and other local units of government. This pass through devolution will drive immigration politics to lower levels of government, generating divergent immigrant policies not just across states but across counties" (Fix & Tumlin, 1997, 5). Such policies will have a particularly deleterious impact on poor immigrants in financially overburdened urban counties such as Los Angeles.

Policies to deny immigrants basic health and social services, to restrict their children's access to public education, or to detain them in relocation camps have not proven to be humane, morally or legally defensible, or good public policy. U.S. immigration policy makes an arbitrary distinction by classifying Cubans as refugees, who can be granted political asylum, and Haitians as economic immigrants, who are immediately deported or detained when they arrive illegally on the Florida coast (Welch, 1999). Human rights advocates suggest that the policy favors Cubans because they are more easily assimilable than Haitians, who are darker, poorer, and less skilled. Just before Christmas in December 1999, a group of Haitian refugees in a detainment camp staged a nonviolent protest, seizing several guards as hostages, and used the incident to publicize their plight to the world.

Recurring waves of anti-immigrant hostility are strongest throughout the nation when the economy is weak, the unemployment rate is high, and the society is undergoing social upheaval (Gutierrez, 1996; Perea, 1997). When the economy is strong and jobs are plentiful, employers are eager to hire immigrants with little concern over the legitimacy of their green cards, but when the economy is weak, immigrants quickly become scapegoats.

### Affirmative Action or Reverse Racism?

California's passage of Proposition 209, to eliminate affirmative action in education, employment, and public contracting, served as a rallying cry for conservatives in numerous other states to roll back progress in equal opportunities for all citizens. The state of Washington soon followed in 1998 with Proposition 200, virtually a clone of Proposition 209 (Broder, 2000). Within a span of four years, two other states, Texas and Florida, proposed ballot initiatives or legislation to repeal affirmative action in any state-supported institutions (Selingo, 2000). Many whites strongly believed that minority groups had achieved parity and were no longer in need of government-sponsored preferential treatment. Many whites were also convinced that affirmative action was a form of "reverse racism" that was unfair to the majority. Despite the reams of statistics documenting major disparities between whites and minorities (except for some groups of Asians), the voters were swayed more by demagogic appeals to their emotions than by rational appeals to their intellect.

The states of Florida and Texas, both governed by Republican governors (the Bush brothers), eliminated affirmative action programs through legislation. In 1996 the Texas legislature passed a bill calling for the guaranteed admission of all students in the top 10 percent of their high school graduating classes to one of the state universities or colleges. This bill was a response to the decision in the 1996 *Hopwood v. Texas* case, in which the U.S. Circuit Court of Appeals in New Orleans outlawed affirmative action in University of Texas Law School admissions policy (Chavez, 1998). In Florida, Governor Jeb Bush preempted the efforts of Ward Connerly to launch a ballot initiative in this state by urging the state cabinet to approve the "One Florida" Initiative that eliminates affirmative action in university admissions and state contracting, but guarantees admission to the top 20 percent of high school graduates to one of the state colleges or universities (Selingo, 2000). Both of these states provided alternative models to the end of race-based preferences by enlarging the total pool of high school graduates eligible for higher education. Although the intention of these programs was to increase diversity, analysts cautioned that neither plan would achieve the same numerical results for the admission of underrepresented minority students, but would expand the pool of low-income students (Lynch, 1999; Price, 2000).

With an economy that has an insatiable need for highly skilled workers and a society that will be at least half people of color by 2050, a retreat from affirmative action will have extremely detrimental consequences on the labor force, will threaten the productivity and competitiveness of the American economy, and will cause further disparities in education and income between whites and people of color. That is a recipe for disaster and could set up an inevitable confrontation between the "haves" and "have nots," making the riots of the 1960s seem like a schoolyard fracas.

### Bilingualism or English Only?

By the end of 1998, twenty-three states had passed some form of "English Only" or "official English" laws, declaring English as the official state language and, in some cases, prohibiting state and local governments from offering bilingual services to residents with limited English proficiency (NEA, 1996). Despite these laws, the federal courts so far have upheld laws requiring officials to provide bilingual ballots in states with significant populations of non-English-speaking voters. Even in some of the states with "English Only" laws, local school districts can offer bilingual services to students, which suggests that there is a disconnection between the ideologies of the states' politicians and the pragmatism of the states' educators. The "English Only" approach has failed to educate thousands of LEP children, not only in California, but also in Arizona, Florida, New Mexico, New York, Texas, and Colorado (Lyons, 1997).

In contrast to California's rejection of bilingual education programs, several other states have developed innovative approaches to address the needs of LEP students. States and local school districts have embraced models of bilingual education from total immersion in English to dual-language approaches that expose students to equal amounts of English and a second language, such as Spanish, Cantonese, Arabic, or Russian (NEA, 1996).

In view of the proliferation of foreign languages currently spoken in urban schools throughout the United States, school districts are financially unable to provide bilingual classes in every language, so they make pragmatic choices about services that will reach the largest numbers of children. For example, over 185 languages or dialects are spoken in New York City schools, and 187 languages are spoken in Fairfax County, Virginia, schools.

The National Education Association (1996) advocates the concept of "English Plus" that supports the preservation of native languages and promotes multilingualism as an economic and diplomatic resource in American society.

In contrast to conservatives' attitudes about bilingual education in America's public schools, most major universities and liberal arts colleges now require proficiency in at least one foreign language and many of them offer students study-abroad programs for the explicit goal of becoming bilingual and learning about another culture. Here again there is a schism between concern over preparing the society's educated elite for future leadership and lack of concern over preparing society's immigrants for successful assimilation into the mainstream.

## PART II: INTERNATIONAL TRENDS

The last half of the twentieth century will be remembered by historians for the birth of the independence movements of colonized countries, subjugated societies, and oppressed minorities around the world. From India and Malaysia in Asia to Ghana and Botswana in Africa, people of color in the so-called "Third World" have thrown off the yoke of colonial domination, declared independence, and established political and cultural autonomy for themselves.

One of the major consequences of the series of civil wars, revolutions, and political confrontations following World War II has been the dispersal of millions of immigrants and refugees around the globe, particularly those seeking new countries where they would not be oppressed by their former enemies or dominated by other ethnic groups. The movement of these displaced populations from developing countries has radically altered the demographic and cultural profile of Western Europe, North America, and Australia, as these nations have become increasingly heterogeneous in race, ethnicity, religion, and culture.

Despite the well-intentioned efforts of countries such as England and Canada to develop policies and programs to ease the adaptation and assimilation of these ethnic minority strangers in their midst, many countries have experienced escalating ethnic, racial, and religious conflicts between their native-born citizens and recent immigrants. As in the United States, those ethnic groups that are most dissimilar from Western European societies in ethnoracial characteristics or religious beliefs have been the slowest to acculturate and the least likely to assimilate, for example, Arabs in France, Pakistanis in England, Turks in Germany, Afro-Caribbeans in Canada (Fenton, 1999; Kymlicka, 1995).

When Joerg Haider, the leader of the far-right Freedom Party in Austria, won 27 percent of the vote in the October 1999 national elections, his opponents accused him of preying on the fears of Austrians about foreigners and exploiting the immigration issue with echoes of Nazi propaganda techniques (Eddy, 1999).

Since 1995 there have been a number of highly publicized incidents of violence against immigrants in France, Italy, Spain, and Germany. Immigrants in all of these countries experience widespread harassment, prejudice, and discrimination in housing, employment, schools, and public accommodations. While these countries may need immigrant labor, their citizens target immigrants as scapegoats for high unemployment, low wages and social problems (Brown, 2000).

Ethnic immigrant and refugee populations in Canada and other Western European countries generally have been subject to discrimination in schools, jobs, housing, and health care (Reitz & Breton, 1994; Small, 1994). With few exceptions, there are wide disparities in educational attainment, occupational status, and annual household income between native-born citizens and first-generation immigrants in these countries. By the second generation, these disparities have narrowed but have not been eliminated except in a few instances.

Low-income immigrants of color have found themselves confined to certain residential areas that have quickly developed into urban or suburban ghettos, with all the social problems accompanying them. Access to health care has been constrained by the lack of adequate hospitals and clinics in these areas, their accessibility to transportation, eligibility criteria, and linguistic and cultural barriers in the delivery of services. Dramatic examples of such barriers to adequate housing and health care are evident among the Arab immigrants in France, the Turkish "guest workers" in Germany, and the Bangladeshis in Great Britain (Kymlicka, 1995; Modood, 1998).

Moreover, social unrest has been tied to economic instability in these countries as interethnic conflict has reflected the cycles of high unemployment, high inflation, and financial uncertainty (Kymlicka, 1995). Immigrants, refugees, and "guest workers" have served as easy scapegoats for the vagaries of the global economy with its insatiable need for cheap labor, low interest rates, new capital, and constant innovation.

### Ethnicity, Crime, and Punishment

The correlation between race, ethnicity, and crime is a pattern found in nearly all Western industrialized societies. In his recent book on *Ethnicity, Crime and Immigration*, Michael Tonry (1997) describes the phenomenon and discusses its manifestations in nine countries in Europe, North America, and Australia. In all of these countries, non-white youth, immigrants, and aboriginal peoples have higher rates of arrests for crimes, higher rates of prosecution, and higher rates of incarceration than native-born whites.

Minority youth, particularly males in the fifteen to twenty-four age group, have also been subjected to discriminatory treatment by the police and differential sentencing in the juvenile and adult criminal justice systems in many countries. Youth of color appear to be targeted by the police in a number of ways that ultimately result in higher rates of criminalization, conviction, and incarceration than those reported for native-born white youth (Reitz & Breton, 1994; Small, 1994; Solomos, 1988; Tonry, 1997). Official reports of police misconduct against people of color occur with alarming frequency, yet lack of police accountability and resistance to changing policing practices against ethnic minority communities sparked urban riots in the 1980s and 1990s in England, Canada, France, and Germany (Solomos, 1988; Tonry, 1997).

Researchers have identified factors such as selective policing practices that target low-income minority communities, lack of opportunities for minority youth, and low tolerance for deviance of minority communities that contribute to both the greater likelihood of involvement of these youth in criminal activities and the higher probability of police criminalizing their behaviors that would be tolerated or excused in members of the dominant society (Tonry, 1997).

Canada and England provide examples of countries with multiethnic populations and technologically advanced economies comparable to the United States. Although the population of blacks in England is much smaller than in the United States (1.6 percent versus 12.8 percent), and primarily of Afro-Caribbean heritage, young West Indian males also have higher rates of arrest and imprisonment than their white peers in the British criminal justice system (Carr-Hill & Drew, 1988; Small, 1983; Solomos, 1988). In the most recent census of the prison population in England and Wales, the combined rates of imprisonment and pretrial detention for all young black males, aged sixteen to nineteen, were over six times higher than for their white counterparts (286.7 versus 45.2 per 10,000). For young adult males, ages twenty to thirty-nine, the rates of incarceration and pretrial detention were more than four times higher for blacks than comparable rates for whites (294.6 versus 67.6) (Smith, 1997).

Since the 1960s there have been numerous reports of police harassment and misconduct against black males of all ages who are more likely than whites or Asian males to be stopped by the British police for "suspicious behavior" (Commission for Racial Equality, 1992; Skogan, 1994; Smith, 1997).

In Canada, where people of color constitute only 11.2 percent of the population, excluding the aboriginal groups, these "visible minorities are overrepresented in rates of offenses, arrests and incarceration" (Roberts & Doob, 1997). Since the Canadian government does not collect statistics on crime by race or ethnicity, it is difficult to gain an overall picture of racial discrimination in the system. However, several provinces collect statistics that show racial disparities and differential treatment of minority offenders, particularly in the more urban provinces of Ontario and Quebec (Roberts & Doob, 1997).

Statistics on aboriginal people indicate that they represent 10 percent of Canada's federal penitentiary population. Aboriginal youth were less likely to win "unconditional release" in a court hearing than members of other groups (Roberts & Doob, 1997, 497). A 1993 study of black and white defendants in Canada found that blacks were more likely to be detained by police, more likely to be denied bail and more likely to be incarcerated, yet these researchers concluded that the critical decision point is made at the point of arrest, when blacks are treated more harshly than white defendants with similar offenses.

## Immigration Control

Since the 1980s, England and Canada have both moved toward more restrictive immigration policies as their populations have become more racially and culturally heterogeneous.

### Great Britain's Immigration Policies: Colonialism Revisited

Due to its history of colonialism and its geographical location, Britain has attracted thousands of immigrants and refugees from Africa, the Caribbean, East Asia, and the Middle East since the end of World War II (Fenton, 1999; Kymlicka, 1995). During the early 1980s, the conflicts between British whites and Caribbean blacks exploded into urban riots in London, Birmingham, Manchester, and Liverpool (Solomos,1989). In the late 1980s and 1990s, Pakistanis, Bangladeshis, Arabs, and Africans became the targets of British racial antipathy (Blackstone, Parekh, & Sanders, 1998; Solomos, 1989).

Political rhetoric in British election campaigns has blamed immigrants of color for high unemployment, poor public schools, deteriorating infrastructure, social problems, and crime (Bhat, Carr-Hill, & Ohri, 1988; Fenton, 1999; Solomos, 1989). In the 1979 general election, conservative Prime Minister Margaret Thatcher warned that "people were rather afraid of being swamped by the introduction of 'non-English' cultural strains that threatened the integrity of the family and cohesive culture-community" (Fenton, 1999, 206). Faced with his Conservative Party's expected defeat in the general election of 1992, Prime Minister John Major once again raised the spectre of the immigrant hordes threatening British civilization to win a surprising victory. More recently, Britain broke its pledge of automatic citizenship to its Asian subjects in Hong Kong, who found their British passports worthless when the territory reverted to Chinese rule in 1997.

British immigration policy currently favors skilled workers through a long-term work permit system, family unification linked to earlier immigrant flows, and a limited refugee admissions program (Papademetriou & Hamilton, 1996). By further restricting access to citizenship and increasing the quotas from non-Commonwealth countries, Britain has effectively closed down most channels of immigration from non-white and third world countries.

Anti-immigration attitudes and policies in Britain are inextricably linked to past colonial relationships, racialized law and order themes, intergroup competition for limited resources, and nostalgia for empire, a combination of factors that scapegoats immigrants of color who are visible, vulnerable, and easily victimized (Fenton, 1999; Kymlicka, 1995; Solomos, 1989). Great Britain, which once prided itself over its benevolent policies toward its former colonial societies, finds itself struggling to incorporate the people of color who seek equality of opportunity and political stability on its shores.

### Canadian Immigration Policies: The Myth of Multiculturalism

The image of Canada as an overwhelmingly white nation is belied by the growing presence of Asians, Hispanics, and Caribbean blacks in the metropolitan areas. In 1990 there were over 100 ethnic groups living in Canada, concentrated in the major cities of Toronto, Montreal, and Vancouver (MacKay, 1999). In 1996 people of color constituted 11.2 percent of the Canadian population and that proportion is expected to grow substantially by the middle of the twenty-first century (Statistics Canada, 1998). Nearly 90 percent of people of color in Canada were foreign-born immigrants in 1990, accounting for about 6 percent of the adult population (Reitz & Breton, 1994). Asians are the largest racial minority group (6.8%) (predominantly Chinese and South Asian immigrants), followed by black Caribbeans as the second largest group (West Indians) (2.0%); most of them arriving in Canada since 1960. In metropolitan areas, such as Montreal, Toronto, and Vancouver, "visible minorities," account for 15 to 25 percent of the population (Li & Bolaria, 1983). Aboriginal groups, including Canadian Indians, Eskimos, and Aleuts, make up 3.9 percent of the total population (Statistics Canada, 1998).

Canada officially adopted a policy of "multiculturalism within a bilingual framework" and "is one of the few countries which has officially recognized and endorsed both polyethnicity and multinationality," as well as recognizing the rights of the aboriginal people to self government (Kymlicka, 1995, 22). But there is a major gap between the appearance of diversity and the reality of inclusion. Tensions between Canadian whites and people of color have escalated over charges of ethnic and racial discrimination in education, housing, employment, and the criminal justice system (Henry, 1994; Reitz & Breton, 1994). Although the educational levels of Asians and Caribbean blacks are higher in Canada than among comparable groups in the United States, the income differentials between these non-white groups and native-born whites are similar in both countries (Henry, 1994; Reitz & Breton, 1994).

Canadian immigration policies became increasingly more restrictive throughout the final quarter of the twentieth century, as Anglo-Canadians began complaining about their high taxes to support social services and education for immigrants and refugees. By the early 1990s, the newly elected liberal government responded to these complaints by passing legislation to reduce immigration levels from 1993 to 2000, to give preference to skilled and professional applicants, and to require sponsors to post a bond to ensure financial support of these newcomers (Li & Bolaria, 1983).

Current immigration policies in Canada include a number of eligibility criteria that reveal thinly veiled preferences for Europeans. In Canada and Great Britain, post–World War II immigration policy has responded to three major forces, that is, the need for skilled and unskilled labor to fuel economic growth, the push/pull relationship of low-income workers in Britain's Commonwealth countries, and the nationalist backlash of conservative political groups threatened by racial and cultural changes (Brubaker, 1989; Fenton, 1999; Kymlicka, 1995).

### Affirmative Action/Equal Opportunity

Since the 1960s, policies to increase equal opportunity for disadvantaged ethnic minorities have been debated, adopted, and modified in several other English-speaking industrialized nations. In England and Canada these policies are respectively called "positive action," or "equity programs," policies

created by legislation or government mandate to counter past discrimination and to increase participation of ethnic minority populations in the educational and economic systems of these countries. The conservative backlash
against affirmative action in the United States has been mirrored in similar
movements throughout Great Britain and Canada.

### Great Britain: Positive Action Programs

Minorities in Great Britain have received some legal protections from a
series of Race Relations Acts, first adopted by Parliament in 1965 and updated in 1968 and 1976. The 1976 law set up a Commission for Racial Equality (CRE) to monitor the implementation of the Race Relations Act, to work
toward eliminating discrimination in employment, to promote equality of
opportunity, and to foster good race relations (Honeyford, 1998; Solomos,
1989). This act was similar in its intentions to the U.S. Civil Rights Act of
1964, but it did not include a strong enforcement mechanism.

In 1984 the Commission for Racial Equality established a Code of Practice "for the elimination of discrimination in employment," strengthening
the implementation of anti-discrimination cases by broadening the criteria
for evidence admissible in hearings, thus making it easier for plaintiffs to
prove their complaints (Solomos, 1989, 81). In 1989 the CRE issued a Code
of Practice for the Elimination of Racial Discrimination in Education after it
concluded ethnic minority children were denied equal educational opportunity and that the underachievement of black students was a function of
"institutional racism" (Honeyford, 1998, 159).

The CRE investigation of racial policies in British schools found that
non-white minority youth are disproportionately found in inner-city
schools with substandard programs, where they are tracked into
nonacademic programs, vocational schools, and commercial or general
courses (Honeyford, 1998). They are also overrepresented in special-educa-
tion classes, or "sin-bins," and have higher rates of disciplinary problems,
suspensions, and dropouts. Teachers tend to stereotype minority students,
have low expectations of their academic ability, and often discourage them
from higher education (Small, 1994; Solomos, 1989). As in the United States,
these processes result in reproducing educational inequality and maintaining racial minorities on the bottom rung of the occupational and socioeconomic hierarchy (Gibbs, 1992; Small, 1994; Solomos, 1989).

Ethnic minority workers in England also occupy the lowest rungs in the
occupational ladder where Afro-Caribbeans are disproportionately found
in service, domestic, and unskilled jobs despite the fact that they have a
higher average educational level than native-born whites (Small, 1994;
Solomos, 1989). Results of the Fourth Labour Force Survey of Britain's ethnic minorities, conducted in 1994 by the Policy Studies Institute, revealed
persistently high rates of unemployment among Caribbeans, Pakistanis,
and Bangladeshis (Modood, 1998). Twenty percent of the minority respon-

dents reported that they had been refused a job on the basis of their race and 75 percent believed that some employers engage in racial discrimination.

In the 1980s, the conservative government of Margaret Thatcher dismantled several programs that were established by the previous Labour government to facilitate the integration of Afro-Caribbeans, Asians, and Arabs in the government schools and in the labor force. With the reelection of the Labour Party in 1997, Asians and blacks have renewed their demands for stronger enforcement of the race relations laws and codes of practice, but the "New" Labour Party under Prime Minister Tony Blair has tried successfully to broaden its appeal to moderates and liberals by focusing on the responsibilities and relative progress of minorities in Britain rather than on their rights and lack of opportunities (Goulbourne, 1998).

### Canada: Employment Equity and Educational Diversity

The Canadian Charter was one of the first national documents to endorse affirmative action for historically disadvantaged groups (Kymlicka, 1995). Subsequently, the Canadian government established education and employment equity programs specifying four categories of disadvantaged people: women, aboriginals (Indians, Aleuts, and Eskimos), visible minorities, and disabled people.

Studies of Afro-Caribbean students in Canada show that they are underrepresented in secondary schools' honors programs and have higher rates of disciplinary actions, yet their rates of high school completion are higher than those of native-born white students (Cummins, 1989; Yon, 1990). Teachers view them as rebellious, disrespectful, and resistant to cultural assimilation, partly based on their use of a Caribbean dialect and their maintenance of a Caribbean cultural and social identity (Gibbs, 1996; Henry, 1994; Solomos, 1988). Recent research suggests that Afro-Caribbean students are screened out from the most competitive colleges and universities and channeled into community colleges and technical schools, thus reinforcing the socioeconomic caste system that limits their employment options.

Although Afro-Caribbeans in Canada have a higher average educational level than native-born Canadians, they have not been able to leverage their educational advantage to gain occupational mobility (Reitz & Breton, 1994). Reports by government agencies and civil rights advocacy groups have identified racism by employers as the major cause of employment discrimination in Canada (Henry, 1994; Small, 1994; Solomos, 1989).

In their 1984 study of simulated "field trials" of black and white job applicants in Toronto, Henry and Ginsberg (1985) found that whites received three times as many job offers as equally qualified blacks. Black youth, ages fifteen to twenty-four, consistently have higher unemployment rates than their white peers and report negative experiences at all phases of the employment process (Gibbs, 1996). The average earnings of Asian and

Afro-Caribbean male and female adults were also lower than earnings of native-born Canadians (Reitz & Breton, 1994).

Opponents of positive action programs have consistently challenged the employment equity guidelines and have attempted to undermine the intention of these programs (Reitz & Breton, 1994). The conservative policy shift occurred in Canada in the early 1990s when the Liberal Party was elected in response to growing anti-immigrant and anti-minority public sentiment (Cardozo & Musto, 1997).

### Bilingual Issues and the Politics of Multiculturalism

Language rights are a fundamental cause of political conflict, even violence, throughout the world, including Canada, Belgium, Spain, Sri Lanka, the Baltics, Bulgaria, Turkey, and many other countries.

D. L. Horowitz (1985, 219–224)

Europeans have found it as difficult and challenging as Americans to integrate newcomers of different races, cultures, and religions into their even more homogeneous societies, schools, and social institutions. In Western industrialized countries with universal access to public education, the schools have assumed the major responsibility for educating and socializing these new arrivals. Invariably, debates over educational policies have pitted the liberals (who advocate special compensatory programs for those who need them) against the conservatives (who oppose any modifications in the traditional curriculum), transforming the educational system into a political battlefield (Blackstone, 1998; Kymlicka, 1995).

Issues of language and national identity increasingly dominate public debate in countries such as Canada and Great Britain. In Canada, language autonomy has become bitterly entwined with the issue of cultural sovereignty in the French-speaking province of Quebec (MacKay, 1999). In England there has been great resistance to the assault on the "Queen's English" by immigrants who speak other languages.

### Canada: The Politics of Bilingualism

Canada's constitution explicitly defines it as a multicultural and bilingual country, designating English and French as the two official languages (Cardozo & Musto, 1997). In the province of Quebec, the separatists voted twice in the last decade to secede from Canada in order to establish a monolingual French state, but they were narrowly defeated both times. English-speaking citizens who have not conformed to the strict French language rules in Quebec have faced legal action, provoking a mass exodus of Anglo-Canadians from that province.

Surveys of foreign language use in Canada have shown a clear decline from the first to the third generation, suggesting that a natural process of language assimilation occurs among immigrants and their descendants over time (Reitz & Breton, 1994). Yet the educational system in Canada has become "the battleground of contested national and ethnic identities" (Fenton, 1999, 176), particularly in the ongoing conflict between French-speaking Quebec and the rest of English-speaking Canada. French Canadians zealously guard their language and distinctive cultural heritage, partly out of pride in their unique identity and partly out of resentment against their history of economic discrimination and social exclusion by the better educated and economically more successful English settlers (Kymlicka, 1995; Reitz & Breton, 1994).

The Canadian policy of promoting multiculturalism supports ethnic languages and celebrations, community centers, and after-school cultural programs. However, the status of English and French as charter languages relegates all other languages to second-class status.

A vocal minority opposed to the policy of fostering multilingualism in Canadian society has been gaining support from those who complain that Canada has no "national identity" because the government has valued multiculturalism over a common cultural heritage (Cardozo & Musto, 1997; Kymlicka, 1995). In the 1990s this group of Canadian nationalists found common cause with the anti-immigration forces to promote more restrictive immigration policies and to challenge the multicultural, multilingual vision of Canadian society (Cardozo & Musto, 1997).

### Great Britain: Tower of Babel

Great Britain, like the United States, only recognizes English as the official language of the country. As a colonial power, the British imposed English as the official language of government, commerce and education, showing little interest in or respect for the indigenous languages of its colonies (Fenton, 1999; Kymlicka, 1995). Since the influx of immigrants from non-white Commonwealth nations, England has become a cultural and linguistic melting pot where over 200 of the world's languages and dialects are spoken (Honeyford, 1998).

The British have reluctantly permitted the establishment of ethnic language schools, ethnic language newspapers and media, and even ethnic advertising (Honeyford, 1998). Although South Asian languages, Arabic, and African languages are widely spoken in the metropolitan areas, newcomers are aware that they must master the Queen's English in order to obtain a job, to succeed in school, and to become socially mobile in British society (Gilroy, 1987; Small, 1994).

The issue of bilingual education is not a very salient issue in British schools, as there is no widespread commitment to teach children in any language other than English. As in the United States, foreign language instruction is viewed as an essential part of a well-rounded curriculum to prepare middle- and upper-class students for college and travel abroad, but these courses are designed for native English speakers and not for those immigrant children who have limited English proficiency.

The role of language in shaping an individual's identity and worldview provides an insight into the deep-seated ethnocentrism about the use of the English language in England and North America. Although some critics have attributed this ethnocentric bias to a sense of Anglo-Saxon superiority, linked to the concept of "empire" in Great Britain and "manifest destiny" in the United States, this preference for English may be partially attributed to a fear that the Anglo-Saxon culture will be destroyed if any other language gains a foothold in these countries. The fear of linguistic pluralism may stem from the same source as the fear of racial and cultural pluralism, that is, the threat of annihilation or extinction as a people, a language, or a culture (Fenton, 1999; Kymlicka, 1995)

Counter-balancing this primal fear of cultural and linguistic annihilation is the movement of the European Union to foster multilingual societies in Europe in order to facilitate international business and communication across national borders (Kymlicka, 1995). This movement has been accelerated throughout the world by the emerging technology of e-mail, the World Wide Web, and cellular telephones that reach around the globe to enable people to communicate at any place at any time. Globalization in business and communications has increased the need for multilingual societies and is fostering an international revolution in education, politics, art, culture, and science. Perhaps, ultimately, as globalism replaces nationalism in the industrialized nations, these societies will view multilingual abilities as a right and responsibility rather than as a privilege and a luxury.

## CHALLENGES OF MULTICULTURALISM

In its final issue of the decade, *Time Magazine* (December 31, 1999) reviewed the major themes and major personalities of the twentieth century. The magazine's editorial board declared that three themes dominated the twentieth century: the triumph of democracy over fascism and communism, the advances of civil and human rights over oppression and discrimination, and the advances in science and technology. The magazine's editors particularly praised Mahatma Ghandi for liberating India from the yoke of British colonialism, Martin Luther King, Jr., for abolishing racial segregation in the United States, and Nelson Mandela for dismantling apartheid in South Africa.

Yet despite the twentieth century's advances in liberating people of color from the tyranny of colonial exploitation and racial discrimination, no single leader or political party has yet been able to solve the long-standing ethnic hostilities between Hindus and Moslems in India, the ingrained patterns of prejudice and racial superiority of whites toward non-whites in the United States, and the traditional tribal conflicts in South Africa. As we enter the first decade of the twenty-first century, interethnic and interracial conflicts are highly visible in America and throughout the world, from indigenous groups in Canada and Australia who are suing their respective governments to reclaim their ancestral lands, to Indian peasants in Central and South America who are demanding full citizenship rights, to tribal groups in Central Africa who are seeking reparations after wars of "ethnic cleansing" in Ruwanda and Burundi.

When we examine these international trends, it is important to recognize the links between economic, political, and cultural trends in America and those in other countries. We now live in an increasingly interdependent global world, linked by satellites that permit the flow of communications and financial instruments around the world on a twenty-four–hour basis, shaped profoundly by international economic forces and political exigencies, and filtered through the lens of an aggressive, intrusive, omnipresent media.

The challenge of the twenty-first century is to transcend the racial and ethnic hostilities of the past by using the power of science and technology to alleviate poverty and to control disease, the power of information and mass communication to foster greater interracial and intercultural understanding among the world's diverse societies, and the power of education and the arts to eliminate prejudice and ethnocentrism and to elevate the human spirit so that ignorance, fear, and hatred will eventually be eradicated from human consciousness.

## REFERENCES

American Civil Liberties Union. (1999). *Driving while black: Racial profiling on our nation's highways*. New York: author.

Amnesty International. (1998). *Shielded from justice*. New York: Amnesty International.

Belluck, P. (1999). As more prisons go private, states seek tighter controls. *New York Times*, April 15, A1.

Bhat, A., Carr-Hill, R., & Ohri, S. (1988). *Britain's Black population: A new perspective*. Aldershot, England: Gower.

Blackstone, T. (1998). Towards a learning society: Can ethnic minorities participate fully? In T. Blackstone, B. Parekh, & P. Sanders (Eds.), *Race relations in Britain* (pp. 96–110). London: Routledge.

Blackstone, T., Parekh, B., & Sanders, P. (Eds.). (1998). *Race relations in Britain*. London: Routledge.

Borjas, G. J. (1990). *Friends or strangers: The impact of immigrants on the U.S. economy*. New York: Basic Books.

Borjas, G. J. (1999). *Heaven's door*. Princeton, NJ: Princeton University Press.

Brimelow, A. (1995). *Alien nation: Common sense about America's immigration disaster*. New York: Random House.

Broder, D. (2000). *Democracy derailed: Initiative campaigns and the power of money*. New York: Harcourt.

Brown, A. (2000). Immigrants walk tightrope in Spain. *San Francisco Chronicle*, August 1, D4.

Brubaker, W. R. (Ed.). (1989). *Immigration and the politics of citizenship in Europe and North America*. Lanham, MD: University Press of America.

Burris, J. L. (1999). *Blue vs. black: Let's end the conflict between cops and minorities*. New York: St. Martin's Press.

Cardozo, A., & Musto, L. (Eds.). (1997). *The battle over multiculturalism*. Ottawa, Ontario: Pearson-Shoyama Institute.

Carr-Hill, R., & Drew, D. (1988). Blacks, police and crime. In A. Bhat, R. Carr-Hill, & S. Ohri (Eds.), *Britain's Black population* (pp. 29–60). Aldershot, England: Gower.

Chavez, L. (1998). *The color bind: California's battle to end affirmative action*. Berkeley: University of California Press.

Christopher Commission. (1991). *Report of the Independent Commission on the Los Angeles Police Department*. Los Angeles: Office of the Mayor.

Commission for Racial Equality. (1992). *Cautions vs. prosecutions: Ethnic monitoring of juveniles by seven police forces*. London: C.R.E.

Congressional Information Service. (1997). *Hate crime statistics, 1997*. Washington, DC: Author.

Cummins, J. (1989). *Education and visible minority youth*. Toronto: Ontario Institute for Studies in Education.

Davidson, J. (1997). Caged cargo. *Emerge*, October, pp. 36–46.

Davis, C., Estes, R., & Schiraldi, V. (1996). *"Three Strikes": The new apartheid*. San Francisco: Center on Juvenile and Criminal Justice.

Davis, M. (1999). Traffic violation. *Emerge*, June, pp. 42–48.

Diamond, S. (1999). Right-wing politics and the anti-immigration cause. In S. Jonas & S. D. Thomas (Eds.), *Immigration: A civil rights issue for the Americas* (pp. 175–189). Wilmington, DE: Scholarly Resources.

Eddy, M. (1999). Europe voices concern over Austria's far-right success. *San Francisco Chronicle*, October 5, A10.

Fenton, S. (1999). *Ethnicity: Racism, class and culture*. Lanham, MD: Rowman & Littlefield.

Fix, M. E., & Tumlin, K. (1997). *Welfare reform and the devolution of immigrant policy*. Series A, No. A–15, October. Washington, DC: The Urban Institute.

Gangi, R., Schiraldi, V., & Ziedenberg, J. (1998). *New York state of mind? Higher education vs. prison funding in the Empire State, 1988–1998*. Washington, DC: Justice Policy Institute.

Gibbs, J. T. (Ed.). (1988). *Young, black and male in America: An endangered species*. Westport, CT: Greenwood Press.

Gibbs, J. T. (1992). *Marginality and mobility: A comparative profile of the socioeconomic status of black youth in England and the United States*. Unpublished monograph. Washington, DC: Joint Center for Political and Economic Studies.

Gibbs, J. T. (1993). British Black and blue. *Focus*, April 3–8. Washington, DC: Joint Center for Political and Economic Studies.

Gibbs, J. T. (1996). Triple marginality: The case of young Afro-Caribbean women in Toronto (Canada) and London (England). *Canadian Social Work Review*, 13(2), 143–156.

Gilroy, P. (1987). *There ain't no Black in the Union Jack: The cultural politics of race and nation.* Chicago: The University of Chicago Press.

Goulbourne, H. (1998). The participation of new minority ethnic groups in British politics. In T. Blackstone, B. Parekh, & P. Sanders (Eds.), *Race relations in Britain* (pp. 181–203). London: Routledge.

Gutierrez, D. G. (Ed.). (1996). *Between two worlds: Mexican immigrants in the United States.* Wilmington, DE: Scholarly Resources.

Hacker, H. (1992). *Two nations: Black and white, separate, hostile, unequal.* New York: Charles Scribner's Sons.

Henry, F. (1994). *The Caribbean diaspora in Toronto: Learning to live with racism.* Toronto: University of Toronto Press.

Henry, F., & Ginsberg, E. (1985). *Who gets the work? A test of racial discrimination in employment.* Toronto: Urban Alliance on Race Relations.

Holmes, S. A. (2000). Race analysis cites disparity in sentencing for narcotics. *New York Times,* June 7, A16.

Honeyford, R. (1998). *The Commission for Racial Equality: British bureaucracy and the multiethnic society.* New Brunswick, NJ: Transaction Publishers.

Horowitz, D. L. (1985). *Ethnic groups in conflict.* Berkeley: University of California Press.

Irwin, J., Schiraldi, V., & Ziedenberg, J. (1999). *America's one million non-violent prisoners.* Washington, DC: Justice Policy Institute.

Jaynes, G. D., & Williams, R. (Eds.) (1989). *A common destiny: Blacks and American society.* Washington, DC: National Academy Press.

Jonas, S., & Thomas, S. D. (1999). *Immigration: A civil rights issue for the Americas.* Wilmington, DE: Scholarly Resources.

Kymlicka, W. (1995). *Multicultural citizenship.* New York: Oxford University Press.

Li, P. S., & Bolaria, B. S. (Eds.). (1983). *Racial minorities in multicultural Canada.* Toronto, Ontario: Garamond Press.

Lynch, M. W. (1999). Davis' 4 percent plan no path to diversity. *San Francisco Chronicle,* February 15, A21.

Lyons, J. J. (1997). Democracy, deception and denial: The 1998 California "English for the Children" initiative. *N.A.B.E. News,* 21(1), 1–4.

MacKay, E. (1999). *The house of difference: Cultural politics and national identity in Canada.* London: Routledge.

Maharidge, D. (1996). *The coming white minority: California, multiculturalism, and America's future.* New York: Vintage Books.

Males, M., & Macallair, D. (2000). *The color of justice: An analysis of juvenile adult court transfers in California.* Washington, D.C.: Building Blocks for Youth, Youth Law Center.

Mauer, M. (1995). *Young Black Americans and the criminal justice system: Five years later.* Washington, DC: The Sentencing Project.

Modood, T. (1992). *Not easy being British: Color, culture, and citizenship.* London: Trentham Books.

Modood, T. (1998). Ethnic diversity and racial disadvantage in employment. In T. Blackstone, B. Parekh, & P. Sanders (Eds.), *Race relations in Britain* (pp. 53–73). London: Routledge.

Mollen Commission. (1994). *Report of the Mollen Commission on the New York City Police Department.* New York: Office of the Mayor.

National Education Association (NEA). (1996). *The debate over English only.* Available online: http://www.nea.org/society/engonly/html

National Urban League. (1999). *The state of Black America.* New York: National Urban League.

Orfield, G., & Ashkinaze, C. (1991). *The closing door: Conservative policy and black opportunity.* Chicago: University of Chicago Press.

Papademetriou, D. G., & Hamilton, K. A. (1996). *Emerging paths to restriction: French, Italian, and British responses to immigration.* Washington: Carnegie Endowment for International Peace.

Perea, J. (Ed.). (1997). *Immigrants out! The new nativism and the anti-immigration impulse in the United States.* New York: New York University Press.

Pimentel, B. (1998). Hate crimes against Asians reported up. *San Francisco Chronicle,* December 18, A25.

Poe-Yamagata, E., & Jones, M. A. (2000). *And justice for some: Differential treatment of minority youth in the justice system.* Washington, DC: Youth Law Center.

Preston, M. B., Cain, B. E., & Bass, S. (Eds.). (1998). *Racial and ethnic politics in California. Vol. II.* Berkeley: Institute of Governmental Studies Press, University of California, Berkeley.

Price, H. B. (2000). The one Florida plan: Counterfeit color-blindness. Press release. New York: National Urban League.

Reitz, J. G., & Breton, J. (1994). *The illusion of difference: Realities of ethnicity in Canada and the United States.* Toronto: C. D. Howe Institute.

Roberts, J. V., & Doob, A. N. (1997). Race, ethnicity and criminal justice in Canada. In M. Tonry (Ed.), *Ethnicity, crime, and immigration* (pp. 469–522). Chicago: University of Chicago Press.

Rojas, A. (1997). Hate crimes on rise against Asian Americans, report says. *San Francisco Chronicle,* September 9, A2.

Sampson, R. J., & Lauritsen, J. L. (1997). Racial and ethnic disparities in crime and criminal justice in the United States. In M. Tonry (Ed.), *Ethnicity, crime and immigration* (pp. 311–374). Chicago: University of Chicago Press.

Schiraldi, Y., & Ambrosio, E. J. (1997). *Striking-out: The crime control impact of "Three Strikes" laws.* Washington, DC: Justice Policy Institute.

Schlesinger, A., Jr. (1992). *The disuniting of America: Reflections on a multicultural society.* New York: W. W. Norton.

Schlosser, E. (1998). The prison-industrial complex. *The Atlantic Monthly,* December, pp. 51–77.

Schrag, P. (1998). *Paradise lost: California's experience, America's future.* Berkeley: University of California Press.

Selingo, J. (2000). Thousands protest Florida plan on racial preferences in admissions. *The Chronicle of Higher Education,* March 17, A38.

Skogan, W. (1994). *Contacts between police and the public: Findings from the 1992 British crime survey.* Research Study no. 134. London: The Home Office.

Skolnick, J. H., & Fyfe, J. J. (1993). *Above the law: Police and the excessive use of force.* New York: Free Press.

Small, S. (1983). *Police and people in London II.* London: Policy Studies Institute.

Small, S. (1994). *Racialized barriers: The black experience in the United States and England in the 1980s.* London: Routledge.

Smith, D. J. (1991). Police and racial minorities. *Policing and Society, 2,* 1–15.

Smith, D. J. (1997). Ethnic origins, crime, and criminal justice in England and Wales. In M. Tonry (Ed.), *Ethnicity, crime and immigration* (pp. 101–182). Chicago: University of Chicago Press.

Solomos, J. (1988). *Black youth, racism and the state*. Cambridge: Cambridge University Press.

Solomos, J. (1989). *Race and racism in contemporary Britain*. London: Macmillan Education.

Southern Poverty Law Center. (2000). The decade in review. *Intelligence Report*. Winter, Issue 97. (Special Report on "Extremism in the New Millennium.")

Statistics Canada. (1998). *Special tabulations from the 1996 National Census*. Ottawa: Statistics Canada.

Stefancic, J. (1997). Funding the nativist agenda. In J. F. Perea (Ed.), *Immigrants out! The new nativism and the anti-immigrant impulse in the United States* (pp. 119–135). New York: New York University Press.

*Time Magazine*. (1999). Special Millennial Issue. December 31.

Tonry, M. (1997). *Ethnicity, crime and immigration*. Chicago: University of Chicago Press.

U.S. Department of Justice. (1997). *Criminal victimization 1996: Changes 1995–96 with trends 1993–96*. Bulletin NCJ-165812. Washington, DC: Bureau of Justice Statistics.

Welch, M. (1999). The immigration crisis: Detention as an emerging mechanism of social control. In S. Jonas & S. D. Thomas (Eds.), *Immigration: A civil rights issue for the Americas*. Wilmington, DE: Scholarly Resources, Inc.

Wilson, W. J. (1987). *The truly disadvantaged*. Chicago: University of Chicago Press.

Yon, D. (1990). Schooling and the politics of ethnicity: A case study of Caribbean students in a Toronto high school. In H. Diaz et al., (Eds.), *Forging identities and patterns of development*. Toronto: Canadian Scholar's Press.

# CHAPTER 9

## The Politics of Identity: Conflict or Coexistence?

There is a religious war going on in our country for the soul of America. It is a cultural war, as critical to the kind of nation we will one day be as was the Cold War itself. . . . As they took back the streets of LA, block by block, so we must take back our cities, and take back our culture, and take back our country.

—Patrick J. Buchanan (qtd. in Takaki, 1994, 296)

The politics of race and ethnicity at the millennium's edge are such that it is no longer useful to conceptualize race and ethnicity only in terms of blacks and whites, especially in California with its unique multicultural society. As a border state, and the first point of entry into the United States for many Asian, Mexican, and Central American immigrants, California has a larger population of ethnic minorities than any other state and hosts a vast multitude of cultures and a complex array of languages and ethnicities (McCarthy & Vernez, 1998). Compared to the rest of the nation, California has more immigrants from Japan, Korea, China, Southeast Asia, and the Phillippines, as well as increasing numbers from India, Thailand, Ethiopia, North Africa, and the Middle East.

By sheer population growth statistics, people of color are expected to outnumber whites in California by the first decade of the twenty-first century, posing a severe threat to the status quo of politics as usual. Extremist political ideologies and xenophobic reactions to these demographic changes were reflected in California's Propositions 184, 187, 209, and 227. All of these propositions were radically conservative and racially divisive, driven by initiatives that cumulatively constituted a backlash to civil rights legislation and affirmative action programs that have been in place since the 1960s. Such nativist, reactionary ideas represent an irrational response of conservative whites to the progress and mobility of people of color, coupled with their mounting anxiety of losing economic ground.

Unique at this time in California's race relations history is the development of the ambiguous "Other." In the "us" versus "them" equation of the political landscape, it is unclear whether or not the "us" is defined as a homogeneous race or socioeconomic group (e.g., white middle class) and the "other" is defined as all people of color or a single targeted ethnic minority group (e.g., Latinos). This sociodemographic schism has created a ripe environment for the evolution of identity politics in the Golden State.

In his 1998 work on *The Possessive Investment in Whiteness: How White People Profit From Identity Politics*, Lipsitz describes the economic value of whiteness in American society. He suggests that this value is significant in formulating public welfare policies as well as private prejudices. Thus, it is not surprising that as the socioeconomic status of ethnic minority groups has improved in California, increasing their share of the American Dream, a strong backlash to laws and programs that further expand opportunity and access for non-whites has emerged. Prevalent stereotypes that people of color are lazy and unmotivated, uneducable, violent, and criminal are pervasive in the popular media, disseminated regularly through conservative radio talk shows. These images reinforce whites' fear of people of color and provide the rationale for public policies that minimize opportunities for minorities to gain access to resources and institutions that would help them to achieve parity and level the playing field with whites.

## IDENTITY POLITICS AT THE MILLENNIUM

"Identity politics" became a politically correct buzz phrase in the 1990s, a decade epitomized by escalating tensions in California between the majority and minority groups, native-born and immigrants, whites and people of color. Identity politics generally has been described as the tendency for each minority group to define issues solely or primarily in terms of their own group interests, values, and priorities (Preston, Cain, & Bass, 1998). With this increasing trend toward defining issues in very narrow ethnocentric terms, ethnic minority groups find themselves frequently at odds not only with the white majority, but also with each other, thus splitting the electorate into a number of special interest groups who are competing for limited resources and circumscribed privileges.

In the United States, ethnic identity traditionally has been linked to religious affiliation, residential area, political affiliation, cultural activities, and community participation. Several examples of this phenomenon are the Irish Catholics in South Boston, Jews in the Lower East Side of New York City, African Americans in Chicago's South Side, and Cubans in Miami, all of whom have substantially shaped the social, economic, and political institutions of their respective communities (Cain, 1998; Mindel & Habenstein, 1981).

But this limited definition of identity politics begs the question of whether ethnic minority groups are the only groups who pursue their own agendas to advance their social, economic, and political goals. Some would argue that identity politics is an enduring feature of American political life, from the growth of the labor union movement in the early twentieth century to the rise of the women's movement in the 1970s and the gay liberation movement in the 1980s. Ironically, any group movement that threatens the power and privilege of the ruling elite is characterized as identity politics, just as any group that attacks the problems of economic inequality and corporate monopolies is deemed a special interest group. Only middle-class white males and entrenched political and business elites avoid being labeled as special interest groups who engage in identity politics because they view themselves as the norm, assume that their values and goals are superior to all other groups, and go to great lengths to protect the status quo in American society (Maharidge, 1996; Schrag, 1998).

Even the U.S. Census has been politicized over the issues of race and ethnicity. Democrats supported a sampling method for the 2000 census enumeration of the nation's population in order to correct for the undercount of minorities in the previous two decennial censuses, but Republicans favored a direct count presumably due to fear of increasing representation from states with large proportions of African American and Latino voters (Kestenbaum, 1998). Although the director of the census and many distinguished statisticians and demographers advocated the sampling method as the most reliable approach to an accurate count of hard-to-reach groups, the Republican majority in Congress prevailed. In an ironic twist, the director of the census announced in early May 2000 that the rate of return from states with large minority populations was higher than expected, indicating that efforts to reach minority voters had proven to be very successful (Holmes, 2000).

In contrast to other sections of the nation, California is the quintessential "melting pot," a culture without roots or a common cultural heritage. Although many whites migrated to California to escape the social limitations and psychological boundaries of their ethnic communities in the East, Midwest, and South, there is a resurgence of interest in common ground and common goals among white Anglo-Americans in California who see themselves as distinct and their goals as divergent from the experiences and goals of Latinos, Asian Americans, and African Americans (Maharidge, 1996; Preston, Cain, & Bass, 1998). It is precisely this shared vision of uniqueness that can be easily exploited and manipulated by political demagogues and special interest groups who wish to maintain the status quo of the dominant majority by fomenting racial and ethnic division, cultural exclusion, and economic and educational inequality between whites and people of color in California.

California represents the apogee of identity politics at the denouement of the twentieth century, an era of explosive social ferment and social change, fueled by a robust economy, a revolution in technology, and a resurgence of ethnic consciousness. Because of its geographical proximity to Mexico and its easy access to Asia, California is the destination of choice for immigrants from Mexico, Central and South America, and the Pacific Rim. With the largest population of Native Americans, California has also become a battleground for issues such as Indian land rights and gaming concessions. Silicon Valley has changed the racial complexion of Northern California by importing thousands of engineers and computer technicians from South Asia, thereby further transforming the San Francisco Bay Area economically and culturally (Nolte, 1999).

## POLITICS OF RACE RELATIONS

Since the 1960s, race relations have changed so radically that the issues of interethnic relations in California are not solely issues of whites and blacks. Asians, Latinos, and newer immigrants and refugees from Africa, the Middle East, and the Indian subcontinent have emerged as visible minority groups with their own ethnocultural perspectives and territorial issues. This new era in racial politics has a much more complex face than in the 1960s with alliances not solely rooted in ethnic identification and racial heritage, but a mixture of identity variables, such as economic status, acculturation level, residential area, immigration status, and political affiliation in influencing voting patterns. However, aging white conservatives continue to be disproportionately represented in voter turnout, but the interests of this dwindling white population are now vastly different from the burgeoning population of youthful minorities. These major demographic differences between the majority of the electorate and the majority of the state's residents suggests a tumultuous future for California when the populations of color become politically active and begin to evaluate the institutionalized injustices resulting from these recent propositions. Analysis of the exit polling after these elections strongly suggests few of these initiatives would have passed if more people of color had voted.

However, voting patterns of people of color are no longer clearly predictable, particularly as these groups become more heterogeneous and more politically sophisticated. African American, Asian American, and La-

tino political leaders are no longer always on the ethnically "politically correct" side of an issue (University of California Regent Ward Connerly's
introduction and support of the anti-affirmative action initiative, Proposition 209, is a good example [Chavez, 1998]). Middle-class people of color,
who historically have voted for Democrats, are now more likely to consider
economic factors when casting their votes, even if this translates into support for Republican candidates.

Historically, public policies that were good for big businesses and driven
by capitalist ideologies were conversely bad for ethnic minorities. Now as
ethnic minorities' economic status improves, the interests of people of color
and the business community are no longer mutually exclusive. However, it
remains true that people of color are still disproportionately low income
and are more likely to be excluded from opinion polls about these policies.
Low-income minorities often do not respond to opinion surveys and political polling due to the history of institutional abuse they have experienced at
the hands of researchers (Jaynes & Williams, 1989).

## IDENTITY POLITICS AND THE CALIFORNIA ELECTORATE

Identity politics can operate through a subtle process of psychological
identification, image manipulation, and symbolic appeals, or it can operate
through overt propaganda, partisan political literature, and media campaigns (Preston, Cain, & Bass, 1998). Whether subtle or overt, the phenomenon of identity politics can best be evaluated in terms of its outcomes: how
effective was its appeal and how well did it achieve its goals?

### Four Examples of Identity Politics

In the three decades preceding the controversial initiatives of the 1990s,
there were three developments that foreshadowed the racial and ethnic
conflicts of the final decade of the twentieth century. In hindsight, each of
these events contained the seeds of the controversies that would fragment
the California electorate over affirmative action, immigration, bilingual education, and urban crime.

In 1964, after a protracted divisive debate over integration and equal
rights for minorities, the California voters passed Proposition 14, a statewide initiative that overturned the Rumford Fair Housing Act that had
eliminated racial discrimination in the sale or rental of housing
(Maharidge, 1996; Sonenshein, 1998). It was a clear stand of the majority
against integrated neighborhoods and the freedom of minorities to buy or
rent a house or apartment of their choice, but its proponents couched their
support in terms of "property values" and "freedom of association" rather
than outright appeals to racism. While the rest of the country was celebrat-

ing the passage of the Civil Rights Act of 1964, the California electorate was sending an unmistakable signal that minorities did not have equal rights to housing in the Golden State.

This successful effort to overturn a piece of important social legislation not only empowered the growing conservative movement in California, but it helped to set the stage for Ronald Reagan's stunning victory over Democratic incumbent Pat Brown in the 1966 gubernatorial election, thereby creating a conservative stranglehold over California politics for most of the next thirty years. In his account of that election, Governor Brown made a prescient observation: "Reagan remains both a force and a symbol of a new and negative type of politics, which could spread outside California and into the future—as the same social conflicts and complexities that have rocked California flair in the rest of the nation" (cited in Maharidge, 1996, 45).

In 1985, Mexican Americans, who constituted nearly two-thirds of the small central coast community of Watsonville, brought a voting rights suit against the city (*Gomez v. City of Watsonville*) to challenge its system of at-large voting to elect the City Council (Saito, 1998). As the agricultural center of Santa Cruz County, Watsonville had long served as a magnet for Mexican farm laborers from western and southern Mexico, but they had endured decades of discrimination and exploitation in the fields and canneries of the area (Zavella, 1997). After a successful strike against the cannery owners in 1985, the leaders of the Mexican American community pressed for greater political representation on the all-white and business-dominated City Council. The courts decided in their favor, instructing the city of Watsonville to replace its existing at-large system with a district system of electing council members, thereby enabling Mexican Americans to nominate and elect two Latino members to the City Council in 1989. As a consequence of these two protracted struggles to improve the economic and political status of Mexican Americans in Watsonville, there was a residue of bitterness and hostility polarizing the white and Latino residents for years afterward, symbolized by ethnic conflicts in the schools, housing discrimination, and economic exclusion in rebuilding the community after the 1989 Loma Prieta earthquake.

In the case of Rodney King, a young black man who was assaulted by four Los Angeles police officers after a high-speed chase in 1991, the majority of Americans disagreed with the "not guilty" jury verdict exonerating three of the four officers and barely slapping the wrist of the fourth officer. But the majority could not understand the rage and anger of the African Americans and Latinos who rioted and looted the stores in South Central Los Angeles for four days and nights after the verdict (Gibbs, 1996; Gooding-Williams, 1993). It was a reprise of the 1965 Watts Riots in Los Angeles, for the same reasons of persistent policy brutality, lack of employment opportunities, housing discrimination, educational inequities, and political disenfranchisement (Christopher Commission, 1991; Glasgow, 1981; Horne, 1995). This time Korean shopkeepers were targeted by the rioters who viewed them as exploitative and racially insensitive. Conservative whites framed the riots in terms of "law and order" and "gang violence," whereas African American and Latino leaders framed the riots in terms of suppressed rage and social justice (Brackman & Erie, 1998; Maharidge, 1996). The irreconcilable views of the majority would ultimately influence the outcome of Proposition 184, designed to appeal to conservatives who value law and order at the price of social justice.

In 1996 Democratic candidate Loretta Sanchez defeated conservative Congressman Robert Dornan in Orange County's forty-sixth congressional district to become the first Latina elected to Congress from California. Latinos, who had literally mushroomed to become over 40 percent of the district, voted as a bloc for Sanchez, prompting Dornan to accuse her campaign of voter fraud by registering hundreds of undocumented immigrants. Although the charges were investigated and proven false, the rancor and recriminations over her victory revealed the depth of anger and resentment of Dornan's supporters toward the Latino community's legitimate electoral triumph (Schrag, 1998). It also reflected the negative attitudes toward the Spanish-speaking community, expressed earlier in the 1995 vote of the Orange County School Board to eliminate bilingual education in their public schools. A closer look at the four propositions examined in previous chapters provides some insights on the manipulation of identity politics in creating or modifying public policy in California.

## IDENTITY POLITICS AND PROPOSITION 184: CALIFORNIA'S "THREE STRIKES" INITIATIVE

Proposition 184, the California "Three Strikes" Initiative, mandating a minimum twenty-five-year sentence for third felony convictions, was passed overwhelmingly in 1994. While the proposition would actually increase grave overcrowding in prisons and create an excessive tax burden for an aging prison population, it passed because negative stereotypes linking criminals to people of color were reinforced by its supporters. In generating support for Proposition 184, the "Three Strikes and You're Out" ballot initiative, supporters were successful in creating an "us versus them" mentality of law-abiding citizens ("us") against career criminals ("them"). However, underlying this generic appeal to the collective superego of the voters was a more subtle theme exploiting the stereotypes and fears of white voters against minority criminals. This theme surfaced particularly in the paid political advertisements on television, but also in political debates and public discourse on radio talk shows, letters to the editor, and op-ed pieces in newspapers (Schrag, 1998).

For example, in the newspaper coverage of the kidnap/murder of twelve-year-old Polly Klaas, one of the two most publicized crimes that prompted the initiative, the accused killer, Richard Allen Davis, was sometimes described as "part-Indian" in early accounts of his arrest. As his trial progressed and, even later, as the initiative gained momentum, reports of his Indian heritage became more frequent with close-ups of his wavy hair and bushy mustache flashed on television (Moore, 1999).

These images of Richard Allen Davis, along with other media images of African American and Latino criminals, clearly were intended to trigger voters' anxieties about crime, linked to their stereotypes of minority males as major perpetrators of violent crime. Unlike the infamous Willie Horton ad in the 1988 Republican presidential campaign, no one could be accused of outright racism with such a low-key, multiethnic message.

California voters still had vivid images of the 1992 civil disorders in Los Angeles following the acquittal of the police officers in the Rodney King assault case. For many whites, these riots had symbolized their greatest fear—the unleashing of black and Latino rage on the white community. For many Asians, the riots had crystalized their ambiguous role as middle-men entrepreneurs and as convenient scapegoats for black and Latino anger against the dominant society (Brackman & Erie, 1998; Cho, 1993; Maharidge, 1996). While it is difficult to measure the direct effect of these destructive riots on voters' attitudes toward the "Three Strikes" initiative, the trauma experienced by so many voters in the Los Angeles area may well have been a factor in overwhelming white and Asian support for Proposition 184.

The marketing of Proposition 184 was so effective that very few California papers challenged the tactics of the campaign committee, thereby failing to confront the divisive racial politics involved in its passage. Once again, the majority of white voters were manipulated into adopting legislation that would result in incarcerating more low-income minority youth for nonviolent offenses, divert money from pressing state needs for education and health care, and promote the growth of the nonproductive prison industry in a state with a shortage of skilled labor (Davis, Estes, & Schiraldi, 1996). Identity politics in this instance pitted whites against non-whites, but it may ultimately prove to be a pyrrhic victory as the prison industry consumes a greater and greater proportion of California's state budget at the very time when its schools are ranked in the lowest tier of the fifty states in terms of per-pupil spending, educational resources, and building facilities (U.S. Department of Education, 1999).

## IDENTITY POLITICS AND PROPOSITION 187: "SAVE OUR STATE" INITIATIVE

Proposition 187, the ballot proposition commonly referred to as the "Save Our State" initiative, further exposed the fault lines between whites and people of color in California. But, in contrast to the "Three Strikes" initiative, this time the issues transcended color lines and revealed schisms between native-born minorities and immigrants from Asia, Mexico, and Latin America. Public debates about the economic and social consequences of immigration obscured the private discussions about the displacement of unskilled African Americans by Mexican, Central American, and Asian immigrants in such urban areas of California as Los Angeles and the San Francisco Bay Area (Rodriguez, 1999).

What is new about initiatives like 187 is that upwardly mobile African Americans, Latinos, and Asian Americans are now central players in race relations issues in California. A higher proportion of middle-class Asians, blacks, and Latinos voted in alliance with conservative whites to pass the measure by a vote of 59 percent versus 41 percent. Thus, the lines of support for anti-immigrant legislation were drawn not only between whites and people of color, but also along an intersecting plane of economic status within ethnic groups, with higher-income African American, Asian American, and Latino voters tending to cast votes reflecting their economic interests rather than their ethnic loyalties (Sowell, 1981; Wilson, 1980).

The class argument was also submerged in a bitter campaign over the rights and responsibilities of immigrants. Unusual alliances were formed between white liberals in Northern California, the agribusiness interests on the Central Coast, and the upper and middle-class suburbanites in Southern California, many of whom opposed Proposition 187 for their own ideological or pragmatic economic reasons (Schockman, 1998; MacDonald & Cain, 1998).

An analysis of voting patterns by county showed that four of the five counties in Northern California with the highest rates of college-educated and most affluent residents posted majority votes against Proposition 187 (MacDonald & Cain, 1998). This study also found that counties with the highest percentage of Asians and Latinos generally had lower support for Proposition 187, thus the more urban racially mixed counties in Northern and Southern California, as well as on the Central Coast, were more likely to reject it or pass it by a slim margin. Noting that there was a substantial overlap between those who voted for Proposition 63, the 1986 ballot initiative declaring English as California's official language, and those who voted for Proposition 187, MacDonald and Cain (1998) concluded that the strong support for the "Save Our State" initiative was due to a combination of factors including "cultural nativism," "racial nativism," economic, and public policy issues.

White liberals were ideologically opposed to restricting the rights of undocumented immigrants as it was antidemocratic and inhumane. Editorial pages in the state's major newspapers revealed they were particularly concerned about the provision that teachers, social workers, and health care professionals would be required to report children and adults who were undocumented, claiming that these professionals would be violating their ethical values by acting like policemen to enforce the law (Schrag, 1998). But white liberals were clearly a minority among the state's voters, as had been demonstrated repeatedly in the state's growing conservatism since the election of Ronald Reagan as governor in 1966.

Agribusiness leaders in the Central Valley and coastal farming areas, which claimed the title of "fruit and salad bowl of the nation," quietly opposed Proposition 187 because of their dependence on itinerant Mexican agricultural laborers, who were willing to work for low wages under less than optimal conditions (Schrag, 1998). Without a steady supply of these workers to plant, cultivate, harvest, and pack or can these fruits and vegetables, these large agricultural operations would quickly face economic disaster, not to mention the negative impact on the nation's food supply. However, agribusiness leaders do not constitute a major voting bloc, and the large corporations were reluctant to flaunt their opposition to an initiative supported by the Republican party leadership.

Middle- and upper-class suburbanites in Northern and Southern California provided another natural constituency to oppose this anti-immigration proposition, particularly since these financially successful professionals, entrepreneurs, and corporate executives depend on a supply of documented (and undocumented) immigrants to provide the myriad services that support their lifestyle—the maids, nannies, gardeners, short-order cooks, and waiters who oil the machinery of their complex lives (Davis, 1992; Rieff, 1991; Schrag, 1998). Unfortunately, these constituents were never organized and never emerged as a cohesive force to champion the cause of the immigrants, perhaps unwilling and unready to articulate their symbiotic relationship with this disenfranchised and disempowered group of noncitizens.

As the campaign for Proposition 187 gained momentum, it also became increasingly clear that many African Americans were supporting it, particularly in Southern California where the inner-city areas of Los Angeles, Long Beach, and San Diego had seen an influx of Latinos and Asian immigrants and refugees since the late 1960s and early 1970s (Gooding-Williams, 1993; Horne, 1995; Maharidge, 1996). Leaders of the African American community had publicly complained that these newcomers had usurped blacks in the low-wage job market, had displaced them in the low-cost housing market, and had changed the culture and character of their neighborhoods (Johnson & Oliver, 1989). Although the major African American civil rights and advocacy organizations, such as the NAACP-Legal Defense and Educational Fund, the Urban League, and the Southern Christian Leadership Conference, voiced their official opposition to Proposition 187, African American voters were clearly more ambivalent and less enthusiastic about rejecting this measure. Ultimately, a majority of blacks voted against Proposition 187 by a slim margin of 53 percent versus 47 percent.

Many Asian Americans felt they were being targeted unfairly by Proposition 187, since most recent Asian newcomers to California were actually refugees rather than immigrants, thus they had entered the United States legally and with certain protections (Nakanishi, 1998). They also expressed their mixed feelings about the initiative by voting against it by the same margin as had African Americans, 53 percent versus 47 percent.

Perhaps the single event that solidified the supporters of the Proposition 187 campaign was the march in Los Angeles on October 16, 1994, when hundreds of Mexican Americans and other Latinos marched to protest the initiative, parading through the streets of the state capital with brightly colored Mexican flags and Spanish banners and Latin American symbols (Maharidge, 1996). Concurrent marches took place in Los Angeles, San Francisco, and San Jose, creating dramatic media images on television across the state and nation. But the march was a tactical error, ill-timed and poorly conceived, resulting in a major backlash of the undecided voters who viewed the marchers as disloyal citizens for displaying the foreign flags. These Latinos paid dearly at the polls a few days after the march when the voters overwhelmingly adopted Proposition 187.

The vote for Proposition 187 represented a watershed moment in California history, for it revealed not only the deep divisions between whites and non-whites, and between native-born and immigrants, but it also revealed the schisms among the three major ethnic groups in terms of their respective agendas, as well as the class divisions that lay submerged under the sanitized rhetoric of the supporters and opponents of the initiative (MacDonald & Cain, 1998; Rodriguez, 1999). This vote epitomized the splintering of the state's electorate by ethnicity, class, and citizenship status, and it proved to be a harbinger of two more divisive propositions that would soon follow.

## IDENTITY POLITICS AND PROPOSITION 209: CALIFORNIA CIVIL RIGHTS INITIATIVE

In 1996, Proposition 209, the anti-affirmative action initiative, put an end to nearly three decades of efforts to create more equitable opportunities in California for underrepresented groups in education, employment, and government contracting. Although African Americans and Latinos lobbied against Proposition 209, which was deceptively marketed as a civil rights initiative, most whites were overwhelming supporters of the initiative that passed by a margin of 54 percent versus 46 percent (Chavez, 1998).

The campaign for Proposition 209 further exacerbated the divisions between whites and people of color in California. From the inception of the initiative, African Americans and Latinos were acutely aware that they had been targeted by the provisions of Proposition 209, outlawing affirmative action in publicly financed education, employment, and government contracting. Much of the media campaign played on the stereotypes that "unqualified" minorities were being admitted to the state universities and being hired for jobs over better qualified white applicants (Chavez, 1998; Preston & Lai, 1998; Schrag, 1998).

Conservative politicians and advocates for Proposition 209 tapped into the growing anxiety of middle-class white males about the economic downturn in California, exploiting their fears of layoffs and stagnant wages (Maharidge, 1996; Preston & Lai, 1998; Schrag, 1998). As in previous eras of economic depression or uncertainty, California politicians were able to manipulate the fears of the majority by scapegoating the minorities (Davis, 1992; Maharidge, 1996; Schrag, 1998).

When the opponents of Proposition 209 began, belatedly, to organize protests against it, they found it was very difficult to marshal support from white women, who had been the principal beneficiaries of affirmative action (Chavez, 1998). It was also difficult to arouse white college students, who had been on the forefront of the civil rights movement in the 1960s. But thirty years later only the most liberal white women and the most radical white students were willing to put themselves on the front line to protest Proposition 209. Apparently, these two groups no longer identified with the discrimination against minorities, especially since the oppression and lack of opportunity so evident in the 1960s was more subtle to observe and more difficult to prove in the 1990s.

That white women did not perceive that they had a vested interest with minorities to oppose Proposition 209 was not too surprising, since they were also the mothers, wives, sisters, and nieces of white males who might possibly be affected adversely by affirmative action in the future. Moreover, by eliminating affirmative action altogether, whites ultimately would be the beneficiaries, as the growing proportion of minority students and workers was clearly a threat to the status quo in California society (Chavez, 1998; Maharidge, 1996; Schrag, 1998).

Since the 1960s, when the University of California at Berkeley had served as the conscience of American college campuses with its take-no-prisoners demonstrations for free speech, civil rights, and antiwar protests, the California campuses had grown decidedly more conservative and less committed to political activism and social change. While minority students on state campuses had led protests against Propositions 187 and 209, the majority of the white students were disengaged politically, focusing on preprofessional courses, social activities, and material goods. It appeared that the goals and interests of the white students on campus were no longer compatible with the goals and interests of the minority students, who, after all, were challenging their presumption of unlimited access to power and privilege, the subtext of an editorial to "End Race and Gender Preferences" published in *The Daily Californian* on November 5, 1996.

Asian Americans found themselves bitterly divided over Proposition 209. Although Asians would be the major beneficiaries of its passage, their support for Proposition 209 would alienate other people of color (Wang, 1998). Asian students formed the largest bloc of students at UC Berkeley and UCLA, the two most selective campuses in the University of California system, and they exceeded the proportion of African Americans and Latinos at several of the other campuses. In fact, Asian students on average had better high school grades and higher SAT scores than whites and all other students, prompting Asian American advocacy organizations to sue the university over admissions criteria that apparently set quotas for the number of Asians admitted as undergraduates (Chavez, 1998; Preston & Lai, 1998).

Asian professionals had made rapid inroads in the fields of science, technology, and business in the 1980s and 1990s, but they complained bitterly about the glass ceiling on their mobility (Edley,1996; Preston & Lai, 1998). Although they constituted about 20 percent of the workforce in Silicon Valley, they accounted for only 2 percent of the top executives in these high technology companies (Nolte, 1999). Perhaps their past experiences of discrimination and exclusion in California made them reluctant to engage in overt protest, but very few Asians joined the mounting multiethnic opposition to Proposition 209.

The opponents of Proposition 209 had not been able to organize an effective coalition of minorities, white women, and liberals to defeat it (Chavez, 1998). These diverse constituencies coalesced around their own narrow identity issues. While white women pursued gender equity and middle-class Asians focused on economic mobility, African Americans and Latinos formed an uneasy alliance to oppose the elimination of affirmative action in California.

However, the opponents were unsuccessful in their efforts to defeat Proposition 209 because they could not overcome the combined problems of an ineffective campaign and the antagonism of the California electorate toward affirmative action. The majority of the state's voters could not identify or empathize with the blacks and Latinos who looked different or spoke a different language, and who seemed to be usurping the American Dream from them and their children (Schrag, 1998).

## IDENTITY POLITICS AND PROPOSITION 227: THE "ENGLISH FOR THE CHILDREN" INITIATIVE

Proposition 227, known as the "English for the Children" initiative, was voted into law in June of 1998. The most recent in a series of anti-immigrant, ethnic-bashing initiatives adopted by California voters, Proposition 227 provoked considerable controversy by severely restricting the use of bilingual programs to teach children in California's public schools. The issue divided native English speakers from nonnative speakers, but it also created unexpected alliances between conservative white supporters of the "English-only" movement with moderate African Americans and assimilationist Asians and Latinos, who viewed bilingual classes as a form of educational marginalization and social disadvantage for immigrant children (Fitzgerald, 1998).

The "English for the Children" initiative found fertile soil in California's growing ambivalence to Asian and Latino immigrants and their diverse languages. English-only legislation historically has been debated in the United Sates during periods of rapid expansion of immigrants, who are frequently characterized by their detractors as a threat to the economic stability and national security of the country (Brimelow, 1995; Perea, 1997). It is no surprise that California, with 25 percent of its students classified as limited English proficient, would be a perfect battle ground for such an initiative's birth.

However, it is too simplistic to portray this current controversy as a conflict between English and non-English speakers or between citizens and immigrants, for it is complicated by issues of class, gender, region, and political affiliation. Among Asian and Latino voters, there was a split between upwardly mobile, acculturated individuals and those who were lower income and less integrated into mainstream society. Northern Californians and Democrats, traditionally more liberal than Southern Californians and Republicans, were more likely to support bilingual programs and vote against Proposition 227, but they were also more likely to be allied with minority voters and to oppose anti-immigration and anti-affirmative measures (MacDonald & Cain, 1998).

In the months preceding the vote on Proposition 227, the proponents of the initiative framed it as a positive strategy to promote acculturation and assimilation, while the opponents framed the initiative as a negative assault on their ethnic identity and autonomy. Coming so soon after Proposition 187, this initiative tapped into the barely suppressed anger and resentment of the native-born whites, African Americans, and other ethnic groups who perceived the more recent Asian and Latino immigrants as interlopers and unfair competitors for pieces of the American Dream (Schrag, 1998).

The passage of Proposition 227 only served to highlight the massive logistical problems of educating the thousands of non-English-speaking students who stream into the California public schools daily from countries as diverse as Cambodia, Iran, and Peru. The political solution to Americanize them by immersion in English-language classes is not necessarily compatible with the social solution to achieve biculturality in a gradually evolving multicultural society (Gibbs, 1996; Maharidge, 1996; Root, 1996).

An observant tourist in California cannot fail to notice the prominent signs of language retention by the state's multiple linguistic minority groups. These signs range from the Spanish botanicas in San Francisco's Mission District, to the Vietnamese grocers in San Jose, to the Chinese markets in Monterey Park, to the Korean strip malls in Los Angeles. More recent waves of immigrants and refugees from Asia, Africa, and South and Central America mark their ethnic enclaves with signs in Hindi in Silicon Valley, Arabic in the Central Valley, and Laotian in Oakland (Maharidge, 1996; Rieff, 1991). So far, most of these groups have not become politically active and have not yet comprehended the power of the ballot box to achieve their objectives. However, as they become better educated and acculturated, they presumably will participate more actively and effectively in electoral politics and may well become more assertive about preserving their languages by teaching them in their local public schools.

## DIVERGENT PATHWAYS TO POWER

Latinos have been called "the sleeping giant" because of their numerical potential to dominate the political process in California. But they lack two essential ingredients for political power: education and wealth. As Latinos develop a middle class and produce a cadre of educated leaders, they will inevitably become a major force in California politics (Guerra, 1998; Maharidge, 1996). Their success in implementing legislation to promote their social and economic agendas will depend largely on their ability to translate their numbers into registered voters with a common vision about the role of Latinos in the future growth of California as a multicultural, multiethnic state.

Asian American voters in California, particularly those from more established groups such as the Chinese and Japanese who have lived in the state for several generations, have tended to ally themselves with people of color on issues of civil rights, but have formed alliances with conservative white voters on those propositions that did not have direct and clearly detrimental effects on their communities (Nakanishi, 1998). Despite their history of discrimination, exploitation, and exclusion by the Californian majority, Asians have kept a low political profile, have avoided confrontation, and have sometimes supported the status quo on controversial social policy issues.

The increasing salience of identity politics is reflected in the growing clout of minority political organizations and advocacy groups. Latinos are becoming more aware of their electoral potential, better organized politically, and willing to exercise their political muscle at the polls (Guerra, 1998; Pachon, 1998). This trend is also apparent in several other states with large Hispanic populations, including Texas, New Mexico, Florida, and New York. Asians in California have had less success at the polls, but they have established networks of successful fund-raisers who have contributed heavily to local, state, and national candidates who are sensitive to their is-sues (Saito, 1998).

The irony of this heightened sense of ethnic politics at the cusp of the twenty-first century is that it has emerged simultaneously as the nation is moving toward a multicultural, multiethnic balance in which no one group will be a clear majority by mid-century (Maharidge, 1996). While many members of minority groups are upwardly mobile and rapidly assimilat-ing into the mainstream culture, newly arriving immigrants and minority youth, seeking a collective ethnic identity, continually swell the ranks of those who are motivated to preserve their traditional values, cultural heri-tages, and behavioral norms as unique entities.

In contrast to Latinos, African Americans have been steadily losing po-litical power in California since the 1980s due to several factors:

1. lack of population growth,
2. economic displacement, and
3. growth of other minority groups.

Concomitant with the increase in the Latino and Asian populations, the black population in California has remained relatively stable at 7 percent. As middle-class blacks have moved out of California's central cities into the suburbs, they have diluted their power as an urban voting block; conse-quently, in the 1990s African Americans lost seats in the state assembly, sev-eral due to term limits, as well as positions as mayor of several large cities including Los Angeles, Oakland, and Berkeley. In 2000 San Francisco was the only major city in California with an African American mayor who won two consecutive terms against less-well-financed and more controversial opponents.

African Americans in California have viewed themselves as targets in initiative campaigns dating back to Proposition 14 in 1964, when the voters overturned the Rumford Fair Housing Law (Maharidge, 1996). Since that time, the black community has been extremely vulnerable to concerted right wing attacks, whether they are masked in the rhetoric of law and or-der as in Proposition 184 or unmasked in the language of anti-affirmative action in Proposition 209.

One of the major challenges to ethnic identity politics in the twenty-first century will not arise from the white community, but from the growing population of racially and ethnically mixed people (Gibbs & Huang, 1998; Root, 1996). Demographers estimate that there will be over 27 million bira-cial and multiracial Americans by 2050 (Gewertz, 2000). These individuals will have dual or triple ties to several ethnic groups, necessarily forging more universal identities and more fluid allegiances to ethnic groups de-pending on the salience of particular issues in specific contexts at different time periods in their lives (Hollinger, 1995; Root, 1996). Perhaps this group of multiracial and multiethnic Americans will serve as a buffer between whites and people of color, mediating their conflicts, modeling more flexible approaches, and creating common ground for diverse viewpoints and competing interests of major ethnic groups (Hollinger, 1995).

Because of their desire to acknowledge their multiple ethnic backgrounds, these multiracial Americans lobbied successfully to revise racial and ethnic categories in the U.S. Census for 2000, so that Americans will now be able to check multiple categories (Holmes, 1998). Although this approach will yield a more accurate portrait of American society in all its diversity, some politicians and civil rights leaders have criticized the new policy as a threat to weakening entitlement programs and voting districts based on racial and ethnic population figures (Schemo, 2000).

## THE MESTIZOIZATION OF CALIFORNIA POLITICS

By 1998 Latino voters had become so numerous and well organized that they were able to place Cruz Bustamante as a Democratic candidate for lieutenant governor on the statewide ballot. Following an overwhelming Democratic victory at the polls in November, twenty-four Latinos were elected to the state legislature and Antonio Villaraigosa was chosen as the first Latino Speaker of the State Assembly in the state's modern history. In April 2000, Villaraigosa resigned in order to run as a candidate for mayor of Los Angeles, a signal that the Latinos were ready to take back the city that they founded in 1781.

However, Latino political candidates still have to contend with the racial polarization that has dominated the public discourse in Los Angeles since the South Central Riots in 1992, the aftermath of the verdict in the Rodney King police brutality case, and the unresolved anger over the "not guilty" verdict in the O. J. Simpson case in 1995 (Brackman & Erie, 1998; Gibbs, 1996; Hahn, 1996). Just a year after the South Central riots, the voters replaced five-term African-American Democrat Tom Bradley with white Republican Richard Riordan as mayor of Los Angeles. Riordan received 85 percent of the white vote, defeating Michael Woo, the Chinese American Democratic candidate, who was the choice of 86 percent of African American and 61 percent of Asian American voters (Hahn, 1996). Multiracial coalitions have become an endangered species in California politics in the 1990s, so Latinos will face formidable challenges in forming coalitions with those voters who are most likely to share their social and economic agenda and their vision for the future of Los Angeles as a multicultural city in which power is shared among whites and people of color (Pachon, 1998; Regalado, 1998).

Los Angeles might take a lesson from its neighbor, Monterey Park, sometimes called "America's first suburban Chinatown" with an ethnically mixed population that shifted from 85 percent white in 1960 to 60 percent Asian, 31 percent Latino, and only 12 percent white by 1990 (Horton, 1999). In his study of political change in Monterey Park, Horton observed that the initial "tendency [of the minority groups] to organize for ethnic representation and against nativist policies and candidates" gradually evolved into "the development of interethnic alliances on candidates and issues in a multiethnic city where no single group would determine political outcomes" (Horton, 1999, 121).

## IMPLICATIONS FOR THE FUTURE

Minorities and majorities increasingly clash over such issues as language rights, regional autonomy, political representation, education curricula, land claims, immigration and naturalization policy, even national symbols. . . . Finding morally defensible and politically viable answers to these issues is the greatest challenge facing democracies today.

Will Kymlicka (1995, 1)

California was colonized by Spanish soldiers and missionaries who imported Indians, mestizos, and mulattoes as farmers and artisans to develop the fertile plains and valleys. While the missionaries proselytized the Indians, the settlers built the rancheros and the towns. Two of the state's largest cities, Los Angeles and San Jose, were founded as missions and settled by this racially mixed group at the end of the eighteenth century (Robinson, 1981; Rolle, 1980). At the beginning of the twenty-first century, California has come full circle with a population reflecting its Spanish, Mexican, African and mestizo roots.

Demographic trends clearly show a dramatic shift in California's population to a majority of people of color shortly after the beginning of the twenty-first century. Latinos will comprise one of three Californians, with Asian Americans and African Americans forming the two other large blocs of non-whites.

The xenophobic and racist roots for immigrant bashing and anti-affirmative action sentiments in California are likely to persist for some time. In an era when what is presented as a civil rights initiative might actually be a civil wrong, the level of deception in developing and launching new initiatives has reached an unprecedented height. Propositions 184, 187, 209, and 227 were misrepresented by their proponents and their full political and financial implications were misunderstood by the voters. All of these initiatives were racially or ethnically divisive in some ways, creating political wedge issues to divide and polarize ethnic groups. Collectively, they provide compelling evidence that people of color were deliberately targeted by whites who are afraid of losing their power and privilege. The authors of these initiatives played directly into the ethnocentrism of white conservatives, the elitism of well-to-do suburbanites, the economic anxieties of the working class, and the fears of the elderly about crime, immigration, affirmative action, and bilingual education.

If California is going to prosper and continue to lead the nation in economic, cultural, and social innovations, this emerging majority of people of color must develop a shared vision and a common agenda with whites, who will continue to occupy the seats of economic and political power for decades to come. With greater educational and occupational mobility, the Latino population inevitably will become more politically sophisticated and more determined to wield their burgeoning political muscle. Likewise, Asian Americans, who have been heretofore reluctant to assert themselves politically, have belatedly learned the pitfalls of passivity and the power of lobbying. The Asian American community in California includes a significant number of highly educated successful engineers and entrepreneurs in the field of high technology, who understand the nexus between politics and business and are eager to become major players in that league. African Americans, on the other hand, will continue to lag behind these other two groups in their rate of growth, their access to power, and their assimilation into the mainstream of California society, so it will be crucial for them to develop more effective leadership and to seek out innovative ways to build multiracial coalitions (Cain, 1998).

Whether or not it will be possible for these three ethnic minority groups to form coalitions and find common ground as they become "the new majority," it will pose an enormous challenge for them to negotiate their relative status vis a vis the whites who currently dominate the state's power structure and control access to its major institutions. If Latinos, African Americans, and Asian Americans are unable to set aside their differences in order to envision an agenda that would be beneficial to all of their communities and would enable people of color and whites to share the benefits and enjoy the rewards of the state's vast material and creative resources, then the California dream will simply become an unfulfilled fantasy for most of its believers.

## REFERENCES

Almaguer, T. (1994). *Racial faultlines: The historical origins of white supremacy in California*. Berkeley: University of California Press.

Borjas, G. J. (1990). *Friends or strangers: The impact of immigrants on the U.S. economy*. New York: Basic Books.

Brackman, H., & Erie, S. P. (1998). At rainbow's end: Empowerment prospects for Latinos and Asian Pacific Americans in Los Angeles. In M. B. Preston, B. E. Cain, & S. Bass (Eds.), *Racial and ethnic politics in California. Vol. II* (pp. 73–107). Berkeley: Institute of Governmental Studies Press, University of California, Berkeley.

Brimelow, A. (1995). *Alien nation: Commonsense about America's immigrant disaster*. New York: Random House.

Cain, B. E. (1998). The politicization of race and ethnicity in the nineties. In M. B. Preston, B. E. Cain, & S. Bass (Eds.), *Racial and ethnic politics in California. Vol. II* (pp. 457–468). Berkeley: Institute of Governmental Studies Press, University of California, Berkeley.

Cain, B. E., & MacDonald, K. (1998). Race and party politics in the 1996 U.S. Presidential election. In M. B. Preston, B. E. Cain, & S. Bass (Eds.), *Racial and ethnic politics in California. Vol. II* (pp. 199–232). Berkeley: Institute of Governmental Studies Press, University of California, Berkeley.

Chavez, L. (1998). *The color bind: California's battle to end affirmative action.* Berkeley: University of California Press.

Cho, S. K. (1993). Korean Americans vs African Americans: Conflict and construction. In R. Gooding-Williams (Ed.), *Reading Rodney King/Reading urban uprising* (pp. 196–211). London: Routledge.

Christopher Commission. (1991). *Report of the Independent Commission on the Los Angeles Police Department.* Los Angeles: Office of the Mayor.

Coleman, J. W. (1998). Affirmative action wars. *Emerge,* March, pp. 30–37.

Davis, C., Estes, R., & Schiraldi, V. (1996). *"Three strikes": The new apartheid.* San Francisco: Center on Juvenile and Criminal Justice.

Davis, M. (1992). *City of quartz: Excavating the future in Los Angeles.* New York: Vintage Books.

Edley, C., Jr. (1996). *Not all black and white: Affirmative action and American values.* New York: Hill and Wang.

End race and gender preferences. (1996). *The Daily Californian,* November 5, p. 3.

Fenton, S. (1999). *Ethnicity: Racism, class and culture.* Lanham, MD: Rowman & Littlefield.

Fitzgerald, M. J. (1998). The making of an initiative. *California Lawyer,* May, pp. 44–87.

Gewertz, K. (2000). Student organized conference to focus on "mixed race experience." *Harvard University Gazette,* April 13, p. 8.

Gibbs, J. T. (1996). *Race and justice: Rodney King and O. J. Simpson in a house divided.* San Francisco: Jossey-Bass.

Gibbs, J. T., & Huang, L. N. (1998). *Children of color: Psychological interventions with culturally diverse youth.* San Francisco: Jossey-Bass.

Glasgow, D. (1981). *The black underclass.* New York: Vintage Books.

Gooding-Williams, R. (Ed.). (1993). *Reading Rodney King/Reading urban uprising.* London: Routledge.

Guerra, F. (1998). Latino politics in California: The necessary conditions for success. In M. B. Preston, B. E. Cain, & S. Bass (Eds.), *Racial and ethnic politics in California. Vol. II* (pp. 439–453). Berkeley: Institute of Governmental Studies Press, University of California, Berkeley.

Hahn, H. (1996). Los Angeles and the future: Uprisings, identity, and new institutions. In M. J. Dear, H. E. Schockman, & G. Hise (Eds.), *Rethinking Los Angeles* (pp. 77–95). Thousand Oaks, CA: Sage Publications.

Hollinger, D. (1995). *Post ethnic America.* New York: Basic Books.

Holmes, S. A. (1998). U.S. officials are struggling to measure multinational heritages. *New York Times,* June 14, A1.

Holmes, S. A. (2000). Stronger response by minorities helps improve census reply rate. *New York Times,* May 4, A1.

Horne, G. (1995). *Fire this time: The Watts uprising and the 1960's*. Charlottesville: University Press of Virginia

Horton, J. (1999). Chinese suburban immigration and political diversity in Monterey Park, California. In S. Jonas & S. D. Thomas (Eds.), *Immigration: A civil rights issue for the Americas* (pp. 119–129). Wilmington, DE: Scholarly Resources.

Jaynes, G. D., & Williams, R. M. (Eds.). (1989). *A common destiny: Blacks and American society*. Washington, DC: National Academy Press.

Johnson, J. H., Jr., & Oliver, M. L. (1989). Interethnic minority conflict in urban America: The effects of economic and social dislocations. *Urban Geography, 10*, 449–463.

Kestenbaum, D. (1998). Census 2000: Where science and politics count equally. *Science, 279*, February 6, pp. 798–799.

Kymlicka, W. (1995). *Multicultural citizenship*. New York: Oxford University Press.

Lipsitz, G. (1998). *The possessive investment in whiteness: How white people profit from identity politics*. Philadelphia: Temple University Press.

MacDonald, K., & Cain, B. E. (1998). Nativism, partisanship, and immigration: An analysis of Prop. 187. In M. B. Preston, B. E. Cain, & S. Bass (Eds.), *Racial and ethnic politics in California. Vol. II* (pp. 277–304). Berkeley: Institute of Governmental Studies Press, University of California, Berkeley.

Maharidge, D. (1996). *The coming white minority: California, multi-culturalism, and America's future*. New York: Vintage Books.

McCarthy, K. F., & Vernez, G. (1998). *Immigration in a changing economy: California's experience—Questions and answers*. Santa Monica, CA: RAND, National Defense Research Institute.

Mindel, C. H., & Habenstein, R. W. (1981). *Ethnic families in America: Patterns and variations*. 2d ed. New York: Elsevier.

Moore, M. (1999). *And justice for all*. Videotape. San Francisco: Porchlight Productions.

Nakanishi, D. T. (1998). When numbers do not add up: Asian Pacific Americans and California politics. In M. B. Preston, B. E. Cain, & S. Bass (Eds.), *Racial and ethnic politics in California. Vol. II* (pp. 3–43). Berkeley: Institute of Governmental Studies Press, University of California, Berkeley.

National Urban League. (1999). *The state of Black America*. New York: author.

Navarro, C., & Acuna, R. (1990). In search of community: A comparative essay on Mexicans in Los Angeles and San Antonio. In N. M. Klein & M. J. Schiesl (Eds.), *20th century Los Angeles: Power, promotion, and social conflict* (pp. 195–226). Claremont, CA: Regina Books.

Nolte, C. (1999). Most changed city is San Jose. *San Francisco Chronicle*, September 2, A1.

Pachon, H. P. (1998). Latino politics in the Golden State: Ready for the 21st century? In M. B. Preston, B. E. Cain, & S. Bass (Eds.), *Racial and ethnic politics in California. Vol. II* (pp. 411–438). Berkeley: Institute of Governmental Studies Press, University of California, Berkeley.

Perea, J. F. (Ed.). (1997). *Immigrants out! The new nativism and the anti-immigration impulse in the United States*. New York: New York University Press.

Pettigrew, T. E., & Alston, D. A. (1988). *Tom Bradley's campaigns for Governor: The dilemmas of race and political strategies*. Washington, DC: Joint Center for Political Studies.

Preston, M. B., Cain, B. E., & Bass, S. (Eds.). (1998). *Racial and ethnic politics in California. Vol. II*. Berkeley: Institute of Governmental Studies Press, University of California, Berkeley.

Preston, M. B., & Lai, J. S. (1998). The symbolic politics of affirmative action. In M. B. Preston, B. E. Cain, & S. Bass (Eds.), *Racial and ethnic politics in California. Vol. II* (pp. 161–198). Berkeley: Institute of Governmental Studies Press, University of California, Berkeley.

Regalado, J. A. (1998). Minority political incorporation in Los Angeles: A broader consideration. In M. B. Preston, B. E. Cain, & S. Bass (Eds.), *Racial and ethnic politics in California Vol. II* (pp. 381–409). Berkeley: Institute of Governmental Studies Press, University of California, Berkeley.

Rieff, D. (1991). *Los Angeles: Capital of the third world*. New York: Simon & Schuster.

Robinson, W. W. (1981). *Los Angeles from the days of the pueblo*. Los Angeles: California Historical Society.

Rodriguez, N. (1999). U.S. immigration and intergroup relations in the late 20th century: African Americans and Latinos. In S. Jonas & S. Dod Thomas (Eds.), *Immigration: A civil rights issue for the Americas* (pp. 131–144). Wilmington, DE: Scholarly Resources.

Rolle, A. F. (1980). *California: A history*. 3rd ed. Arlington Heights, IL: AHM Publishing Corporation.

Romanucci-Ross, L., & DeVos, G. A. (Eds.). (1995). *Ethnic identity: Creation, conflict and accommodation*. Walnut Creek, CA: Alta Mira Press.

Root, M. P. (Ed.). (1992). *Racially mixed people in America*. Newbury Park, CA: Sage Publications.

Root, M. P. (Ed.). (1996). *The multiracial experience: Racial borders as the new frontier*. Thousand Oaks, CA: Sage Publications.

Saito, L. T. (1998). Beyond numbers: Asian American and Latino politics in Los Angeles' San Gabriel Valley. In M. B. Preston, B. E. Cain, & S. Bass (Eds.), *Racial and ethnic politics in California. Vol. II* (pp. 45–727). Berkeley: Institute of Governmental Studies Press, University of California, Berkeley.

Salett, E. P., & Koslow, D. R. (Eds.). (1994). *Race, ethnicity, and self: Identity in multicultural perspective*. Washington, DC: National Multicultural Institute.

Schemo, D. J. (2000). Despite options on census, many to check "black" only. *New York Times*, February 12, A1.

Schiraldi, V., Sussman, P. Y., & Hyland, L. (1994). *Three strikes: The unintended victims*. San Francisco: Center on Juvenile and Criminal Justice.

Schlesinger, A., Jr. (1992). *The disuniting of America: Reflections on a multicultural society*. New York: W. W. Norton.

Schockman, H. E. (1998). California's ethnic experiment and the unsolvable immigration issue: Proposition 187 and beyond. In M. B. Preston, B. E. Cain, & S. Bass (Eds.), *Racial and ethnic politics in California. Vol. II* (pp. 233–276). Berkeley: Institute of Governmental Studies Press, University of California, Berkeley.

Schrag, P. (1998). *Paradise lost: California's experience, America's future*. Berkeley: University of California Press.

Sonenshein, R. (1993). *Politics in Black and white: Race and power in Los Angeles*. Princeton, NJ: Princeton University Press.

Sonenshein, R. (1998). Jewish participation in California politics: A revisit in the 1990s. In M. B. Preston, B. E. Cain, & S. Bass (Eds.), *Racial and ethnic politics in California. Vol. II* (pp. 109–136). Berkeley: Institute of Governmental Studies Press, University of California, Berkeley.

Sowell, T. (1981). *Ethnic America*. New York: Basic Books.

Streisand, B. (1997). Is it "hasta la vista" for bilingual ed? *U.S. News and World Report, 123*, 36–38.

Takaki, R. (Ed.). (1994). *From different shores: Perspectives on race and ethnicity in America*. 2d ed. Boston: Little, Brown, and Company.

U.S. Department of Education. (1999). *Digest of education statistics 1999*. Washington, DC: National Center for Education Statistics.

Wang, J. (1998). How affirmative action hurts Asians. *San Francisco Chronicle*, January 28, A21.

Wilson, W. J. (1980). *The declining significance of race*. Chicago: University of Chicago Press.

Zavella, P. (1997). The tables are turned: Immigration, poverty, and social conflict in California communities. In J. F. Perea (Ed.), *Immigrants out! The new nativism and the anti-immigration impulse in the United States* (pp. 136–161). New York: New York University Press.

# CHAPTER 10

# *Meeting the Millennium: Making Multiculturalism Work*

California is a window into the future. The powerful, almost incomprehensible new forces that are reshaping the lives of men everywhere are at their strongest here; the traditional patterns of institutions, community and class (which hold back change) are at their weakest. California presents the promise and the challenge contained at the very heart of the original American dream; here, probably more than at any other place or time, the shackles of the past are broken.

—George Leonard (1962, 31)

On January 27, 2000, President William Clinton concluded his final State of the Union speech with these words: "Within 10 years there will be no majority race in our largest state California. In a little more than 50 years, there will be no majority race in America. In a more interconnected world, this diversity can be our greatest strength. . . . Therefore, we must do more than tolerate diversity—we must honor it and celebrate it" (Text, 2000, A17).

Although President Clinton's race initiative floundered on the shoals of political correctness and bureaucratic missteps, he still reminded his fellow Americans that the goals of racial equality and racial reconciliation were far from being realized (Edley, 1996). The president proceeded to lay out his vision for a comprehensive public policy agenda that would increase educational and economic opportunities for low-income and minority youth, improve the economic and health status of their families, and reduce urban crime and social pathologies. Presumably, these policies would contribute significantly to the nation's continued economic prosperity, political stability, and well-being, thereby indirectly contributing to a reduction in interracial and interethnic conflicts.

President Clinton indirectly acknowledged the challenge created by the demographic imperative of the nation's rapidly changing population, dominated by people of color who are multiracial, multiethnic, and multilingual. Sometimes referred to as the "browning of America," the population of the twenty-first century will be much more diverse, with deeper roots in the developing countries of Asia, Africa, the Caribbean, South America, and the Middle East. As the proportion of racially and ethnically mixed families increases, racial identity itself will become so ambiguous and so specific that it will seem irrelevant as a salient characteristic for many (Gibbs, 1998; Hollinger, 1995; Root, 1996).

Current projections of the population by mid-century dramatically highlight these demographic changes. The U.S. Bureau of the Census (1999), using medium-range estimates, has projected that by 2050, non-Hispanic whites will constitute 52.8 percent of the nation's population, with ethnic minorities comprising 47.2 percent. One of every 4 Americans (24.5 percent) will be of Hispanic descent, one of 7 (13.6 percent) will be African American, one of 12 (8.2 percent) will be Asian American, and about one of 100 (0.09 percent) will be American Indian, Eskimo, or Aleut. These projections do not include the millions of people who will be racially or ethnically mixed and do not fit neatly into any single category.

Recent events in California graphically epitomize these demographic changes: the election of a Latino lieutenant governor and Speaker of the House in November 1998; the media salute to the first African American to coach a Rose Bowl team (Stanford University versus University of Wisconsin) on New Year's Day, 2000; the appointment of the first Chinese American police chief in San Francisco in January 1995; and the prominence of Asian Indian immigrant entrepreneurs in Silicon Valley high technology firms. These highly visible minority achievers in the worlds of politics, sports, criminal justice, and business may be in the vanguard of social change in California, but they are also emblematic of developments throughout the rest of the American society.

In the 1990s, the nation has witnessed an explosion of Latino music and culture, a resurgence of American Indian demands for self-government and economic empowerment, a revival of African American civil rights struggles, an awakening of Asian American political solidarity, and a demand for a multiracial census designation. The voices and visions of these communities of color are clamoring to be heard, to be respected, and to be validated. What they seek is not conflict or division, but cooperation and inclusion on their own terms, not as outsiders or strangers in this society, but as integral members of the American mosaic and legitimate heirs to the American Dream.

California must be viewed as the harbinger of this multicultural future in America, the repository of the hopes, aspirations, and dreams of a diverse democracy. California is a mirror of the social, economic, and cultural trends of the nation and, as such, a barometer of how these trends will reshape and reconfigure the social relationships and social institutions of the twenty-first century (Gibbs, 1998; Hollinger, 1995; Maharidge, 1996; Schrag, 1998).

With its destined role as a demographic trend-setter, California can also become a model for the transition from a monolingual homogeneous society to a multilingual heterogeneous society in which multicultural diversity will be viewed as a strength and an asset. Political, professional, and business leaders face the challenge of pioneering constructive and humane public policies and social programs that will be informed by rational debate, grounded in principles of fairness and equity, and motivated by the goals of inclusion, equal opportunity, and equal justice for all citizens.

## CURRENT ISSUES IN CALIFORNIA

At the beginning of the millennial year 2000, the nation's economy was enjoying its longest period of economic growth in history ("Jobless rate falls," 2000). California, along with the rest of the nation, basked in its robust economy, booming real estate market, fast- growing high-tech companies, and mushrooming media and entertainment. It was a time of unparalleled economic prosperity, political stability, and social complacency, yet there were invisible pockets of poverty, incidents of racial tension, and some underlying signs of social anxiety.

Amid all the affluence and the innovation were some deeper symptoms of discontent and disaffection from those who felt threatened by the pace of change and from those who had been bypassed by the California Dream. There was a widening income gap between high and low income families, even greater in California than in the rest of the nation as manifested in the lack of affordable housing, the poor condition of urban schools, the "digital divide" in access to computers and the World Wide Web, and unequal access to health care and public transportation (Clausing, 1999; Zinko, 1999). These low income groups continue to be disproportionately immigrants and people of color.

Escalating racial and ethnic tensions surfaced in a rise in hate crimes and hate speech in communities from San Diego in the south to Crockett in the north. California holds the distinction of serving as headquarters to a disproportionate number of organized hate groups and extreme right wing organizations, so there were people who burned crosses, posted hate speech on the Internet, and scrawled racial graffiti on homes and churches (Southern Poverty Law Center, 2000). In February 2000, Governor Gray Davis introduced a package of hate-crime legislation, proposing laws that would increase penalties for attacks against persons because of their race or ethnicity, add hate crimes to the list of violent felonies with additional three-year prison sentences, strengthen anti-hate education, and curtail hate speech on the Internet ("Gov. Davis," 2000, A1).

A bill to investigate racial profiling, the practice of police targeting of African American and Latino drivers, was introduced in the California State Assembly in 1999 after the American Civil Liberties Union filed a lawsuit against the California Highway Patrol, but was subsequently vetoed by democratic Governor Gray Davis in September 1999 (Lucas,1999). A year later, after harsh criticism from liberals and minority groups, Governor Davis finally pledged to sign a bill on racial profiling, but the bill was largely symbolic since the state and local police were not required to record the race or ethnicity of the motorists they stopped (Lucas, 2000, A3). On August 31, the final day of the 2000 legislative session, the California State Legislature adopted a compromise bill requiring "cultural diversity" training for all police officers and sheriff's deputies and a legislative study of voluntary data collected on traffic stops by police in several jurisdictions around the state (Lucas & Gledhill, 2000). It was a clear victory for law and order, but a bitter defeat for minorities and civil libertarians.

After a four-year investigation of alleged civil rights violations and police misconduct in the Los Angeles Police Department, the U.S. Justice Department advised the LAPD in May 2000 that they would have to make a number of significant reforms in police training and procedures or the Justice Department would initiate a federal lawsuit to oversee the administration of the city's police force (Purdum, 2000a, 2000c).

Immigrant bashing was alive and well as California entered the twenty-first century. Anti-immigrant rhetoric did not subside substantially after the passage of Proposition 187, but was ignited again after most of the proposition was overturned in the federal courts. Latinos were still being harassed at the Mexican border, targeted by the police, discriminated against by employers, and treated rudely in retail stores and public settings (Welch, 1999). Corrupt police officers from the Rampart Division in Los Angeles were also accused of preying on illegal immigrants, then reporting them to the INS for deportation if they complained of being assaulted.

Not surprisingly, California again set the pace for the nation, challenging the theory that racism and xenophobia are inversely correlated with economic prosperity. Throughout the nation, the patterns of increased income inequity, rising hate crimes, persistent police misconduct, and immigrant bashing have proliferated and have proven to be stubbornly resistant to government intervention, judicial rulings, or public opprobrium.

Clearly the time is opportune for California to eschew the "politics of division" and adopt the "politics of inclusion." Having waged successful campaigns to polarize voters around the issues of crime control, immigration, affirmative action, and bilingual education, the political leaders of California now have a golden opportunity to reverse the politics that target ethnic minorities and immigrants of color in discriminatory ways to criminalize and incarcerate them (Proposition 184), to exclude them and deny their fundamental civil rights (Proposition 187), to deny them educational and employment opportunities (Proposition 209), and to deprive them of their linguistic birthright and consign them to educational failure (Proposition 227). With the Latino population soon to become the majority in the state's population as well as in its public schools, these policies will marginalize and disempower them; thus, they are insulting, inhospitable, and indefensible.

Through financial control of the political process and a clever manipulation of the media, right wing forces in California succeeded in adopting their long-term agenda of preserving the power and the privilege of the state's declining Anglo-American population through a series of divisive propositions that increased racial antagonisms between whites and non-whites, increased ethnic hostilities between citizens and immigrants, increased conflicts between ethnic minority groups, and increased competition within ethnic groups for access to equal opportunities and distribution of limited resources. This agenda, as we have documented in previous chapters, was promoted by ambitious conservative politicians and angry community leaders; financed largely by the Republican Party, various corporate interests, and wealthy right wing individuals and advocacy groups; supported by an uninformed and easily manipulated electorate; ratified by an ineffective and irresponsible state legislature; and implemented by a conservative and cautious judiciary.

As moderate politicians gain more power and more visibility in California, they are in a prime position to initiate more progressive policies that will unite the state's diverse population groups. In the following section, we propose a set of principles that should guide public policies in the twenty-first century, as well as a limited number of proposals in the areas of crime control, immigration control, affirmative action, and bilingual education, the four principal foci of this book.

## PUBLIC POLICIES FOR THE TWENTY-FIRST CENTURY

The principles guiding the development of public policy for an ethnically and culturally diverse state must be cognizant of the competing needs of these groups for access to equal educational and economic opportunities, the equitable distribution of resources and social benefits, and the goals of a truly democratic society based on freedom, justice, and respect for human rights and human dignity (Bacon, 1999; Walzer, 1983).

These principles must themselves be rooted in an understanding and re-spect for the integrity of all cultures, the validity of their worldview, and the resiliency of their families and social institutions (Fenton, 1999; Gibbs & Huang, 1998). Language needs to be understood, not merely as a tool of communication, but as an essential aspect of a group's ethnic identity to be nurtured and preserved. Religious beliefs, dietary restrictions, child-rear-ing practices, marriage customs, ethical values—all are potential areas of misinterpretation and conflict that must be viewed in the context of their intrinsic cultural meanings and functions.

### Goals of Public Policies

The goals of the proposed alternative public policy options are the fol-lowing:

1. to build a multiethnic, multiracial society in California and the nation based on equal opportunity, equal justice under the law, and protection of civil rights and human rights for citizens as well as "non-citizens";
2. to promote greater *inclusion* and tolerance of diversity rather than *exclusion* and xenophobic fears of differences;
3. to increase mutual understanding and trust between whites and people of color, between citizens and immigrants, and among ethnic minority groups;
4. to reduce intraethnic and interethnic conflicts over the unequal distribu-tion of resources, the widening income inequality and the growing gap in technology and training between the "haves" and the "have nots," the majority of whom are low-income people of color and immigrants.

In his book describing the intensive assessment of affirmative action pol-icies by the Clinton Administration, Christopher Edley (1996) presents three alternative goals for policies addressing the status of minority groups in the United States, that is, correcting the effects of past discrimination, preventing future discrimination, or fostering diversity as a societal goal. In his concluding chapter on "Values and Community," Edley suggests that all policy choices have a moral dimension and ultimately reflect the funda-mental values of a society toward its most vulnerable members. Thus, one of the basic criteria for evaluating any proposed public policy is whether the benefits accorded to one group will outweigh the losses imposed on an-other group by said policy.

### The Criminal Justice System and "Three Strikes" Laws

As we noted in Chapter 4, the state of California spent more of its budget on building prisons than on building schools in the late 1990s. Along with

New York, Texas, and Georgia, it is in the forefront of incarcerating juvenile and adult offenders for long periods of time, responding to the demands of a fearful public and a powerful prison lobby. The stark reality that the United States has the highest rate of incarceration in the industrialized world, with a prison population disproportionately made up of African American and Latino males, raises some fundamental questions about crime and punishment in American society. Experts in criminology have warned that: "Until racial disparities in crime and justice are reduced, the social stability of the criminal justice system—and perhaps the social structure of the United States—will remain in doubt" (Sampson & Lauritsen, 1997, 366).

Recent studies have debunked the notion that more punitive laws such as "Three Strikes, You're Out," serve as a deterrent to violent crime or as a long-term solution to recidivism (Schiraldi & Ambrosio, 1997). There have been major problems in the implementation of the "Three Strikes" law in California across legal jurisdictions due to inconsistent applications of the law to different classes of defendants, and active opposition to the law by liberal prosecutors and judges. However, as described in Chapter 4, the major problem has been the severe financial impact of incarcerating nonviolent offenders for lengthy periods, during which they are not economically productive yet are draining valuable tax dollars for their support and security. Moreover, as these prisoners age in the system, they are at higher risk for chronic health problems, AIDS, injuries, and mental disorders, none of which prisons are equipped to manage adequately or effectively.

Governor Gray Davis, who was elected as a moderate Democrat in 1998, has surprised and disappointed many of his supporters with his staunch advocacy of punitive law and order policies, such as trying juvenile offenders as adults, refusing early release to model prisoners for parole, blocking efforts to modify the "Three Strikes" law, and supporting the death penalty. A critical article about Davis in the *New York Times* in May 2000 described him: "the governor is establishing himself as more of a conservative on criminal justice issues than his Republican predecessors, or any other elected official in California—if not the nation" (Nieves, 2000, 1A).

As the level of crime declines and the proportion of young people employed rises, at the beginning of this new millennium, it presents an opportunity to reexamine the criminal justice system, its underlying philosophy, its function in a democratic society, and its ultimate goals. Does this society want to maintain the current system that operates with bias toward the poor, the powerless, and the minorities; a system that rarely holds police accountable for their misconduct and brutality toward these groups; a system that is riddled with political patronage, incompetence, and judicial malfeasance; a system that protects the wealthy and punishes the disadvantaged; a system in which race is the major predictor of the death penalty?

## Alternative Policy Options

Critics of the "Three Strikes" laws have complained that, due to systemic racial and socioeconomic inequities in the criminal justice system, ethnic minority offenders will be overrepresented among those prisoners convicted of a third strike.

Second, the function of incarceration in an enlightened democratic society should be to rehabilitate offenders rather than to wreak revenge on them. Moreover, the punishment should be in proportion to the nature of the crime itself. To sentence a young man to twenty-five years in prison for stealing a bicycle or a piece of pizza, regardless of his previous convictions, seems blatantly disproportionate, and a form of cruel and unusual punishment. If there were a social consensus that rehabilitation is the major function of imprisonment, then the prison system could use the public's tax monies to establish or strengthen comprehensive educational programs, skills training for contemporary high-tech industries, psychological counseling to address issues of low self-esteem and anger, and conflict mediation to reduce recidivism rates. Most importantly, correctional institutions must develop and support internal substance abuse treatment programs, since over 40 percent of the prisoners in California are addicted to alcohol and other drugs, a figure that is replicated in national crime statistics (Foote, 1993).

Several specific proposals have been advanced by advocates and policy makers in California, such as the expansion of special drug courts to handle the volume of drug-related cases. The chief justice of the California Supreme Court supports this proposal because these courts offer an array of services to offenders such as counseling, substance abuse treatment, and intensive supervision, a combination that has proven effective in reducing rates of recidivism in this population. The Center on Juvenile and Criminal Justice has also proposed the establishment of a sentencing commission to revamp California's Penal Code to "reserve prison space for violent-recalcitrant offenders"; to enact a Community Corrections Act that would compensate counties for placing low-level offenders in "intensive supervision and/or drug treatment programs"; and "to address the serious and worsening racial and ethnic disparity evident in California's criminal justice system" by promoting collaborative relationships between the county district attorneys, civil rights organizations, and communities of color throughout the state (Davis, Estes, & Schiraldi, 1996, 6).

Finally, the goal of the prison system should be the ultimate return of prisoners to the general population with improved skills, self-insight, and self-discipline to become productive members of society. They can only achieve this goal if prisons assess the educational, vocational, and psychological needs of each prisoner; establish programs to help each prisoner to become literate, to develop some marketable skills, and to monitor their moods and manage their impulses more effectively; and help place released prisoners in halfway houses and community settings where they can make transitions to appropriate training programs, jobs, or educational institutions that will enable them to be self-sufficient, self-respecting, and stable members of the community.

## Immigration Reform and Immigrants' Rights

In his book *Spheres of Justice*, Michael Walzer (1983) emphasizes the critical importance of defining membership in a society. He asserts that "the principle of political justice is this; that the processes of self-determination through which a democratic state shapes its internal life, must be equally open to all those men and women who live within its territory, work in the local economy, and are subject to local law. . . . No democratic state can tolerate the establishment of a fixed status between citizen and foreigner" (60–61).

As Walzer (1983) points out: "The denial of membership is always the first of a long train of abuses" in excluding devalued groups (e.g., immigrants, minorities, guest workers) from equal access to the goods and benefits of a society. He concludes: "The determination of aliens and guests by an exclusive band of citizens (or of slaves by masters, of women by men, of blacks by whites, or conquered peoples by their conquerors) is not communal freedom but oppression" (62).

The current immigration policies of the United States are a complex maze of bureaucratic rules and regulations, based on an outdated obsession with cold-war security concerns, and are totally ineffective to secure its borders (Jonas, 1999; Welch, 1999). The inconsistent application of our policies in this hemisphere has created diplomatic crises, ill will, and retaliatory policies toward the United States, resulting in negative publicity and endless litigation. The disparities in the treatment of immigrants from Cuba and Haiti has been well documented, but there is also justifiable criticism over the U.S. State Department's rather arbitrary distinction between "immigrants" and "refugees" and between those who are seeking asylum for reasons of economic or political repression from Central and Latin America (Bacon, 1999).

### Alternative Policy Options

Several authors have proposed that American immigration policy should be formulated in a regional framework in the context of North and South American interests with the U.S. government acknowledging the relationship between immigration policy and foreign policy, as well as the connections between financial policies, economic growth, environmental issues, and social development (Jonas, 1999; Sassen, 1999). Jonas proposes a new conception of citizenship that transcends national borders and recognizes the realities of cross-border economic and social contacts. Underlying this conception of citizenship is the view that it is an issue of human rights and that "undocumented immigrants are not simply noncitizens with no rights, but are socially de facto citizens of more than one state" (108). As she points out, immigrants are already "transnational citizens of the 21st century" and are "most vulnerable to human rights and civil rights violations" (108), thus countries with large numbers of immigrants (documented and undocumented) are obligated to address their basic human needs (also see Bacon, 1999).

U.S. immigration policy should also cooperate with other countries in the hemisphere to develop legal protection for immigrants in terms of labor laws, wages and working conditions, health and education benefits, and civil rights for the undocumented, particularly at border crossings (Bacon, 1999; Jonas, 1999). Although the North American Free Trade Agreement (NAFTA), adopted by Congress in 1994 after a prolonged debate, will gradually eliminate trade barriers between the United States, Canada, and Mexico, it does not provide adequate legal and social protections for workers in other countries (Acevedo & Espenshade, 1996).

Rather than continuing to pursue punitive policies that often endanger the lives and families of immigrants, the U.S. government could reinforce efforts of these newcomers to build stable families in this country while helping to foster linkages between immigrants and their extended families in the sending countries, which benefit greatly from regular remittances of money, goods, and the infusion of new ideas and technology in these communities (Jonas, 1999; Sassen, 1999).

The U.S. government should also take a leading role in developing agreements on the rights of migrant workers, both regionally and internationally (Jonas, 1999; Sassen, 1999). The plight of workers who move across and within borders is one of the most neglected issues of civil and human rights. Now that the economy is indeed global, it is essential to reach agreement on the movement of labor, just as nations have established rules and standards governing the movement of capital, information and technology, and arts and culture across international borders.

Following the example of the European Union, the United States should cooperate with its regional neighbors to develop a comprehensive policy on social health and well-being for immigrants and their families (Jonas, 1999). Due to their undocumented status in the United States, many immigrants avoid seeking health care, social welfare, or legal assistance, even when it might be legally available. Such a policy would ensure that immigrants are eligible for basic services that would maintain their health and enhance their social functioning, as well as reduce the risks of spreading infectious diseases in their adopted communities. Moreover, these policies should address the reality that the majority of children of illegal immigrants are U.S. citizens, but current policies divide families into those who are eligible for benefits and those who are not, creating unnecessary bureaucratic difficulties.

Finally, current U.S. immigration policy also creates two classes of immigrants, those who are valued for their education and occupational skills, and those who are exploited for their unskilled labor and service jobs. The former category is given priorities for visas under a special congressional quota, while the latter groups are often harassed to show their green cards, deported without due process, and demonized in the media. This differential treatment not only reeks of hypocrisy, but also negates the true value of the thousands of unskilled and semiskilled laborers, domestic servants, gardeners, and restaurant workers who support the lifestyle of the middle and upper classes, fill the dirty and dangerous jobs that no one else wants, and enrich the economy with their taxes, spending, and savings. At the very least, the nation should recognize their contribution and encourage their participation in American society with proactive and humane policies.

In the fall of 1999, the Clinton Administration proposed granting amnesty to over 500,000 illegal immigrants who were in the United States during the previous amnesty in 1986, but did not file applications in time. The AFL-CIO labor organization supports this proposal and has also called for an end to sanctions for employers who hire these undocumented workers. These proposals are reasonable and may lay the foundation for a comprehensive reform of the nation's unfair and inflexible immigration policies (Greenhouse, 2000b).

When Vicente Fox Quesada, the new President-Elect of Mexico, visited the United States in August 2000, he articulated his vision of a radical change in U.S. immigration policies that would recognize open borders between the two countries, improve working conditions for migrant laborers, and invest in job training programs to improve the skills of immigrants from Mexico (Thompson, 2000). While U.S. officials expressed skepticism about his proposals, he succeeded in initiating a serious dialogue about revamping U.S. immigration policy.

### Affirmative Action: Opportunity versus Entitlement

Before the heated debate over affirmative action in the campaign for Proposition 209, the Clinton administration had set up a White House task force in 1994 to examine current federal affirmative action laws and policies and to evaluate their effectiveness (Edley, 1996).

After months of collecting data on the impact of affirmative action on employment, education, and government contracting, gauging public opinion through polls and focus groups, and weighing the political implications of any policy shift, the Clinton Administration concluded that affirmative action policies had benefitted disadvantaged minority groups enormously by significantly increasing their access to educational and employment opportunities, expanding their access to entrepreneurial opportunities through government contracts, and fostering equal opportunities in the armed services (Edley, 1996).

However, the report also concluded that minorities' access to capital was still quite limited, that court decisions had severely curtailed their access to government contracts, and that there were still significant gaps in opportunity and equality between whites and minorities (Edley, 1996). Debunking the claim that affirmative action goals had substantially harmed white males, the report cited evidence that "court records do not bear out the claim that white males or any other group have suffered widespread 'reverse discrimination'" (Edley, 1996, 203).

After thoroughly weighing the report's evaluation of affirmative action programs, President Clinton arrived at a Solomonic decision to "mend it, but don't end it," which he announced in an address to the nation at the National Archives in July 1995.

One of the major dilemmas in supporting the need for affirmative action programs is justifying some types of remediation for groups previously disadvantaged or disenfranchised by government policies at the risk of depriving other groups who were not responsible for the government's actions. A second major dilemma in formulating affirmative action remedies is the trade-off between mandating goals for minority admissions to colleges and universities, minority employment, and minority contracts at the expense of equally or better-qualified white students, employers, and entrepreneurs for these same slots (Bowen & Bok, 1998; Edley, 1996).

In his book *The Big Test*, Nicholas Lemann (1999) tackles the controversial issue of "meritocracy" based on objective criteria, such as college board test scores. In this critical analysis of the history and purpose of these achievement tests, Lemann asserts that the tests themselves were developed to reflect, reinforce, and maintain the status quo of the Anglo-American upper-class establishment. By creating a series of tests that measure the academic information available in well-equipped and well-endowed public and private schools, as well as the vocabulary and skills that reflect a middle-class lifestyle with its exposure to books, cultural activities, travel, and leisure pursuits (e.g., "regatta"), the authors of the Scholastic Achievement Test (SAT) helped to perpetuate an educational elite who attend the most selective institutions of higher education and replicate themselves generation after generation.

Studies have shown that students can improve their scores on the SAT examinations by taking them several times before their senior year in high school, as well as by enrolling in SAT review courses prior to the crucial final opportunity to take the test (Bowen & Bok, 1998; Lemann, 1999). Higher-income students who attend highly competitive public and private high schools have clear advantages over lower-income white and minority students because they can afford to pay fees to take the SAT exam repeatedly on practice trials, to afford the high cost of SAT review courses, and to pay private tutors in their weakest subjects. These advantages may produce far more merit scholars among middle- and upper-income students, but it certainly does not indicate that they are inherently smarter or more deserving of "merit" for their performance than other students who were not practiced, coached, or tutored to elevate their scores.

As Lemann and other social scientists have observed, this so-called "meritocracy" reproduces itself, not because of any innate intellectual superiority, but because of the competitive advantages operating from birth that enable these privileged youth to gain admission to the most prestigious preparatory schools, colleges, and graduate schools, allowing them to develop a network of friends, colleagues, and mentors who, in turn, help them to find positions in elite law firms, corporations, banks and brokerages, universities and foundations, and all the other institutions that are linked through family connections, boardrooms, and private clubs to form a national establishment (Bowen & Bok, 1998).

As outsiders to this extensive network of powerful people and institutions, minorities are generally excluded from the decision making and overlooked in implementing policy changes. Without some form of external intervention such as affirmative action, minorities would be severely handicapped in their ability to compete for the slots that could potentially afford them access to those very institutions of power and influence.

This potential for social mobility and access to institutional power is discussed by Bowen and Bok in their 1998 book *The Shape of the River*, which examines the long-term consequences of affirmative action in college admissions. Their study followed a cohort of over 45,000 students who entered as freshmen in twenty-eight selective private and public universities in three cohorts from 1951, 1976, and 1989. The study was designed to chart the pathways of these students from their freshman year in college through graduate or professional school, examining the subsequent employment patterns, earnings, and job satisfaction, and measuring their civic participation, life satisfaction, and perspectives on their college experiences.

Among the major findings of this study were the following:

1. black enrollment at these selective colleges increased by 50 to 70 percent through the use of affirmative action admissions policies;
2. over three-fourths of all African American and Hispanic students graduated from these schools within six years, a higher rate than from member institutions of the National Collegiate Athletic Association;
3. graduation rates for underrepresented minority students were highest at the top tiers of the *most selective institutions* in the sample, despite the deficiencies in pre-college preparation and the lower college grades for most of these students;

4. black and white graduates of these institutions earned graduate and professional degrees in about the same proportions, despite blacks' lower SAT scores, lower socioeconomic status, and lower grades as undergraduates;

5. black graduates of these selective schools were more involved than their white classmates in community activities, assuming positions of leadership in a range of civic, political, and arts organizations.

Bowen and Bok (1998) conclude that affirmative action in college admissions has produced a number of positive outcomes not only for the minority students themselves but also for the entire nation, both by broadening the base of an educated and well-trained society and by contributing to the formation of a stable middle class among African Americans.

### Alternative Policy Options

In the continuing debate over "color-blind" or "race neutral" policies versus affirmative action, Bowen and Bok (1998) offer a number of recommendations that are applicable to educational institutions and employment settings.

First, it is important to redefine "merit" from the narrowly conceived measures of test scores and grade-point averages to a broader assessment of abilities, enriching life experiences, motivation, and perseverance, all qualities that enhance a person's potential to work hard, overcome adversity, and excel. Grades and test scores may be valid predictors of a student's performance in the first year of college, but after that other factors are better indicators of students' overall academic success.

Second, diversity in and of itself is an important value and a worthwhile goal in institutions of higher education, particularly in a multiethnic, multicultural society (Turner et al., 1996). Just as colleges have traditionally sought to admit a cross-section of applicants from athletes to alumni "legacies," they ought to have the flexibility to use race or ethnicity as one additional factor in producing a diverse class, particularly since research has shown that diverse groups on campus produce a greater range of viewpoints and create a more dynamic and stimulating learning environment (Meacham, 1996; Turner et al., 1996). Diversity also contributes to greater understanding of racial and cultural differences among students as they prepare for adult roles in a multicultural society. As the proportion of non-white students is predicted to swell to 37 percent of the growth of the total enrollment, diversity will be a reality in higher education, irrespective of any policies to prevent or promote it (Wilgoren, 2000).

Third, affirmative action is important to address long-term societal needs, such as the growth of a professional class to serve underserved areas as health professionals, lawyers, teachers, and social workers. Increasing the number of well-educated people of color will also ensure the continued growth of a middle class among African Americans and Latinos, an essential development to reduce the income inequality between whites and non-whites and to increase access to capital for economic development and empowerment in ethnic minority communities.

Fourth, Edley (1996) suggests any system of race-based preferences "must be 1) carefully justified and 2) tailored in means and duration to fit that justification" (160) in order to balance the benefits of affirmative action against the costs of race-conscious policies. Additionally, the Supreme Court has established guidelines of a "compelling governmental interest" for public sector measures and a "manifest imbalance" in racial representation for private-sector affirmative action, both of which should prevent potential abuses of these policies.

Edley (1996) further proposes a set of criteria that clearly define the purpose or scope of the measures and identify the class of victims targeted by affirmative action in order to weigh the benefits and costs of the remedy. For example, the scope of the remedial action can be very narrow to address complaints of a few specific victims, or they can be broad to apply to an entire class of victims (e.g., minority police officers), or they can be totally inclusive to cover an entire ethnic or racial group (e.g., all African Americans).

Using another dimension of "opportunity versus results," Edley (1996) examines a continuum of mechanisms that will yield different outcomes in different policy contexts. For example, these mechanisms can range from outreach and recruitment, advantages or preferences, set-asides, to goals or quotas in the areas of education, employment, and government contracting. In selecting a particular remedy, he emphasizes the need for policy makers to articulate the values that guide the choice and the vision of society that is the ultimate goal of such a remedy.

It is not productive to frame the issue as affirmative action versus race-neutral policies, but rather to determine what measures are appropriate, for which policy arenas, and then to determine how they should be tailored to target which group of victims, under what specific circumstances, and for what period of time? Polls have shown that the majority of the American public believe in equal opportunity and will support targeted measures to redress past disadvantage and discrimination based on race or ethnicity.

Finally, as Justice Blackman once said: "To get beyond racism, we must first take account of race . . . and in order to treat some persons equally, we must treat them differently" (Edley, 1996, 269). Despite all attempts to justify the elimination of affirmative action by conservative adversaries such as Thomas Sowell (1981) and Arthur Schlesinger (1992), the data incontrovertibly demonstrate that there is still a huge gap between African Americans, Latinos, and whites in educational attainment, occupational status, income, wealth, home ownership, access to healthcare, access to capital, and even longevity. For example, in May 2000 the American Civil Liberties

Union filed a suit against California state education officials on the grounds that students attending schools in low-income and minority neighborhoods were being deprived of educational opportunity because their schools lacked basic resources such as qualified teachers, books, and properly maintained facilities (Purdum, 2000b). Without continued remediation to reduce these inequities through a range of affirmative action strategies, disadvantaged people of color will lose the gains won during the civil rights struggles of the 1960s and 1970s. Consequently, interracial and interethnic conflicts over limited resources could escalate, and the nation would ultimately lose the benefits of increased productivity, effective participation, and enhanced well-being of all of its citizens.

## Bilingualism: Right or Privilege?

In 1988 the National Education Association's publication *Official English/English Only: More Than Meets the Eye* was highly critical of the English-only movement's goal to ban bilingual education in public schools. The NEA (1988) summarized its objections as follows:

> The English Language Amendment is the wrong remedy for whatever of America's ills it tries to solve—for five reasons. It ignores our country's civil rights tradition; it fails to promote the integration of language minority citizens into the American mainstream; it neglects the need for American merchants to communicate with foreign markets; it restricts the government's ability to reach all citizens; and it raises constitutional concerns (1).

The NEA concluded that the English-only proposed amendment would "disenfranchise minority citizens; it promotes divisiveness and hostility toward those whose first language is not English" (NEA, 1996, 2). As an alternative policy, the NEA proposed "English Plus," which would address the language needs of both limited English proficient (LEP) persons and native English speakers who wish to learn a foreign language.

In the state of California, where over 100 languages and dialects are spoken, bilingualism and multilingualism are viewed by some as a valuable linguistic resource and by others as a cultural threat. Those who view bilingualism as a resource see its utility in giving California a competitive edge in international business and diplomacy with the state's trading partners in Mexico, Latin America, and Asia-Pacific Rim nations. They also understand the importance of language in preserving the cultural traditions of the state's diverse ethnic groups, whose cultural contributions of food, music, and art have shaped the dynamic eclecticism of the California lifestyle.

By contrast, those who view bilingualism as a threat to American culture express hostility to it on the grounds that it undermines English as a common language, subverts the dominant Anglo-American culture, and slows the process of acculturation and assimilation of immigrants into American society.

However, neither of these views should be determinative of public policy on bilingual education, since they are based on opinions rather than factual evidence on the role of bilingual education in facilitating either set of goals. For policy makers to formulate good public policy, it is first necessary to evaluate the research on bilingual programs to determine what kinds of approaches are most effective in teaching English to non-English-speaking students, at what age, and under what kinds of pedagogical situations. Unfortunately, Proposition 227, the "English for the Children" initiative, was not based on sound research, was not crafted by experts on bilingual education, and did not reflect the informed views of educators and policy makers in this field.

### Alternative Policy Options

Since the number of LEP students in California has more than doubled between 1988 and 1997, and two-thirds of these students are in grades K through six, the need for bilingual programs in the state's elementary schools is obviously crucial, particularly because these students must learn to read as well as to master a new language before they can proceed to secondary school (Ed Source, 1998). Because the LEP students are heavily concentrated in urban school districts like Los Angeles, San Francisco, and San Jose, as well as agricultural communities in the Central Valley and Central Coast with large farm worker populations, it is important that school districts maintain considerable flexibility to allow them to tailor the bilingual programs according to the needs of their school population. In April 1998 the state Board of Education granted this flexibility to local school districts, as long as they met the federal guidelines for bilingual instruction (Ed Source, 1998). However, Proposition 227 superceded this decision, removing the flexibility and mandating a standardized form of "sheltered English" for all the state's schools.

According to Hakuta (1984) and other linguists, it takes a minimum of five years for young children to learn another language well enough so they can master the subject content of their classes. If this is the case, then a "sheltered immersion" program of one year, as mandated by Proposition 227, would simply be inadequate and ineffective for most of the LEP children in California elementary schools. If they do not learn to read English by the third grade, this will place them in academic jeopardy for their remaining elementary school years and place them at high risk of dropping out of school long before they complete high school. Since Spanish-speaking students already have the highest dropout rates of any group in the California schools, any bilingual program that fails to teach them English will be a grave disservice and a sure ticket to academic failure for these students.

As Michael Kirst, a Stanford University professor of education, has warned: Latino students are not attending college in anywhere near the numbers of whites, blacks, or Asians, and they are relegated to low-wage, dead-end jobs. This creates an enormous challenge for schools and is potentially a very big social problem that could further bifurcate society along racial lines. (Guthrie, 1997, 1)

Since research and evaluation studies of bilingual programs have consistently demonstrated that non-English-speaking children who receive instruction in their native language, while simultaneously learning English, perform at higher levels of achievement in core subjects such as English, mathematics, and reading, educational policy makers should advocate for these types of programs for LEP students.

The two types of program models that have proven to be the most effective in terms of teaching English as a second language, as well as achieving mastery of core academic subjects at the elementary school level, are the native language instruction model and the two-way bilingual program model (Ed Source, 1998). Students in native language instruction programs are taught most subjects in their primary language, with classroom materials and books in that language and in English. Such programs can be "early-exit" (K–third grade) or "late exit" (K–fifth grade), but research has shown that students in the "late exit" programs performed better academically than students in "early exit" programs (Ramirez, Yuen, & Ramey, 1991).

The two-way bilingual program has gained considerable popularity in recent years, as it is used in regular classrooms to facilitate bilingualism in English-speaking and non-English-speaking students. This model has many advantages in that it does not segregate the LEP students into separate classrooms, it does not stigmatize their language as a less desirable language, and it affords a natural opportunity for children to cooperate and share in learning each other's languages.

Two-way bilingual programs are particularly suitable for California classrooms, where there are too many languages for an equitable distribution of bilingual programs. Moreover, English-speaking children who attend schools and live in neighborhoods with high percentages of Spanish, Vietnamese, or Filipino children casually pick up phrases in these other languages, so transferring these interactions in a more structured way to the classroom would be a natural development. This solution would benefit all children and prepare them more effectively for a rapidly changing global economy.

On March 15, 2000, Secretary Richard Riley proposed that public school districts around the nation should create 1,000 new "dual-language" schools, where children would be taught in English and another language such as Spanish (McQueen, 2000). According to Secretary Riley "dual language instruction has proven to help Latino children do better academically as well as to preserve children's heritage and promote the bilingualism all students need in a global economy" (McQueen, 2000, 1A). As the spokesman for official government policy in public education, Riley placed himself squarely on the side of linguistic experts who support dual-language instruction as the most effective and efficient method of promoting bilingual proficiency in English-speaking and non-English-speaking students.

Notwithstanding the dire predictions about the impact of Proposition 227 on the educational performance of students classified as "limited English proficient" (LEP), these students have performed surprisingly well on statewide standardized tests since the passage of the "English for the Children" initiative in June 1998. In the most recent tests in reading and math administered to elementary and high school students, LEP students made impressive gains in their scores and rankings in nationwide comparisons (Steinberg, 2000). However, critics of the virtual ban on bilingual instruction point out that these improved scores could be attributed to a number of factors including recently-mandated smaller class sizes, greater efforts of teachers to devise effective strategies for LEP students to learn English, and more time spent in preparation for the specific statewide tests (Steinberg, 2000).

Ultimately, whatever teaching method is adopted, bilingualism will be a tremendous asset in the twenty-first century as the state and the nation become increasingly multicultural, as borders between countries are breached by floods of immigrants and refugees, and as globalization displaces national economic activities and influences political agendas. Bilingualism is no longer simply the luxury of the upper classes or the passport to acculturation for the immigrant, but a pragmatic necessity for business executives, scientists, politicians, scholars, and financiers in the twenty-first century.

## THE LATINIZATION OF CALIFORNIA

In February 2000, the Field Institute poll released an updated demographic poll of California Latino voters (Garcia, 2000). Constituting 16 percent of the state's electorate, these 2.4 million Latino voters included nearly half newly registered voters who were younger, poorer, more likely to be first-generation immigrants, and less well-educated than the more established residents. Among the newer voters, 58 percent registered as Democrats, 22 percent as Republicans, and 20 percent as Independents or third-party affiliates. The surge in Latino voters of one million voters between 1990 and 2000, half of whom are immigrants, can be traced directly to the passage of Proposition 187, with additional surges after the passage of Propositions 209 and 227. Although only 39 percent of all Latinos in California were registered to vote at the beginning of 2000, they still form a critical swing vote in any election. In the wake of the three initiatives that clearly targeted immigrants during Governor Wilson's Republican tenure in Sacramento, Latinos have mobilized their communities, rejected the Republican Party, and are awakening "the sleeping giant" with a great reservoir of anger, resentment, and resolve to flex their political power and improve their economic status in the state they founded. Latinos, at their current rate of population growth, will soon be poised to reclaim California as their native state, revitalize it with their mestizo culture, and reinvent it with their Hispanic language.

In early April, thousands of janitors, mainly Latino and Asian, went on strike in Los Angeles to protest low wages and poor benefits (Greenhouse, 2000a). Union leaders claimed that janitors in Los Angeles were the lowest paid of any major city in the United States with average hourly wages of $6.80–7.90 per hour, compared to a top rate of $13.00 per hour in other cities, largely due to the huge labor pool of immigrants willing to work for low wages. Gaining the support of Cardinal Roger Mahony and many of the city's political and civic leaders, the janitors won a raise of 26 percent over three years, an unprecedented victory for unskilled workers. As the janitors' strike spread across the nation to Chicago, New York, and other large cities, two factors emerged from the large demonstrations and the heated rhetoric: first, Latinos were flexing their muscles in a newly discovered militancy reflecting their high visibility in the service sector of many American cities, and second, these cities are heavily dependent on immigrant service and domestic workers and could not function effectively for very long without them (Greenhouse, 2000a). As Mike Garcia, president of the Los Angeles local for the Service Employees International Union, declared after the strike, "with Los Angeles as the backdrop, with its huge disparity between rich and poor, with all the uninsured and immigrant workers, we wanted to show that a group of workers can organize and lift themselves out of poverty if they bring enough pressure" (Greenhouse, 2000a, A12).

In early May 2000, the U.S. Census announced that minority groups had responded to the 2000 census at higher rates than whites, citing California as posting the largest growth rate of any state in responding to the census questionnaires between 1990 and 2000. The 68 percent response rate from California was largely credited to the unexpectedly high response from the state's Latinos and African Americans, who reported "high levels of exposure" to the Census Bureau's campaign to reach minority households (Holmes, 2000). It appeared that minorities had gotten the Census Bureau's message to "make yourself count" ("hagase contar") in a state where they had been on the receiving end of four propositions with the explicit message that they really didn't count.

## MEETING THE MILLENNIUM: WHERE DO WE GO FROM HERE?

As we enter the twenty-first century, it is important to understand that the seismic changes in technology are mirrored in the seismic changes in demography. Yet American society is far more comfortable about accepting the technological changes and far more anxious about confronting the demographic changes.

However, these two major changes are inextricably linked, as experts predict that 60 percent of the new jobs in the early twenty-first century will be in the fields of information technology and the communications industry. Thus, those who master and control the new technology will be to the twenty-first century what those who controlled capital and labor were to the twentieth century. This link obviously creates an imperative to educate ethnic minority youth and prepare them for highly skilled jobs in order to maintain California's preeminence in the high technology field and America's leadership in the global economy.

Even more compelling is the argument of demographers that, in the first decade of this century, 85 percent of the workers entering the labor force will be ethnic minorities and women while only 15 percent will be non-Hispanic white males (Reid, 1998). By 2025, 38 percent of the working population will be African American, Latino, or Asian but nearly 75 percent of the elderly population will be white (Tilove, 1997). Thus, a predominantly youthful labor force of people of color will bear the economic burden of supporting the social security system for a largely white aging population. The need to educate this current cohort of youth to succeed in the economy of high technology, information processing, and specialized services presents a demographic imperative and a political challenge for American society. Without such education and training, coupled with equal social resources and equal opportunity, the vision for a peaceful and prosperious multiethnic society will not be easily achieved.

As William Julius Wilson (1978) has noted, class has increasingly become more important than race in determining access to opportunities, power, and privilege in American society. Wilson's controversial conclusion has been supported by a very recent Urban Institute report documenting the trend of wage rate differences that are widening by education, but narrowing by race and gender (Lerman, 1997). If these findings are valid, one would predict that, as more people of color enter the middle class, barriers to their social mobility will fall and interracial conflicts will ultimately diminish. Likewise, as immigrants of color become more acculturated, cultural distinctions will either blend or coexist with the mainstream society, creating a truly equalitarian, multicultural society. That is, of course, a very optimistic scenario for the future of race and ethnic relations in California, but certainly preferable to a pessimistic prediction that the largest and most diverse state in the nation could become another Yugoslavia, rent with ethnic and racial conflicts that could easily escalate into armed confrontations and urban guerilla warfare.

Finally, to acknowledge that California is the crucible where these ethnic and racial tensions are heating up and threatening to boil over is also to recognize that California must lead the nation in developing viable solutions to these issues. Unless California's political, business, and professional leaders want the crucible to become a cauldron, they should heed the warning of Harvard Professor Cornel West (1993) after the Los Angeles riots:

> Whoever our leaders will be as we approach the twenty-first century, their challenges will be to help America determine whether a genuine multiracial democracy can be created and sustained in an era of global economies and a moment of xenophobic frenzy: Let's hope and pray that the vast intelligence, imagination, humor, and courage in this country will not fail us. Either we learn a new language of empathy and compassion, or the fire this time will consume us all. (13)

If these problems cannot be solved in California, there is very little hope that they will be solved anywhere else in this nation.

## REFERENCES

Acevedo, D., & Espenshade, T. J. (1996). Implications of the North American Free Trade Agreement for Mexican migration into the United States. In D. Gutierrez (Ed.), *Between two worlds: Mexican immigrants in the United States* (pp. 229–245). Wilmington, DE: Scholarly Resources.

Bacon, D. (1999). For an immigration policy based on human rights. In S. Jonas & S. D. Thomas (Eds.), *Immigration: A civil rights issue for the Americas* (pp. 157–173). Wilmington, DE: Scholarly Resources.

Bowen, W. G., & Bok, D. (1998). *The shape of the river: Long-term consequences of considering race in college and university admissions*. Princeton, NJ: Princeton University Press.

Clausing, J. (1999). A push to narrow disparities in training and access to Web. *New York Times*, December 10, A12.

Davis, C., Estes, R., & Schiraldi, V. (1996). *"Three Strikes": The new apartheid*. San Francisco: Center on Juvenile and Criminal Justice.

Edley, C. (1996). *Not all Black and white: Affirmative action and American values*. New York: Hill and Wang.

Ed Source. (1998). *Bilingual education in California*. Palo Alto, CA: Ed Source.

Fenton, S. (1999). *Ethnicity: Racism, class and culture*. Lanham, MD: Rowman & Littlefield.

Foote, C. (1993). *The prison population explosion: California's rogue elephant*. San Francisco: Center on Juvenile and Criminal Justice.

Garcia, E. (2000). Latino electorate changing rapidly. *San Jose Mercury*, February 18, p. 1.

Gibbs, J. T. (1998). *The California crucible: Toward a new paradigm of race and ethnic relations*. San Francisco: Study Center Press.

Gibbs, J. T., & Huang, L. N. (1998). *Children of color: Psychological interventions with culturally diverse youth*. San Francisco: Jossey-Bass.

Gov. Davis seeks to increase penalties for hate crimes. (2000). *San Francisco Chronicle*, February 22, A1.

Greenhouse, S. (2000a). Janitors, long paid little, demand a larger slice. *New York Times*, April 28, A12.

Greenhouse, S. (2000b). Unions urge amnesty for illegal immigrants. *San Francisco Chronicle*, February 17, A3.

Guthrie, J. (1997). 21st century test for schools: Millions of students with limited English. *San Francisco Examiner*, May 15, p. 1.

Hakuta, K. (1984). *The mirror of language*. New York: Basic Books.

Hollinger, D. A. (1995). *Post-ethnic America*. New York: Basic Books.

Holmes, S. A. (2000). Stronger response by minorities helps improve census reply rate. *New York Times*, May 4, A1.

Jobless rate falls to lowest level in 30 years. (2000). *San Francisco Chronicle*, February 5, A1.

Jonas, S. (1999). Rethinking immigration policy and citizenship in the Americas: A regional framework. In S. Jonas & S. D. Thomas (Eds.), *Immigration: A civil rights issue for the Americas*. Wilmington, DE: Scholarly Resources.

Lemann, N. (1999). *The big test: The secret history of the American meritocracy*. New York: Farrar, Straus & Giroux.

Leonard, G. (1962). California. *Look Magazine*, September 18, p. 31.

Lerman, R. I. (1997). Meritocracy without rising inequality? Wage rate differences are widening by education and narrowing by gender and race. *Urban Institute*, 2, 1–5.

Lucas, G. (1999). Davis vetoes bill to track drivers' race. *San Francisco Chronicle*, September 29, A1.

Lucas, G. (2000). State racial profiling bill gutted at Davis' request. *San Francisco Chronicle*, April 28, A1.

Lucas, G., & Gledhill, L. (2000). Davis, legislators reach deal on race-profiling measure. *San Francisco Chronicle*, September 1, A1.

Maharidge, D. (1996). *The coming white minority: California, multiculturalism, and America's future*. New York: Vintage Books.

McQueen, A. (2000). Education chief calls for bilingual schools. *San Francisco Chronicle*, March 16, A3.

Meacham, J. (Ed.) (1996). Multiculturalism and diversity in higher education. *American Behavioral Scientist*, 40(2), 112–241. Special Issue.

National Education Association. (1988). *Official English/English only: More than meets the eye*. Washington, DC: Author.

National Education Association (NEA). (1996). The debate over English only. Available online: http://www.nea.org/society/engonly.html

Nieves, E. (2000). California governor building a "tough on crime" record. *New York Times*, May 23, A1.

Purdum, T. S. (2000a). Justice department warns Los Angeles police. *New York Times*, May 9, A14.

Purdum, T. S. (2000b). Rights groups sue California public schools. *New York Times*, May 16, A16.

Purdum, T. S. (2000c). Washington tries to right a stumbling Los Angeles. *New York Times*, May 15, A12.

Ramirez, J. D., Yuen, S. D., & Ramey, D. R. (1991). *Longitudinal study of structured English immersion strategy, early-exit, and late-exit transitional bilingual education programs for language-minority children.* Washington, DC: U.S. Department of Education.

Reid, M. J. (1998). Profit motivates corporate diversity effort. *San Francisco Sunday Examiner and Chronicle*, March 15, W42.

Root, M. P. (Ed.) (1996). *Racially-mixed people in America.* Newbury Park, CA: Sage Publications.

Sampson, R. J., & Lauritsen, J. L. (1997). Racial and ethnic disparities in crime and criminal justice in the United States. In M. Tonry (Ed.), *Ethnicity, crime and immigration* (pp. 311–372). Chicago: University of Chicago Press.

Sassen, S. (1999). Beyond sovereignty: Immigration policy making today. In S. Jonas & S. D. Thomas (Eds.), *Immigration: A civil rights issue for the Americas* (pp. 15–26). Wilmington, DE: Scholarly Resources.

Schiraldi, V., & Ambrosio, T. J. (1997). *Striking out: The crime control impact of "Three Strikes" laws.* Washington, DC: Justice Policy Institute.

Schlesinger, A., Jr. (1992). *The disuniting of America: Reflections on a multicultural society.* New York: W. W. Norton.

Schrag, P. (1998). *Paradise lost: California's experience, America's future.* Berkeley: University of California Press.

Southern Poverty Law Center. (2000). *The decade in review—Intelligence Report.* Winter, Issue 97. (Special Report on "Extremism in the new Millennium.")

Sowell, T. (1981). *Ethnic America: A history.* New York: Basic Books.

Steinberg, J. (2000). Test scores rise, surprising critics of bilingual ban. *New York Times*, August 20, p. 1.

The Text of President Clinton's State of the Union Address to Congress. (2000). *New York Times*, January 28, A16.

Thompson, G. (2000). Mexican leader visits U.S. with a vision to sell. *New York Times*, August 24, A3.

Tilove, J. (1997). Generation gap becoming racial gap. *San Francisco Sunday Examiner and Chronicle*, November 23, A17.

Turner, C., Garcia, M., Nora, A., & Pendon, L. I. (Eds.). (1996). *Racial and ethnic diversity in higher education.* New York: Simon & Schuster Custom Publishing.

U.S. Bureau of the Census. (1999). *Statistical abstract of the United States* (119th ed.). Washington, DC: U.S. Department of Commerce.

Walzer, M. (1983). *Spheres of justice.* New York: Basic Books.

Welch, M. (1999). The immigration crisis: Detention as an emerging mechanism of social control. In S. Jonas & S. D. Thomas (Eds.), *Immigration: A civil rights issue for the Americas* (pp. 191–206). Wilmington, DE: Scholarly Resources.

West, C. (1993). Learning to talk of race. In R. Gooding-Williams (Ed.), *Reading Rodney King/Reading urban uprising.* New York: Routledge.

Wilgoren, J. (2000). Swell of minority students is predicted at colleges. *New York Times*, May 24, A14.

Wilson, W. J. (1978). *The declining significance of race.* Chicago: University of Chicago Press.

Zinko, C. (1999). State study finds ethnic gap in computer use. *San Francisco Chronicle*, September 13, A17.

# For Further Reading

Almaguer, T. (1994). *Racial faultlines: The historical origins of white supremacy in California*. Bekeley: University of California Press.

Bowen, W. G., & Bok, D. (1998). *The shape of the river: Long-term consequences of considering race in college and university admissions*. Princeton, NJ: Princeton University Press.

Broder, D. (2000). *Democracy derailed: Initiative campaigns and the power of money*. New York: Harcourt, Inc.

Chavez, L. (1998). *The color bind: California's battle to end affirmative action*. Berkeley: University of California Press.

Crawford, J. (1989). *Bilingual education: History, politics, theory, and practice*. Trenton, NJ: Crane Publishing Company, Inc.

Davis, M. (1992). *City of quartz: Excavating the future in Los Angeles*. New York: Vintage Books.

Dear, M. J., Schockman, H. E., & Hise, G. (Eds.). (1996). *Rethinking Los Angeles*. Thousand Oaks, CA: Sage Publications.

Edley, C., Jr. (1996). *Not all black and white: Affirmative action and American values*. New York: Hill and Wang.

Fenton, S. (1999). *Ethnicity: Racism, class, and culture*. Lanham, MD: Rowman & Littlefield Publishers Inc.

Gibbs, J. T. (1996). *Race and justice: Rodney King and O. J. Simpson in a house divided*. San Francisco: Jossey-Bass Publishers, Inc.

Gibbs, J. T. (Ed.). (1988). *Young, Black and male in America: An endangered species*. Westport, CT: Greenwood Press.

Gooding-Williams, R. (Ed.). (1993). *Reading Rodney King/Reading urban uprising*. New York: Routledge.

Gutierrez, D. (Ed.). (1996). *Between two worlds: Mexican immigrants in the United States*. Wilmington, DE: Scholarly Resources, Inc.

Hollinger, D. (1995). *Post-ethnic America*. New York: Basic Books.

Jaynes, G. D., & Williams, R. M. (Eds.). (1989). *A common destiny: Blacks and American society*. Washington, DC: National Academy Press.

Jonas, S., & Thomas, S. D. (Eds.). (1999). *Immigration: A civil rights issue for the Americas*. Wilmington, DE: Scholarly Resources, Inc.

Klein, N. M., & Schiesl, M. J. (Eds.). (1990). *20th century Los Angeles: Power, promotion, and social conflict*. Claremont, CA: Regina Books.

Kymlicka, W. (1995). *Multicultural citizenship*. New York: Oxford University Press, Inc.

Lemann, N. N. (1999). *The big test: The secret history of the American meritocracy*. New York: Farrar, Straus & Giroux.

Lipsitz, G. (1998). *The possessive investment in whiteness: How white people profit from identity politics*. Philadelphia: Temple University Press.

Maharidge, D. (1996). *The coming white minority: California, multiculturalism, and America's future*. New York: Vintage Books.

McCarthy, K. F., & Vernez, G. (1998). *Immigration in a changing economy: California's experience—Questions and answers*. Santa Monica, CA: RAND, National Defense Research Institute.

Orfield, G., & Ashkinaze, C. (1991). *The closing door: Conservative policy and black opportunity*. Chicago: University of Chicago Press.

Perea, J. F. (Ed.). (1997). *Immigrants out!: The new nativism and the anti-immigrant impulse in the United States*. New York: New York University Press.

Preston, M. B., Cain, B. E., & Bass, S. (Eds.). (1998). *Racial and ethnic politics in California. Vol. II*. Berkeley: Institute of Governmental Studies Press, University of California, Berkeley.

Reitz, J. G., & Breton, J. (1994). *The illusion of difference: Realities of ethnicity in Canada and the United States*. Toronto: C. D. Howe Institute.

Reiff, D. (1991). *Los Angeles: Capital of the third world*. New York: Simon & Schuster.

Schlesinger, A., Jr. (1992). *The disuniting of America: Reflections on a multicultural society*. New York: W. W. Norton.

Schrag, P. (1998). *Paradise lost: California's experience, America's future*. Berkeley: University of California Press.

Skolnick, J. H., & Fyfe, J. J. (1993). *Above the law: Police and the excessive use of force*. New York: Free Press.

Small, S. (1994). *Racialized barriers: The black experience in the United States and England in the 1980s*. London: Routledge.

Smith, J. P., & Edmonston, B. (Eds.). (1997). *The new America: Economic, demographic and fiscal effects of immigration*. Washington, DC: National Academy Press.

Takaki, R. (Ed.). (1994). *From different shores: Perspectives on race and ethnicity in America*. 2nd ed. Boston: Little, Brown and Company.

Tonry, M. (Ed.). (1997). *Ethnicity, crime, and immigration*. Chicago: University of Chicago Press.

Wildmon, S. (Ed.). (1996). *Privilege revealed: How invisible preference undermines America*. New York: New York University Press.

# Index

## About the Authors

JEWELLE TAYLOR GIBBS is the Zellerbach Family Fund Professor of Social Policy, Community Change, and Practice Emerita at the School of Social Work, University of California at Berkeley. In addition she is a licensed clinical psychologist. Gibbs is editor of *Young, Black, and Male in America: An Endangered Species* (Auburn House, 1988), author of *Race and Justice: Rodney King and O. J. Simpson in a House Divided* (1996), and co-author of *Children of Color: Psychological Interventions with Culturally Diverse Youth* (1998).

TEIAHSHA BANKHEAD is a doctoral candidate at the School of Social Welfare at the University of California at Berkeley. She is the former Development Director of the Bayview Hunters Point Foundation for Community Improvement in San Francisco.